From Third World to World Class

The Future of Emerging Markets in the Global Economy

PETER MARBER

PERSEUS BOOKS
Reading, Massachusetts

Perseus Books is a member of the Perseus Books Group

Cover design by Suzanne Heiser
Text design by Pagesetters/IPA
Set in 11-point Stempel Garamond by Pagesetters

123456789-MA-02010099

Perseus Books are available at special discounts for bulk purchases
in the U.S. by corporations, institutions, and other organizations.
For more information, please contact the Special Markets Department at
HarperCollins Publishers, 10 East 53rd Street, New York, NY 10022,
or call 1-212-207-7528.

Find us on the World Wide Web at
http://www.aw.com/gb/

Contents

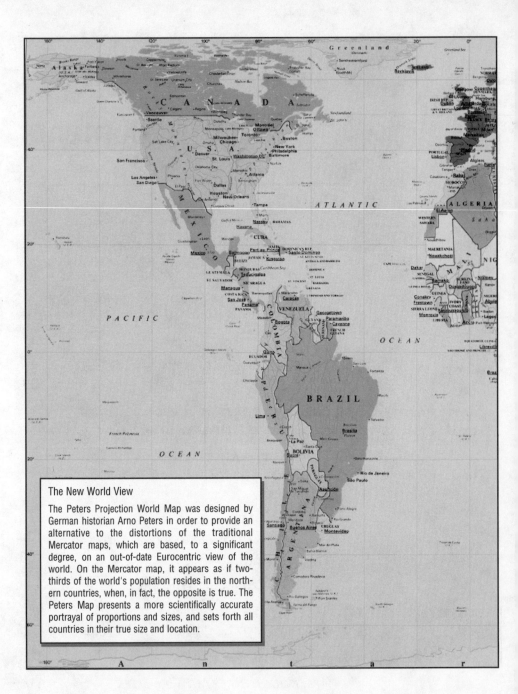

The New World View

The Peters Projection World Map was designed by German historian Arno Peters in order to provide an alternative to the distortions of the traditional Mercator maps, which are based, to a significant degree, on an out-of-date Eurocentric view of the world. On the Mercator map, it appears as if two-thirds of the world's population resides in the northern countries, when, in fact, the opposite is true. The Peters Map presents a more scientifically accurate portrayal of proportions and sizes, and sets forth all countries in their true size and location.

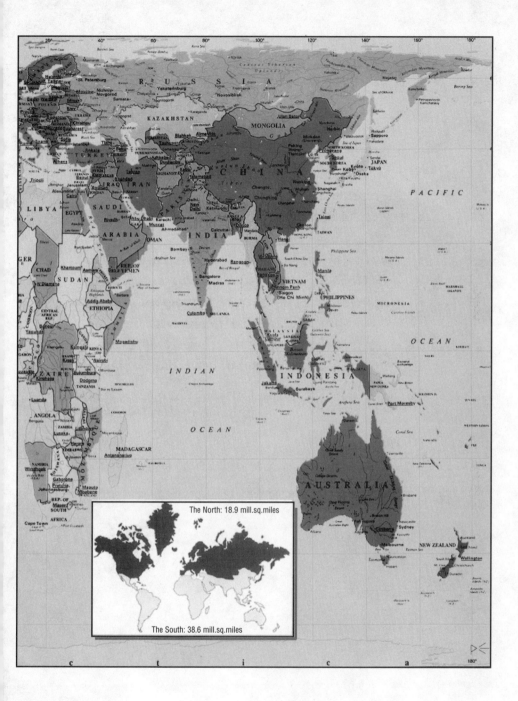

The North: 18.9 mill.sq.miles

The South: 38.6 mill.sq.miles

From the earliest times of which we have record—back, say, to two thousand years before Christ—down to the beginning of the 18th century, there was no very great change in the standard life of the average man living in civilised centres of the earth. Ups and downs certainly. Visitation of plague, famine, and war. Golden intervals. But no progressive, violent change. . . . This slow rate of progress, or lack of progress, was due to two reasons—to the remarkable absence of technical improvements and to the failure of capital to accumulate.

—JOHN MAYNARD KEYNES,
ESSAYS IN PERSUASION (1930)

Acknowledgments

A BOOK THAT tries to explain what's happening to six billion people needs an awful lot of help. This one is no exception.

First, a note of thanks to my partners Mike Gagliardi and Hernando Perez, who have indulged this project for the last year and a half, as well as contributed greatly to my general knowledge and understanding of emerging markets over the last twelve years. My other close colleagues—particularly Luke Imperator, Carlos Ordonez, Denise Simon, Lisa Sherk, and Clay Kingsbery—also have provided strong encouragement. I am eternally grateful to new and old friends at Columbia University's School of International and Public Affairs, particularly Lisa Anderson, Steven Cohen, Karin Lissakers, and John Ruggie, along with Gailen Hite and Safwan Masri of Columbia Business School, whose support has provided a platform for my writing and teaching over the years.

My sister Lisa Marber-Rich was instrumental in pushing the book forward, particularly in finding my agent, Maria Massie of Witherspoon Associates. Thanks is also owed to Perseus Books and specifically to my editor, Nick Philipson. They have boldly taken a chance on a first-time author with an ambitious topic, and for that I am forever grateful. In this respect, Henning Gutman deserves immense credit for seeing the value in such a book initially.

Many have helped with my writing and research. Jon Beckmann has served as an excellent project manager, line editor, cheerleader, and drill sergeant. Camilla Bustani, a long-time collaborator, has added immense sophistication to several arguments and has substantially increased the book's intellectual heft. Various former students and colleagues have also burned midnight oil for the book, including Nicole Beinstein, Arah Erickson, Jenny Kim, Julie Mak, Maura

McIntire, Beth Michelson, Bruce Schoenfeld, and Bill Young. Larry Codraro and Emily Burg particularly have gone above and beyond the call of duty helping both hardcover and paperback editions move to print.

So much of the material in this book comes from years of interaction with Wall Street and World Bank professionals; there have been so many contributors, their names alone would fill a book. A few, however, stand out. For years Mark Jurish has greatly increased my knowledge and understanding of market inefficiencies and the funds business. Jae Park has been an excellent soundboard on practical and theoretical portfolio management. Michael Howell has been a strong shaper of my own investment approach and many of his thoughts are strewn throughout the book. I have many long-time market friends— Alden Brewster, Gabriel Buteler, Marta Cabrera, Player Crosby, Peter Frey, Scott Gordon, Marc Helie, Rich Lotto, Price Lowenstein, Ted Merz, Ron Molloy, Ricardo Mora, Juan Peralta-Ramos, Romulo Perez-Segnini, Kurt Schmid, Steven Schoenfeld, Mike Smith, and Robin Willoughby—who all have provided key emerging market insights over the years that have laced several arguments in the book. A special thanks is owed to Giacomo DeFillippis, one of the more thoughtful and generous minds on Wall Street, who has dispensed more pearls of wisdom to me than he knows.

Finally, my family deserves much praise. My parents and in-laws have always had great faith in my abilities and have rarely hidden it. But the greatest inspiration has come from my wife, Andrea, and my two daughters—Sinclaire and Haley—beautiful, wise women who for years have suffered with a man obsessed with weighty questions, worldly endeavors, and wildly gyrating markets. Andrea, this book is to put the legend to rest and, until disproved, shall remain the law.

Preface to the
Paperback Edition

THE SCHOLAR GEORGE Thompson has suggested that writing was first invented to facilitate trade; ironically, in my particular case it is trading that has facilitated writing. This book has been in development for most of my adult life, the culmination of years investing throughout the developing world, as well as teaching graduate school classes. Working simultaneously in the worlds of Wall Street and the Academy has been no easy feat; at various times I have felt like both prisoner of and guard to these powerful institutions. But understanding developing countries and how they affect the lives of those in the First World requires both a theoretical and a practical grounding. This is what makes studying the developing world so interesting: it's part art, part science. So much of investing in these new emerging markets hinges on confidence, and this confidence needs to be based on information and sentiment. If this book has one purpose, it is to build the reader's confidence about the tremendous contribution the developing world can and will make to the global economy.

For centuries trade with exotic-sounding places like Casablanca, São Paulo, Djakarta, and Shanghai has conjured up images of caravans of Marco Polo–like explorers bartering trinkets in bazaars for spices, precious stones, and silk. As we head into the next century these once faraway and strange lands are moving closer and becoming more tightly entwined with the West than ever before. Technological innovations in transportation and communication have given birth to a truly global economy. Our romantic visions of bazaars should be replaced with more familiar images of noisy construction sites, smoggy traffic jams, and banks buzzing with telephones and blinking computer screens. The West has always maintained an ego-centric and distorted view of the world, starting with Mercator maps first drawn up in the sixteenth century in which the countries of the "North" are depicted as being twice as big as the "South." This book will show that the true stature and potential of these countries are just the opposite.

I have had a unique window onto the developing world. My family has manufactured and sold winter gloves for most of this century; through this business I have seen theoretical comparative advantage displayed in its simplest form. Making gloves has changed little in the last few decades. For gloves, twenty-odd pieces of material are assembled by hand at a sewing machine; it has gotten no simpler than that. The leather was cut, stretched, and sewn by hand at my family's company here in the U.S. for the first half of the twentieth century. However, by the 1950s these processes were being done by cheaper labor in Japan and Italy. That phase lasted until the 1960s, when my family moved some production to Puerto Rico (fueled by U.S. tax incentives) and later to the Philippines. The 1970s saw many Asian island countries offer reasonably priced production—South Korea and Taiwan being my family's choice sites. By the early 1980s mainland China began glove production, and it has been pretty dominant for the last ten years. But my father tells me that several of his largest competitors have been shifting some production to Bangladesh and Vietnam, and some adventurous types have been looking into former Soviet republics like Georgia and Kazakhstan.

The glove business has always been simple and small; however, it provided an interesting glimpse into what more complicated companies like Nike or IBM must consider when thinking about the future. These companies constantly address how to produce cheaper goods while maintaining quality standards. And while my family never really thought about selling overseas into the markets where they were manufacturing, Nike and IBM do; their production sites today become their new markets tomorrow. That process is perpetual.

It is the same for Wall Street. I have traded assets from more than fifty developing countries for the last decade. I have seen that the investment world is driven by windows of new opportunities opening and closing, the way manufacturing opportunities open and close.

Isolated financial opportunities occur from country to country—Mexico one year, Poland the next—and may individually be perceived as Wall Street fads. However, taken together they form a *trend*. And the trend toward globalization in finance, I believe, is irreversible. Wall Street channels money from savers to borrowers. For financiers, today's emerging market borrowers are tomorrow's savers. In that respect, the globalization of finance is also inevitable, the result of the world's increasingly trade-linked economies.

And technology is driving this globalization of finance and commerce. The rapid proliferation of information technology—computing and telecommunications—has torn down barriers of entry and has linked buyers and sellers like never before. The fact that five companies—Microsoft, Cisco, Intel, Lucent and Dell—comprise more than 10% of S&P 500 stock market capitalization trumpets where the future of business lies. Since access to information technology is much cheaper than previous milestone technologies such as electricity or railroads, one would expect the resulting new business applications to multiply, thus accelerating global integration of the marketplace.

I am hardly the first to see such large trends. Unfortunately, current debate about the global economy at the end of this century has become increasingly provincial. From one side, many First Worlders sense an end to their prosperity, and politicians are slaves to their constituents' fears. Free-trade agreements are being resisted by everyone from blue-collar workers to environmentalists. Third World politicians lash out at Wall Street for speculating in and ruining their financial markets. Countries caught in between point fingers in both directions. These myopic views are focused on the bark—not even the trees, and certainly not the whole forest. This is truly unfortunate, because in the developing world's emerging markets unprecedented opportunities for all are waiting to be seized.

Sophisticated multinational corporations and investment banks know this. That is why they are expanding globally as fast as possible. Ask Fortune 500 chief executive officers about future growth plans and they'll point you to the developing world. While many politicians can also see the economic future, their ability to promote it is constrained by their local constituencies. In the short run, economic globalization hurts, particularly those who have enjoyed advantages for a long time. But in the long run, to resist globalization will spell economic stagnation for everyone.

The benefits of world trade are astounding. One needs only to see how much better lives in the developing world have become in the last few decades. According to CARE, the percentage of developing world people living in poverty has halved since 1960. In all corners of the planet, many now have hope that their children's futures will be filled with promise, not endless squalor. While that alone may be enough reason to embrace globalist policies, our own self-interest should also lead us to engage these regions: they are the outlets for our capital and the buyers of our wares. That is how we in the First World will continue prospering.

RECENT CRISES AND BEYOND

The economic volatility experienced by the world since the hardcover edition of this book was completed in late 1997 confirms the inevitability of global integration and its associated costs and benefits. In this new global system, the pool of international private capital has far outstripped the amounts that government can muster, and technology whirls around such money faster than ever before, making the increasingly important financial markets even more volatile. The new system was put to the test early in August 1997, as the Asian economic crisis reverberated globally in the financial markets. While IMF aid packages seemed to be slowly patching up tattered nations like Thailand, three fairly large economies were still to be hit with unprecedented liquidity squeezes: South Korea in late 1997, Indonesia in early 1998, and Russia in August 1998—all of which rocked First World stock markets.

As in all crises, a little hindsight shows that problems had been brewing for some time and, indeed, the problems underscored just how globalized the world had become. In Asia, Japan (the second most powerful economy and key growth engine in the Pacific Rim for nearly fifty years) had been mired in a structural recession for most of the 1990s. Its inability to extricate itself from its malaise resulted in the yen weakening from below 80 yen to the U.S. dollar in early 1995 to more than 130 yen by the summer of 1997. Since many Asian economies had pegged their currencies largely to the U.S. dollar, the Japanese gained tremendous competitive ground on South Korea, Thailand, Indonesia, Malaysia, and the Philippines, among others. The weak yen policy signaled a traditional response to Japanese economic slowdowns—export the economy out of recession. However, Asia's problems were also exacerbated by China, a country which attracted over $150 billion in foreign direct investment to modernize its industrial infrastructure in the 1990s. Over the decade, many low-end labor intensive businesses—e.g., apparel, metalwork, and plastics—suddenly sprouted up on the Mainland to compete with Asian island economies. As a result, the global productivity paradigm was being silently jumbled, with Japan pressuring down from the high end of the marketplace, and China up from the low end. Many Pacific Rim countries became the casualties of this competitive sandwiching. Even today, nearly two years after the initial trouble signs in Asia, many economies in that part of the world are still mired in an economic identity crisis.

Russia (and those who had invested there) also fell victim to downside of globalization, no thanks to Russia's lagging domestic reform. As the world economy grew after the former Soviet Union disbanded in 1991, Russia benefited from stable commodity exports and a steady stream of foreign capital to assist its transition from state to market economy. When Asia's growth slowed and commodity prices collapsed, Russia—itself, suffering from a hard currency shortage—borrowed aggressively from international and domestic markets to close fiscal gaps while trying to maintain a stable, dollar-linked currency. To attract capital and prevent capital flight, local ruble interest rates hit 150%; after a while, the Russians had no choice but to go to the International Monetary Fund (IMF) for cheaper money, as the Indonesians, Koreans and Thais had done previously. The IMF quickly agreed to a $22 billion package, but when the Russians came back for more aid they were flatly refused. Many speculate that the First World could have mobilized a rescue effort, but that would have been unpopular domestically. In the U.S., President Bill Clinton was mired in the Lewinsky affair only weeks before the mid-term Congressional elections of 1998. Japan, with its widely publicized troubled economy and banking system, could offer no leadership. The logical spearhead would have been Germany, one of Russia's largest trading partners. But Helmut Kohl, trailing in his bid for presidential re-election and preparing Germany for the single currency, was also in no position to muster support. Foreign bailouts are never politically popular, and Russia—a country accused of poor tax collection, crony-ism, and Mafia rule—was certainly not high on the list of countries to be saved. Refused additional aid, the Russians committed what some consider financial suicide by defaulting on *domestic* debt, an unlikely political act considering the sovereign ability to print money and pay off such obligations.

The Asian and Russian crises, as well as the fallout that has blown southwestward to Brazil (following the increasingly familiar pattern of its predecessors almost like clockwork), illustrate the degree to which the global economy is already integrated. In response to Mex-ico's peso crisis in early 1995, the U.S. government quickly stepped in with a heroic rescue plan, notably protecting American financial and strategic investments in Mexico. Similarly, when Asia's unsustainable banking sectors began to leak and many Asian currencies came under attack, the Group of 7 (G7) immediately appreciated that the region represented billions in U.S., European, and Japanese exposure through factories, cross-border loans, and portfolio investment, and that the Pacific Rim economies in crisis represented a large component of global GDP. To allow the crisis to fester would have spelled trouble for the entire global economy. Russia's collapse, however, did not gener-ate the same enthusiasm, no doubt because the direct economic stakes for the G7 and Russia's contribution to the world economy were comparably small. In an attempt to halt the currency contagion's spread into Latin America—a vital trading partner for the U.S.—Washington quickly garnered support for Brazil in late 1998 through $40+ billion IMF package and several public support statements from the Clinton Administration.

These crises will certainly not be the last; on the contrary, they most likely will be the beginning of frequent economic and financial dislocations precipitated by an ever-globalizing and more competitive world system. The mixed results of these collective $200+ billion bailouts demonstrate that the world has not completely discovered the best formula for filling such economic potholes. So while the world indeed grows more prosperous, it has also become more volatile. The recent IMF led bailouts, while not the perfect solutions, still positively underscore the G7 countries' acknowledgment of how they are already, and practically inextricably, tied into the same global economy of many large developing countries. For any one component of this integrated economic machine to prosper, the machine itself, and each of its components, must be in good working order.

When I originally conceived of *From Third World to World Class*, it was intended to distill my professional trading experience for prospective investors, as well as to reflect many of the ideas discussed in my emerging markets investing class at Columbia University. As the writing progressed, however, it went beyond the often arcane complexities of Wall Street or the Academy and attempted to discuss issues relevant to a broader readership. This book tries to make sense out of today's frenetic currents: turbulent global politics, volatile economies and financial markets, and technologies that seem to change hourly. In the end, my conclusions are as uncomplicated as my family's gloves: vast economic and political changes are afoot, and everyone can benefit. The coming decades should provide the most enriching ride for more people than ever before in history. Get on board confidently, embrace the trends, and prosper.

P. M.
February 1999

Darkest Before Dawn?

EVER SINCE OSWALD Spengler penned *The Decline of the West* nearly one hundred years ago, many distinguished scholars and academics have made careers for themselves as harbingers of Western civilization's demise. Recent doomsayers cite the plundering of the earth's natural resources, the growing inequality between the wealthy and poor, the decay of moral fiber and family values—among others— as the causes of this impending meltdown. The newest focus of our supposed imminent collapse is developing countries: those rogue nations who steal our jobs with cheap labor, dump inferior goods in our markets, hollow out our industrial sectors with unfair trade practices, and subject our capital to assorted financial crises.

This is unfortunate, for the truth is that there now exists such a clear, unprecedented economic opportunity for the First World (once referred to as the "West" but which must now include such Asian powers as Japan) that to wallow in our supposed collective woes denies the future that we have laboriously created for ourselves over the last three centuries: a truly global economy and international capital market. We all can profit from embracing the economic forces that the doomsayers reject. Rather than accept the downward spiral of Western society, we should look instead to the economies of the developing countries that are being integrated into the First World's economies, and to the redistribution of economic and political power as we enter the third millennium. Instead of lamenting our purported decline, we should prepare ourselves to take advantage of the growth in Asia, Latin America, the former Soviet Union, and Africa.

THE ERA OF BAD FEELINGS

During the last thirty-odd years "Western decline" literature has proliferated not only in the United States but in most of the industrialized world. The pessimism has been economic: raging inflation in the late 1970s, factory closures and the impoverishment of farmers in the early 1980s, unemployment, growing urban poverty, and rising crime rates in the 1990s—these are but a few of the problems cited by American pessimists. In Europe, it is the overburdened welfare state, compounded by low economic growth rates, worsening unemployment, and the alleged erosion of national identities through further integration into the Common Market. In Germany, matters have been aggravated by the effects of having to absorb 17 million East Germans into the economy after unification; in England, the economic crisis was underscored by the pulverization of the pound under the fist of a single international investor; and in France, a 14% unemployment rate has led to a cultural dismay over *"l'horreur économique."* The economic pessimism is not limited to the West. Even Japan, the postwar miracle nation, its stock market at this writing trading at less than half its historic high, now suffers from a socioeconomic identity crisis as it struggles to regain its financial luster. South Korea, too, experiencing its worst financial crisis in thirty years, laments a future amid greater competition from less-developed neighbors, such as China and Vietnam.

In recent years, scores of books have espoused economic pessimism, warning us that the era of great prosperity is over; the West is losing its competitiveness; our governments operate with intolerably high deficits; we fail to save enough; economic inequality is growing; we are losing our industries to Third World nations. This list goes on.*

---

* Such doomsayers, among others, and their works include Ravi Batra (*The Great Depression of 1990*, written in 1987), Paul Ehrlich (*The End of Affluence*, 1995), Robert Frank and Philip Cook (*Winner-Take-All Society*, 1995), William Greider

This anxiety is understandable; there is an unsettling of the First World's economies as we prepare to leap into the next century. But these facts remain clear: inflation is historically low, our collective stock markets are strong, economic growth has been fairly consistent, living standards throughout the world are at their highest at any point in history, and more people live under economic and political freedom than ever before.

But the pessimism has also become political and social. Paul Kennedy's *Rise and Fall of the Great Powers* (1987) outlined America's grim fate in a historical context of overstretched imperialism. Others have announced the twilight of democracy, the end of affluence, and increased racial strife—all of which are rooted in the notion that we are in economic decline. Our so-called deterioration has led to the rise of nationalistic movements and pundits in America, such as Pat Buchanan, David Duke, Pierre Rinfret, and the Institute for Historical Review in California, as well as abroad: Jean-Marie Le Pen and the National Front in France, the National Front in Britain, neofascists in Italy, skinheads in Germany, Georg Haider in Austria.

The pessimism has also been cultural, with many commentators expressing dismay at the effects of advanced capitalism, what Jerry Mander describes in *The Case Against the Global Economy* (1996) as the "global homogenization of culture, lifestyle, and levels of techno-logical immersion, with the corresponding deterioration of local tradi-tions and economies. Soon, every place will look and feel like every place else, with the same restaurants and hotels, the same clothes, the same malls and superstores, and the same streets crowded with cars"— what author Benjamin Barber has categorized as "McWorld." Similar critics in France bemoan developments such as EuroDisney as a com-mercial terrorist attack on the culture of Voltaire.

(*Who Will Tell the People,* 1993; *One World, Ready or Not,* 1996), Christopher Lasch (*The Age of Narcissism,* 1979), Edward Luttwak (*The Endangered American Dream,* 1994), Kevin Phillips (*Arrogant Capital,* 1995; *Boiling Point,* 1993), Lester Thurow (*The Zero Sum Society,* 1980), Cornell West (*Race Matters,* 1993), and Bill Wolman (*The Judas Economy,* 1997). Taken to the extreme, the list might even include the infamous Unabomber manifesto, the ultimate pessimistic outpouring on technology and society.

In general, these sentiments seem to reflect what author and social critic Thomas Byrne Edsall has called the "Era of Bad Feelings." While the observations of social dislocation seem somewhat accurate, they are only a part of the larger picture and, therefore, fail to lead to accurate future forecasting. But the earth continues to turn; as the sun sets for someone, it rises for someone else. I have seen such pessimism before. In my experience on Wall Street, it has always been darkest before dawn; that is, markets are typically poised for upturns just after they have oversold. Thus, a few simple words of investment advice to the pessimists: *cover your shorts* and *go long.*

While it is fair to say that some of the pessimists' observations are correct, taken as an aggregate, they are incomplete. Arthur Herman has written in *The Idea of Decline in Western History* (1996) that "pessimism and optimism are attitudes the scholar brings to his analysis of events, not conclusions that arise from that analysis." What is certainly true is that all of us, the pessimists as well as the apparently less prolific optimists, have been experiencing change on a scale never before experienced in a single generation. Whereas population has always grown, it has never grown at the rate witnessed in the last two generations. Whereas technological change has always worked to unemploy those in backward industries, technological changes have never taken place at the rate and on the scale we are seeing today. The Agricultural Revolution that changed the nature of land use over the span of the seventeenth and eighteenth centuries could more accurately be termed an evolution. The Industrial Revolution's impact was more concentrated, bringing rapid urbanization and centralized production, and eliminating many cottage industries, all *in a single generation.* The Information Revolution, in turn, is producing innovations that profoundly impact our lives *every year.*

Today it is no longer possible for a country to insulate itself from the rest of the world. Economic developments, technological developments, and even ideological developments—both good and bad—have a *global* impact. The technology-capital-labor dynamic that changed England—first in the form of the Agricultural Revolution—and then altered all of Europe and crossed the Atlantic to stimulate technological innovations such as Eli Whitney's cotton gin (during the Industrial Revolution) today transforms the whole world by connecting the world's computer users (the Information Revolution). Change can no longer be contained. And because the effects of events ripple across the world, to confine one's observations, as the pessimists generally do, to a single country or even a single region, let alone a single segment of a society, is to depict fragments of reality and underestimate the opportunity before us.

The pessimists' inadequate picture also leaves out the dramatic improvements to human life already achieved, not only in the industrialized countries but also in those countries thought to be backward. These improvements can be measured by increased rates of literacy, daily caloric intake, and life expectancy, and decreased rates of infant mortality, for instance. Pessimists fail to recognize that what is perceived as the decline of the industrialized world is merely the narrowing of the gap between it and the erstwhile laggards, and that further integration, not inward-looking protectionism (whether economic or cultural), is what will in fact *prevent* the decline they fear.

Most multinational corporations are already capitalizing on the benefits of this economic integration. While they have always had global operations, their presence abroad has increased exponentially in recent years. Their profits from global operations are at unprecedented levels and often outstrip their profits from domestic business. Cheaper labor elsewhere has shifted production and assembly away from the multinationals' home countries, and trade arrangements and organizations such as NAFTA, GATT, and WTO have only intensified this trend. McDonald's has always had restaurants abroad, but the startling rate of its expansion (with a plan to open 1,200 to 1,500 new restaurants each year, two-thirds of which will be outside the U.S.) is mind-boggling to today's cautious and critical observers. Whereas these kinds of changes have been occurring, in some form, for the last three centuries, they never happened quickly, and the depth of their impact often went unnoticed and was taken for granted. The *accelerated pace of change* is what disturbs the pessimists, because *they can see it happening.* Their fear puts blinders on their perception of the world around them and leads them to warn us of the threats to traditional ways of life, to existing global positions of power, to cultural identities to which we have all grown accustomed. Their discomfort arises from challenges to the comfort of the familiar.

Economics is no longer, if it ever was, a zero-sum game. Although the almost unqualified economic dominance of the "West" is apparently being challenged, this does not imply the West's decline. Growth in the economies of Asia, Latin America, the Middle East, Africa, and the former Soviet Union does not signal the erosion of Western living standards because jobs are being lost to cheaper labor markets. In the late nineteenth century, 90% of Americans were farmers, yet as transportation improved and trade opened up, leading to increased importation of cheaper agricultural goods, the number of farmers decreased; today only 3% remain. However, at no point was there mass unemployment; rather, industrialization was the next wave, and factories quickly absorbed a newly urbanized labor force, resulting in a huge increase in living standards. Today, we are seeing a similar phenomenon, only it is industrial jobs that are being challenged, and the industrialized countries' new comparative advantage—largely rooted in technology and capital—has to be tapped. And there is evidence that advanced capitalist countries may also have an infrastructural advantage to prosper in the rapidly changing world. Just visit Silicon Valley, the center of global innovation and the seat of America's comparative advantage. The developing world may be prospering from high growth rates, but it is the First World that still possesses "the wealth of notions"—the true essence of innovation, capital accumulation, and economic expansion.

Unprecedented technological innovation is clearly behind this latest wave of change. To ride it, the industrialized countries will have to continue to be innovators and boost productivity. As *The Economist* notes: "the new jobs in tomorrow's industries, in manufacturing and services alike, will call for more than button-pressing automatons. They will require workers that are literate, numerate, adaptable, and trainable—in a word, 'educated.' " Rather than follow the pessimists' prescription of protectionism, factory workers will have to invest in acquiring computer skills in anticipation of the day when their jobs in Detroit will migrate to Guadalajara, at which point they will be able to migrate to Silicon Valley (or to any of the multiple technology clusters that have sprouted around the country in the last decade). As American factory workers move to California, their Mexican colleagues will be moving into Guadalajara from the surrounding countryside to take up jobs at the Ford assembly plant. As they move to factory jobs, their salaries will increase until one day they too will be able to own a Ford. At this point, Ford will have contributed to the growth of a new consumer market, increasing its sales, and allowing Ford to increase its investment into research and development, currently being carried out by former American factory workers. Meanwhile, Ford's stock prices will reflect greater global sales and increased investment in R&D, so its shareholders will be receiving heftier dividends. For over two hundred years capitalism has thrived like this on differentiated national economies based on comparative advantage. As simplistic as this "virtuous circle" of capital and technological accumulation appears, it provides a glimpse into the benefits of embracing, rather than rejecting, the latest wave of economic integration.

PREPARING FOR THE BEST, NOT THE WORST

Despite the anxieties in the industrialized world, technological progress marches on. The late twentieth century has bequeathed products and processes that are dramatically altering the way people work, consume, and live. The most visible advances have been in the information sector. Silicon Valley and the Internet have become the symbols of this new engine's potential. Progress comes in the form of pure information technologies, such as microprocessors, that allow machines to process millions of instructions per second. And in the telecommunications sector, advances in cable and wireless technologies allow for greater flows of information than ever before. These innovations are affecting business just as electricity and railroads did in previous generations. Each day advances are being made in medicine and agriculture that dramatically improve the quality and duration of life. The advent of preventative medicines and vaccines, the product of research in biotechnology, allows us to fortify our health. Agrotechnology allows us to maximize our natural resources, enhancing and expanding food production. Together, these technologies create a world in which people can live longer, healthier lives and have more opportunities to improve their quality of life.

Few countries will be left untouched by these advances, and the world economy is rapidly integrating and being integrated by these technologies. The industrialized world, particularly the United States, is blazing the new economic trail—with Wall Street helping to finance the new industrial infrastructure. Change typically yields opportunities, and rather than lamenting the passing of old business and industrial paradigms, many industrial and less industrialized nations are maximizing their comparative advantage to align with these monumental shifts. This is the dynamic we will examine.

THE TERRITORY AHEAD

In many respects, the developing world is unknown economic and financial territory. This book is designed to help act as a compass in such frontier lands. Chapters 1, 2, and 3 describe how technology has impacted economic development and capital accumulation. What we have witnessed over time is that the West's early lead and technological push forward has created opportunities, and will continue to do so in the future. Technological innovation has always been the engine of the global economy, and there are indications that recent breakthroughs in information technology are poised to fuel unprecedented growth in the world. In addition, we will see how these technological changes help integrate different economies and produce welcome benefits for all participating. Moreover, coupled with technological changes, ideological shifts in the Third World allow more countries to seize opportunities in the new economic order. We have seen the abandonment of socialist and state-planned economies throughout the developing world, some inevitable and some coincidental. China and the former Soviet Union represent the most visible of these ideological flip-flops, but there are other less publicized but equally important developments in parts of Africa, the Middle East, and Latin America. Even successful Asian countries are being forced to adopt more free market reforms in the wake of recent financial crises and reexamine traditionally opaque business practices. These ideological shifts help accelerate the developing world's economic integration with advanced capitalist nations, moves that make them competitive within the global economy.

Next, Chapters 4, 5, and 6 focus specifically on the net benefits of these changes and how they accumulate. First World multinational corporations are indeed seizing economic opportunities in developing countries in the never-ending quest to lower production costs to boost margins and to increase sales in home markets. But more important, in the long run they will sell more products in *new* marketplaces that are not as saturated as those in the advanced societies. Moreover, First World investors are reaping rewards in the growing financial markets of these integrated developing countries, with the savviest ones profiting from both booms and busts that characterize emerging markets. Capital from these investments, coupled with growing domestic financial markets, are helping to fuel the inevitable expansion of these developing regions, and the benefits accrue to *all* participating.

Finally, in Chapter 7 the global socioeconomic landscape of the future is examined. New winners, along with new losers, will be evident. Some peoples and nations will stagnate or fall behind, the way some languished and lagged after the Agricultural and Industrial Revolutions. Dominant technology shifts also will make some First World workers obsolete or expensive relative to workers in the developing world. Increasingly, the First World workers must go "upscale" to remain active and competitive. Some advanced countries, such as the United States, understand this shift and are adapting well in terms of productivity and innovation, while others (Japan and some European countries) suffer under culturally induced structural labor problems (including rigid unions, sticky wages, burdensome regulations et al.) that will make the transition more difficult. Education, therefore, will become increasingly important in maintaining an innovative edge, and, again, not all advanced nations will thrive in this new environment.

Nor will all developing countries advance equally or quickly in the future. Many old success stories may stall and/or face huge setbacks in their growth paths, as we have recently seen in Northern and Southeast Asia. The financial crises that erupted in these historically high growth regions remind us that the world constantly changes and that countries at every economic strata are subject to the new order of globalized capital and competition. As comparative advantages are exploited, the gaps between many middle-income and lower-income nations will most likely grow. This differentiation is inevitable and, according to many theorists, will actually aid development in the long run by allowing regional trade to flourish, encouraging newly advanced countries to invest in less developed neighbors.

While global economic integration is inevitable, its greatest obstacle is *protectionism*. Traditionally, when a country's way of life is threatened economically (and hence politically and culturally), protectionist measures are enacted, as was the case in Latin America in the 1970s. Immigration issues become more politically charged as well, and cultural backlashes may ensue: First Worlders may feel uneasy about giving up old ways of life, while newly industrialized nations may see globalistic (neé Western) influences as modern forms of colonialism.

Given all these developments, tomorrow's world may not be an extension of our Western-dominated past. The twenty-first century will be populated by many strong industrialized economies not based in the Western Hemisphere. While the world may indeed grow wealthier, it may not necessarily grow more "Western." For example, the trends in modernization and capitalism do not certainly imply the spread of liberal democratization (at least in the American and European sense), as we have learned from certain Asian nations such as Singapore. We should prepare for a world in which our values may not be dominant or universal. For the last few hundred years, Western culture has shaped and dominated not only global economics, but politics as well. As the economic might of the developing world increases, Western concerns for human rights and other freedoms are often taking a back seat to economic opportunities. This is particularly clear in China, which currently has greater hard currency reserves than England or Germany, and whose new market orientation should propel its economy past that of Western Europe within two decades. What makes China so interesting is that it has a modernizing economy alongside a rich, non-Western cultural heritage predating ancient Greece, and distinct from the West's. The resulting cultural—or what Samuel P. Huntington has called "civilizational"—clash (based on, among other things, incomparable interpretations of human and civil rights) may be the basis for global political conflict in the twenty-first century. Preparation for this conflict should be the dominant theme of the current debate about our future, not the pessimistic outpourings that line our bookstore shelves.

Make no mistake: those who ignore these historic trends will be left behind like a horse and buggy hopelessly trailing a sports car. Yes, the industrialized world is restructuring itself in dramatic fashion, but that alone should lead us to be optimistic. Change is taking place. The resulting social, cultural, and economic anxieties are the result, I believe, of *too many* opportunities, not too few. We are now confronted with critical decisions daily about the basics of life—where to live, what job to choose, which school to select for our children—all in a rapidly changing environment. It can only get more complicated, and isolating ourselves or longing for the past seems fruitless if not foolish. After all, there are billions of people in the developing world who are becoming economically enfranchised as never before in history. To maintain high living standards, as well as to increase them for generations to come, the earth's advanced societies must capitalize on these burgeoning new markets, remain technologically superior, enhance their financial savvy, and embrace the competitive world of the twenty-first century.

As the World Turns: Evolutions and Revolutions Affecting the Global Economy

As WE PREPARE to enter the third millennium, at a time when West-erners daily see headlines proclaiming chaos, disorder, and global turmoil, we tend to ignore the news that our species is blessed by technological miracles that alter life for the better every day. Living standards—measured not only by Net Disposable Income or Gross Domestic Product per capita, but by life expectancy, daily caloric intake, infant mortality, and literacy rates—have improved to levels unprecedented in history. The West has for centuries been the leader in these statistics, and the gap between it and most of the developing world has historically been enormous.[1] That is because, by and large, most of the planet has not even begun to participate in the quality modernization that has characterized the West's history over the last three hundred years, let alone become integrated with the (Western-dominated) global economy.

But dynamic geopolitics are redrawing the global economic map. The world our children will inherit most likely will *not* revolve around North America and its Western European counterparts, but rather around the currently developing nations of Africa, Asia, Latin America, and the former Soviet Union. And for good reason.

TABLE 1.1
A CHANGED AND CHANGING WORLD, 1950–2050

Economic Indicators	1950	2000 (est.)	2050 (est.)
Population of developing world	1.2 billion	4.8 billion	9.5 billion
% of total world population	55%	85%	90%
World GDP %	5%	25%	50%
Stock market capitalization	less than $100 million	$2.5 trillion	$250+ trillion
% of global stock market capitalization	less than 1%	15%	40+%

SOURCES: Economist Intelligence Unit; World Bank; United Nations; author's estimates

TABLE 1.2
QUALITY OF LIFE INDICATORS

	Developing World 1950	Developing World 2000 (est.)	Developing World 2050 (est.)	First World 1950	First World 2000 (est.)	First World 2050 (est.)
Life expectancy	43	63	76	65	77	82
Daily caloric intake	1215	2000	2400	2200	2800	2900
Infant mortality (per 1,000)	140	63	12	30	8	4
Literacy rate %	33	64	90	95	98	99

SOURCES: Economist Intelligence Unit; World Bank; United Nations; author's estimates

At this writing, developing countries comprise approximately 85% of the world's population, 77% of the earth's land mass, and 63% of global commodity production, but their economies constitute less than 22% of world income and only 12% of global stock market capitalization. Yet, institutional investors from the First World have only invested less than 2% of their assets in these nations. But these numbers have dramatically changed since 1950, as indicated in Tables 1.1 and 1.2, and will continue to change over the coming decades.

SHIFTS IN MOMENTUM

As Tables 1.1 and 1.2 indicate, there has been a huge shift in human progress over the last fifty-odd years, and the developing world's slice of the global pie grows daily. It is these countries that now have and will maintain greater economic momentum than Organization for Economic Cooperation and Development (OECD) nations. In fact, the World Bank notes that developing economies are growing at more than 6% per annum, more than double the 2.5% projected growth rate for the First World. There are many reasons for this difference in economic momentum, including long-term trends in labor and technology, demographic shifts, and political reorientations. But a simpler and more intuitive perspective is this: Third World countries with average per capita Gross Domestic Product of $1,000 to $2,000 grow at 6% more easily than a $30,000 GDP country grows at 2.5% because of diminishing returns in the West. Diminishing returns are the result of what Lenin called "overripe capitalism," whereby rich countries saturate their own markets and become victims of their own success.[2] To maintain living standards, rich countries seek to exploit lower production costs outside their home borders, as well as to sell goods to underserved and undersupplied consumers in less developed nations.

Historically, one dominant global economy has been the forerunner of another. The British Empire begat America in the twentieth century, as the Dutch economy begat the British two centuries earlier, and the Spanish begat the Dutch a century before that. We have already witnessed the modern Japanese economy spring from its rela-

FIGURE 1.1
REAL GLOBAL GDP GROWTH RATE
1990–1996

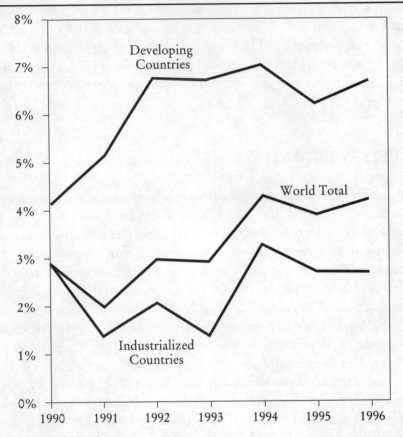

SOURCE: World Bank

tionship with America, and we are beginning to see the emergence of new powers on the horizon. Now we have the second and third generations of cross-pollination: in Asia, Japan has emerged a full-fledged economic power and is now itself a progenitor. What used to be the arithmetic addition of single economic influences has now become a multiplicative process that promises to integrate the economies of most of the planet. The exploitation of free market principles first postulated by Adam Smith, based on notions of comparative advantage as defined by David Ricardo, is fueling tremendous global

FIGURE 1.1
WORLD GROWTH FORECASTS
1997–2005*

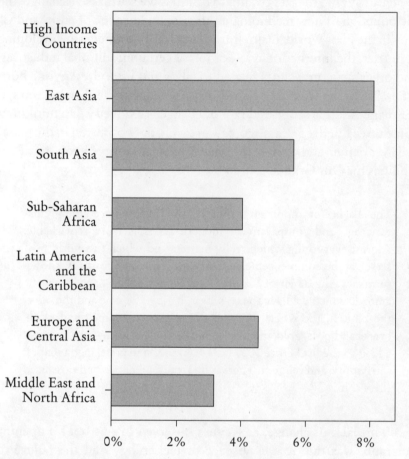

* The forecast for total World Growth for this period is 3.5%.
SOURCE: World Bank

economic integration and is spawning new economies. Indeed, it is estimated that world trade will grow from $308 billion in 1950 to an estimated $4 trillion by the end of the millennium.[3] In the last ten years, annual foreign direct investment from the First to the Third World has swelled from $11.3 billion to more than $90 billion, and aggregate annual capital flows to the developing countries now total some $350 billion, compared to less than $100 billion in 1985.[4]

NEW PARADIGM FOR THE NEW WORLD

When analyzing the late twentieth century, we see massive change: the introduction of new technologies, the rise and decline of entire industries in the First World, major infrastructural investments in developing countries, the international relocation of certain traditional industries, and other structural shifts related to labor and lifestyle. Anyone born after 1900 in the West has become accustomed to these changes, though for mankind, this scope and rate of change is a novelty. Up until only some three hundred years ago, few great changes occurred in the material lives of men and women. Keynes noted in his essay "Economic Possibilities for Our Grandchildren":

> The absence of important technical inventions between the prehistoric age and comparatively modern times is truly remarkable. Almost everything which really matters and which the world possessed at the commencement of the modern age was already known to man at the dawn of history. Language, fire, the same domestic animals which we have today, wheat, barley, the vine and the olive, the plough, the wheel, the oar, the sail, leather, linen and cloth, bricks and pots, gold and silver, copper, tin and lead—and iron was added to the list before 1000 BC—banking, statecraft, mathematics, astronomy, and religion. There is no record when we first possessed these things.[5]

This lack of change, as Keynes observed in this book's opening epigraph, was due to the absence of technology and the failure to accumulate capital. Most preindustrial societies were economically rigid, if not zero-sum games. According to most historical records, there was little economic growth anywhere on earth until the late Middle Ages. Subsistence agrarian life allowed few to accumulate wealth and prosper. In fact, crude estimates by *The Economist* suggest that for thirteen hundred years, until 1800, Western European GDP rose by only 0.1% to 0.2% per year. At that pace, living standards barely changed in one's lifetime, with real incomes taking some five hundred years to double.[6]

FIGURE 1.2

ECONOMIC PROGRESS THROUGHOUT HISTORY:
REAL GDP PER PERSON IN OECD COUNTRIES

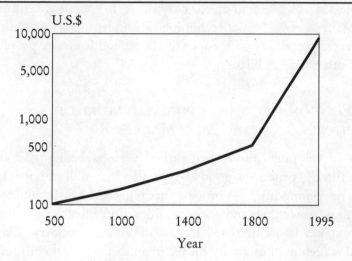

SOURCE: Economist Intelligence Unit

As a result, in most preindustrial civilizations sparse economic growth limited social mobility, because someone's increased wealth was generally achieved at someone else's expense. This may have been the source of the frequent wars and battles for much of recorded history; without industrialization and the subsequent advent of a competitive, mercantilist society, theft, conquest, and inheritance were virtually the only ways to become richer. In preindustrial societies, the notion of wealth was that it *existed.* Our more experienced view is that wealth is *created.* This notion has had a profound sociocultural impact on life.

Most preindustrialized civilizations (circa 1700 and earlier) reflected the former perspective, and it may be that many economic and social strata developed along these lines. Until approximately three hundred and fifty years ago in the West (and for billions of people still today), virtually everyone lived for per diem subsistence—working daily in order to feed, clothe, and shelter themselves. Flatly stated, in the last ²⁄₁₀₀ths of 1% of mankind's existence, a small percentage of our species has been able to contemplate and achieve a better, longer existence within their lifetime. Undeniably, it has been the marriage of technology and capital that has led to the raising of human living standards to their highest levels ever. In this respect, the West has been first blessed. As we stand on the cusp of the twenty-first century, it is the potent combination of technological and financial power that has accelerated our ability to enhance life faster and for more people than at any other time in history.

THE ECONOMICALLY INTEGRATIVE NATURE OF TECHNOLOGY, CAPITAL, AND MARKETS

When a developing country first enters the global economy, it exports competitively produced goods—typically low-skill, labor-intensive goods or commodities—a process that reflects the differentiated cost structures of wealthier and poorer nations. Trade develops, and capital from exports is accumulated by the developing country. This new capital is then used to satisfy local demand and expand consumption, resulting in the importation of consumer goods—foodstuffs, beverages, health products, etc.—from advanced countries.

Eventually, domestic production of the consumer goods previously imported begins in the developing country, using the expanded local consumer market as an outlet. The developing country is no longer importing consumer goods, since it now produces them domestically, but rather capital goods that it does not produce.* In turn, it begins to export the consumer goods it once imported but now produces to less developed countries. This pattern is repeated with capital goods, through high tech, ad infinitum. Such is the technological chain of economic integration through comparative advantage and trade.[7]

The big shift we witnessed in the Industrial Age was that economic production became *destined for markets, not personal consumption*. Industrialization, in principle, means the standardization of

---

* Capital goods are goods that produce other goods, such as textile looms.

Comparative Advantage: The Religion of Economics Key Commandment

When economists or businesspeople discuss Adam Smith or David Ricardo, it is with a reverence that is normally reserved for deities. Among capitalists, there is no debate about the importance of their theories—they are believed in with an undying faith akin to the veneration of the Old and New Testaments, the Koran, or the Bhagavadgita. Among the economic Ten Commandments, one of the most important—if not *the* most important—is comparative advantage.

Comparative advantage states that all people should produce goods or services in which they have either an absolute or a relative advantage. For example, let's assume a lawyer can bill time at $100 per hour. This talented lawyer can also type 100 words a minute. If the lawyer spends 20 hours a week typing, some $2,000 in legal billings might be forgone because of the time he spends typing. However, the lawyer can maximize his comparative advantage by hiring a typist who can type 80 words a minute and paying $15 dollars an hour for that service. While the typist takes 25 hours to do the same typing the lawyer would do in 20, it still makes economic sense for the lawyer to hire the typist. For the typing, the lawyer pays 25 × $15, or $375 per week. However, the lawyer is now free to bill $2,000 in hours that were previously spent typing, resulting in a potential $1,625 profit. The lawyer needs to bill only four extra hours a week to cover his typist's cost. So while the lawyer is actually the better typist, the economic utility of practicing law is more valuable. It is a win-win situation for both parties.

The same goes for countries. While the U.S. may be the best producer of low-skill products (like stuffed animals or gloves), in the long run it pays for the U.S. to produce high-skill products (like aircraft or biotechnology) and let other countries produce the low-skill goods. In making this choice, the U.S. can earn the most money producing what it can produce best, while simultaneously making room in the global production paradigm for developing countries to produce and profit from the goods that they are skilled in making. Thus we have a win-win situation, as in the lawyer/typist example.

This is why technological innovation is so important in a global economy. As new technologies are introduced, comparative advantage in the world is effectively altered, creating opportunities for some countries and anxieties for others. Given the speed at which today's technologies are changing, countries must continually upgrade their productivity to remain competitive.

products and specialization of labor to produce them, not for the producer's consumption but for the market itself. What happened in the late eighteenth and early nineteenth centuries provoked and promoted a large complex of economic, social, political, and cultural changes, which have in turn influenced the rate and course of technological development.[8] As certain countries evolved from subsistence agriculture to production for *other people's consumption*, there was a greater reliance on the market to function as the arena for economic exchange. And while there have been documented markets for the last four thousand years, the use of the market was subordinate to the social or religio-cultural goals of those old agrarian societies.[9] Industrialization changed this forever by adopting money—capital—as the market's medium of exchange.

With the multiple advances in technology in the seventeenth century came new forms of industrial organization and capital to invest in these new labor-saving technologies. The Industrial Revolution changed the face of labor and economics in the West forever, and this industrialist, capitalist framework is being overlaid on the world's remaining agrarian societies today. The power of technology to integrate economies is at least as important as the individual advances it produces. The mass marketing of technology and its applications, along with the profits from its sale, drives greater technological advances. It is technology that turns the once exotic and dear into a cheap household item. Historian David Landes noted that "it took the Industrial Revolution to make tea and coffee, the banana of Central America, and the pineapple of Hawaii everyday foods."[10] Over time, different technologies have dramatically altered the global production paradigm, creating new opportunities for production, consumption, and profit. In doing so, economies have become more integrated.

MARKETS RULE, NOT KINGS

Many countries around the globe have been drawn into the money system in the post–World War II period, including India, China, and, in the last decade, the former Soviet Union. The market now largely dictates social and political goals. Commercial values over the last two centuries have become central to all societies; economic growth is the primary goal of governments, whether fully capitalist, socialist, or somewhere in between.[11] The market—that self-empowering, self-reinforcing, and sometimes self-crippling institution—has encouraged and will continue to promote greater expansion overseas, greater efficiencies, and greater productivity. Again it is technology that has set this self-perpetuating process in motion. As Alvin Toffler notes, "the obsessive concern with money, goods, or capitalism is a reflection not of capitalism or socialism, but of industrialism. It is a reflection of the central role of the marketplace in *all* societies in which production is divorced from consumption, in which everyone is dependent on the marketplace rather than his or her own productive skills for the necessities in life."[12] When people wake up every day, they go to work to produce goods for *others* in exchange for paper money, the medium of exchange, *not* for their immediate personal benefit. The accumulation of capital becomes the paramount concern, and investment and innovation its favorite engines of growth. With the introduction of technology into the economic equation, the whole nature of risk and investment is altered. Prior to the Industrial Revolution, almost all the costs of manufacturing depended on two variables—raw materials and labor; technology meant that the variables of plant, property, and equipment became equally essential in calculating investments. The skillful use of capital is now just as important to profit margins as producing and selling goods, making the management of a business far more complex than in the past.

After the Industrial Revolution, farming was condemned to die a slow death in England and the West. Whereas 95% of the English population were farmers in the late 1700s, by 1912 the number had declined to 12%.[13] As the runner behind Britain in the seventeenth and eighteenth centuries, the U.S. was 80% agrarian by the late 1890s;

today only 2.8% of the population works in agriculture, not only for U.S. consumption, but also for export. And indeed the U.S. also imports food produced by other countries. This process in the last five decades has also begun to erode the West's manufacturing base, relocating some of it to developing countries, such as Mexico, while generating a rise in domestic service-sector jobs—recent evidence of how technological change alters comparative advantage.

WAVE THEORIES AND GENIUS TECHNOLOGIES

Many economists have seen recent history as a series of cycles that interweave technology, surplus capital, and markets; Karl Marx and Nobelist Joseph Schumpeter have made some of the most important contributions to the subject. One of the more interesting theorists who postulated that the *economic* and *financial markets* determine who produces and who consumes technology is a little-known Russian economist named Nikolai Kondratieff, born in 1892. In a series of papers written in the 1920s, Kondratieff developed a long wave theory of economic growth that was quite controversial in post-czarist Russia and led to his forced exile to Siberia, where he died at age forty-six. It took decades for his works to be published in English, but his thoughts have greatly affected many scholars and economists who have theorized on both long-term and short-term patterns of economic growth and development, including Simon Kuznets, Paul Samuelson, Gerhard Mensch, and Walt Rostow. In fact, Kondratieff has inspired the Systems Dynamic Group at the Sloan School of the Massachusetts Institute of Technology to study long economic cycles.[14]

Kondratieff's theory, in its most basic form, states that the development of modern civilization since the Industrial Revolution has been based on "long economic cycles" of roughly fifty years in duration. Provoked by the introduction of new technologies, each cycle consists of a period of economic development and progress lasting approximately twenty-five years followed by approximately twenty-five years of economic decline, and each cycle exhibits identifiable common characteristics.

FIGURE 1.3

THE CHANGING FACE OF FIRST WORLD LABOR

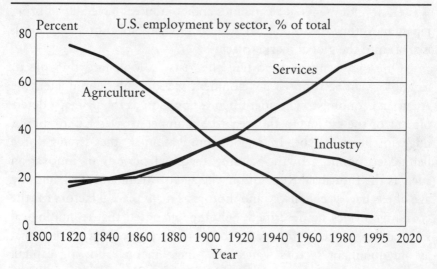

SOURCES: OECD; U.S. Department of Commerce, as cited in, *The Economist*, 28 September 1996, p. 7.

Each new long cycle begins with the development of a new technology—what I call "Genius Technology"—that radically alters the cost and speed of producing goods and getting them to market. Each cycle is also characterized by the integration of new countries and regions into the global production paradigm and economic system to exploit shifts in comparative advantage and provide new markets into which to sell Genius Technologies. For example, the Industrial Revolution, fueled by the development of steam power, led to new and more efficient forms of production, particularly in the textile industry. These developments led to the emergence of Britain as the leader in the global economy. Similarly, the expansion of the railroads in the United States in the mid-nineteenth century and the development of efficient transcontinental and international transportation, including shipping (and airplanes later in the twentieth century), helped integrate the U.S. as a leader into the global economy. The early twentieth century witnessed the development of electricity and automobiles, which facilitated the integration of Australia, Canada, and South Africa into the global economy, former colonies that became adept traders after generations of producing solely for their mother country. Since World War II, developments in electronics and computers have helped bring Japan and other Asian countries (e.g., Taiwan, Singapore, and South Korea) into the global marketplace.

One of the more important theorists to look into the role of technology in relation to development was Joseph Schumpeter, the Austrian economist, who identified innovation as the primary determinant of the cycles. In this regard Schumpeter owes Kondratieff a huge intellectual debt. In tagging innovation as the driving force behind economic growth, Schumpeter cited periods of innovation such as the Industrial Revolution, the age of steam and steel, and the age of electricity, chemistry and motors as major causal factors for the economic cycles he described. Schumpeter noted that technological innovations generally follow a process of "creative destruction," that as old dominant sectors wane, new ones emerge, allowing capital, ideas, and people to be reallocated both nationally and, now, internationally. Today's Genius Technologies—largely in the information and telecommunications sectors—dramatically accelerate this process because they are applicable to so many processes in so many sectors, creating more opportunities for industrialized countries to build new industries (and thus accumulate more capital), while allowing older technologies to be exploited by developing countries (which also accumulate capital in the process).

What is compelling about these cycle theories is the basic hypothesis that political, social, economic, and financial developments are inextricably linked. This helps to explain both the state of the world today and the state from which it has evolved. As technologies saturate markets, there is a consequent business decline. The inherent lack of investment opportunities during the decline leads to increased savings (accumulation of capital), which in turn will finance the development of new technologies, during the next upward phase.

In addition to the economic and financial indicators just noted, social indicators are essential to the qualitative analysis of long cycles. Such transition periods, as many have argued, are characterized by increased incidences of conflict among nations and social upheaval— much like our world today. As Toffler hyperbolically notes:

FIGURE 1.4
CYCLES OF GENIUS TECHNOLOGY

♦ Most historic economic upturns have been characterized by
  • New Genius Technologies
  • New Markets
♦ The next cycle will be no different

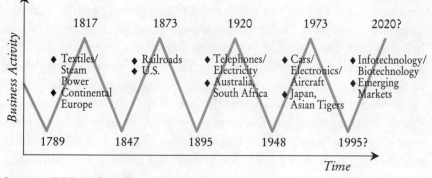

SOURCE: ING-Barings

> When a society is struck by two or more giant waves of change, and none is yet clearly dominant, the image of the future is fractured. It becomes extremely difficult to sort out the meaning of the changes and conflicts that arise. The collision of wave fronts creates a raging ocean, full of clashing currents, eddies, and maelstroms which conceal the more important historic tides.[15]

It should be noted that the actual time of the beginning or end of long cycles is exceedingly difficult to pin down. Indeed, Kondratieff, Kuznets, and other cycle theorists don't really use the long cycle theory as a predictive model, but rather as empirical evidence that such long cycles actually exist.[16] Exactly when a cycle begins is not important. What is important is to recognize that such cycles exist and to understand how they work. One needs only to look at the rapid advances in information technology, embodied in Intel and Microsoft, or the strides in biotechnology (such as the recent cloning of sheep) to know that the world has witnessed historic breakthrough innovations in recent years. Indeed, there seems to be strong evidence that the world is involved in a technological upswing and that developing countries are being absorbed into the world economy as we speak.

THE DEVELOPING WORLD: THE NEXT BLESSED

It is interesting to note how Third World countries were written off a generation ago. During the 1960s and 1970s, a global pessimism arose, based on a neo-Malthusian concern over population growth. Many believed that uncontrolled population expansion, especially in what were considered less developed countries, would lead to the depletion of food and natural resources. In fact, the enormous population increase in developing countries in the late twentieth century is akin to that in the eighteenth and nineteenth centuries, when industrialization swept over Europe and the United States. There is overwhelming evidence not only that population growth has actually contributed to further economic progress in the developing world, but also, according to the Danish economist Ester Boserup, that it may even be a causal element in its current expansion. She notes that a certain high population density actually facilitates market development and makes markets more efficient, as has been witnessed in the West as well as in Japan, Singapore, and Hong Kong.[17] In addition, the earth's food supply is far more abundant than ever before, despite being produced on less land. As Figure 1.5 and its accompanying table note, even with the doubling of the earth's population (the bulk coming from the developing world), food production has actually *increased* on a per capita basis for the last four decades.

Beginning in 1950, developing regions experienced a dramatic upswing in population growth, largely because of a decrease in infant mortality rates, which extended average life expectancy some 50%, from forty-three years to sixty-four years. When one steps back and looks at the milestones of human progress, they seem to be marked by three key variables: an increase in human population and density, the buildup and dissemination of knowledge and technology, and a rise in living standards. At the end of the twentieth century, more people are synthesizing these elements in their lives than ever before. As the late sociologist and "doomslayer" Julian Simon noted, "People alive now are living in the midst of what may well be the most extraordinary three or four centuries in human history."[18] Far from mass starvation and resource depletion, the world has witnessed the triumph of technology in the form of higher living standards for more people than Malthus or any recent doomsayer could possibly have imagined. Indeed, the developing world's cup is far fuller than it has ever been, and it seems to be filling fast.

FIGURE 1.5

A HUGE GROWTH IN POPULATION ...

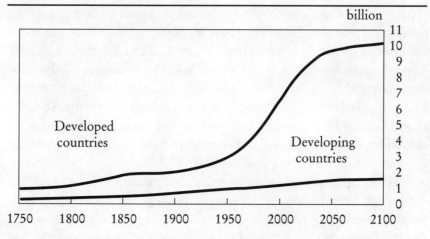

... ACCOMPANIED BY INCREASING FOOD OUTPUT

	1950	*1997*
Grain production (per capita)	247 kg	322 kg
Total grain yield per hectare (tons)	1.06	2.7
Soybean production (per capita)	7 kg	26 kg
Fertilizer use (per capita)	5.5 kg	22.4 kg
Meat production (per capita)	17.2 kg	36.1 kg
Fish catch (per capita)	8.6 kg	16 kg (1996)
World population	2.5 billion	5.8 billion

SOURCES: Economist Intelligence Unit, USDA; Lester R. Brown, Michael Renner, and Christopher Flavin, *Vital Signs 1998* (New York: W. W. Norton, 1998).

CURRENT ECONOMIC MOMENTUM AND INTEGRATION

To date, the story of developing countries and their attraction for First World capitalists has focused primarily on the fundamental economic aspects of early-stage industrialization: cheaper labor and lower operating costs. In a theoretically borderless world, the market leader in every global industry should be the lowest-cost producer. With the advent of global competition, a scramble has developed for low-cost inputs, and scramblers seek to relocate nearer these low-cost resources.[19] Just as British capital once owned nearly half of the cheaper, more efficient productive base of nineteenth century America, the U.S., Western Europe, and Japan are now rapidly deploying investments throughout the developing world and fueling unprecedented growth. The countries of the developing world can narrow the gap: "Indeed, all of the so-called 'growth miracles' in the post–World War II period from Taiwan to Germany and from Singapore to Japan are examples of past economic catch-ups. Today it is the turn of the runners from the former socialist economies [of East Europe, Asia, Africa, and Latin America] who are throwing off the leg-irons of bureaucracy, discarding the chains of state intervention and sprinting into the lead."[20]

From 1973 to 1993, economic growth, measured in real GDP, in the industrialized countries averaged roughly 2.5%. Over the same period, developing countries averaged 3.5% growth. Over the next decade, however, as the First World continues to struggle, expanding modestly, the developing-country economies are expected to grow between 5% and 6% annually. When the so-called economies in transition, those of the former Soviet Union and communist Eastern Europe, are excluded from the calculations, growth in the developing countries is expected to average over 6% annually.[21]

As a result of the rapid economic growth currently underway in many developing countries, it is projected that by 2010 these countries will produce more than 27% of total world output.[22] This still represents a relatively small proportion of global output given the aggregate total of world population, but, when expressed in terms of *purchasing power parity* (PPP), this increase becomes highly significant as the developing countries are expected to produce more than 50% of total global output.

HOW BIG IS AN ECONOMY?
THE BIG MAC KNOWS

It is very difficult to assess the actual size of an economy. Straight GDP figures tell us only one part of the story—the dollar size of the economy—which tells us the amount of dollars spent, but not what that amount actually buys. What a dollar buys in the U.S. is typically *less* than what it would buy in a developing country. Because of this, GDP estimations tend to misrepresent national income, thus distorting real per capita purchasing potential. Purchasing power parity (PPP) is used to compare developing countries with industrialized countries on a whole range of economic measures such as income levels, exports, and industrial output. For example, China's GDP per capita is $654 on the traditional exchange rate basis and as high as $1,000 using PPP adjustments.

PPP can more accurately estimate income levels of developing countries by taking into account differences in local living standards. PPP is calculated by determining the number of units of a country's currency required to purchase the same amounts of goods in the domestic market as, for example, one dollar would buy in America. In the long run, PPP advocates argue, exchange rates between any two currencies should be such that the cost of identical goods in those countries is equal.

PPP analysis is often used to forecast long-term currency exchange rates. PPP also helps compare GDP and other national income measurements by converting national currencies to a common currency as a basis of comparison. The key assumptions of PPP are that the goods in question are identical and that there are no trade barriers and no transportation costs.

Some economists believe PPP to be flawed in that it ignores the role of domestic preferences in determining local demand (and hence costs), that trade barriers do exist and therefore distort prices in different countries, that different tax policies result in poor price comparisons, and that PPP does not take into account the differences in the costs of nontradable services (e.g., rent and labor) that are present in different economies. The World Bank believes that comparisons of economies based solely on PPP "should be treated with some care," because PPP calculations "place a much higher weight on the part of developing country output that is not tradable (mainly services), so as to reflect their higher prices in industrial countries" (*Global Economic Prospects and the Developing Countries, 1995* [Washington, D.C.: World Bank, 1995], p. 66).

The Economist uses its Big Mac index to demonstrate PPP, a humorous attempt to analyze current dollar exchange rates based on the price of a Big Mac in thirty-two countries. The Big Mac index is calculated by dividing the local currency cost of a Big Mac by the cost of a Big Mac in the U.S. If this value (the implied PPP exchange rate) is greater than the actual exchange rate, then the currency is overvalued against the dollar; if it is lower, then the currency is undervalued. For example, the cost of a Big Mac in the U.S. was $2.36 in 1996. However, in Poland it costs zloty 3.80, which is actually $1.44, which suggests that the zloty is undervalued. In Switzerland it costs SFr 5.90, or $4.80, which suggests that the SFr is overvalued. Although PPP can be useful for comparative purposes, it should not necessarily be treated as an absolutely reliable tool.

Country	GDP Per Capita	GDP Per Capita on a PPP Basis (1996)
Brazil	$4,664	$3,451
China	$654	$998
Mexico	$2,995	$3,414
Russia	$4,088	$4,824
Country	$2,993	$3,592

SOURCES: Economist Intelligence Unit; The Futures Group

The economic integration of new countries into the global economic system is a key element of our collective future. The liberalization of global trading patterns over the last several years, evidenced by the successful conclusion of the Uruguay Round of GATT and the creation of the World Trade Organization, as well as by the emergence of various regional free trade agreements such as the North American Free Trade Agreement (NAFTA), the European Union (EU), MERCOSUR (the Latin American free trade regime), and ASEAN (Association of South East Asian Nations), has resulted in significant trade gains for the developing countries. Indeed, developing countries' contribution to global trade growth is expected to increase from 20% to 30% over the next fifteen years, and may top 50% by 2020, according to the World Bank.

Part of this economic expansion will be fueled by mushrooming financial markets. Capital investment is considered by most economists to be necessary for economic growth. With the greater securitization of financial assets, emerging stock markets are increasingly the funnel through which investment funds, both foreign and domestic, flow to the economies of developing countries. While the industrial modernization story in the Third World warrants interest, the more exciting and less reported tale is financial marketization and its relationship to consumerism in developing countries. Industrialization typically begins at annual income levels of approximately $500 to $1,000 per capita. Mass consumption starts at $3,000, and the demand for banking and financial products at $5,000. It is at this point, when countries have begun to amass capital to propel their economies up toward First World levels, that the story of developing countries gets interesting. With many Third World countries generating savings rates of between 20% and 45% versus 5% to 15% in the OECD, capital accumulation is being accomplished at a rapid rate. Without a doubt, financial power is a prerequisite for continued economic progress.[23]

The incredible growth of emerging market stock markets over the past ten years indicates the extremes to which more money, including overseas portfolio investment, is also being pumped into emerging market economies. From 1985 to 1995, stock market capitalization in these economies swelled from approximately $239 billion to nearly $2 trillion.[24] Recent statistics on foreign direct investment indicate that a virtual tidal wave of funds has been pouring into developing countries. Between 1992 and 1994, developing countries received roughly 40% of all foreign direct investment, up from about 20% in 1987 in absolute terms.[25] With increasing trade and financial liberalization, this figure is expected to top 50% by 2010. Furthermore, from 1985 to 1995, foreign direct investment in emerging markets increased by 800%. These investment funds will, in turn, contribute to further economic growth in the developing countries. This is perhaps the most encouraging long-term indication of the future economic potential of the Third World.

MEANWHILE, IN THE FIRST WORLD . . .

In contrast to the sharp economic ascension of developing countries, the First World's fortunes seem to be stagnating, a perception that has been the root of so much of the economic pessimism and anxiety in recent years. Shifts in demography and consumption are rapidly undermining the West's political and social infrastructures: mature capitalism in the developed world is reflected in the saturation of consumer markets and the related increase in mergers and acquisitions. In addition, wealthy First World countries typically have lower birth rates, which contribute to the aging or "graying" of the population. Gray populations tend to spend differently than younger populations, with a greater emphasis on services than on goods. With flat growth prospects in the OECD, corporations try to increase profits through consolidation, largely in order to cut expenses rather than grow sales. This, along with regulatory changes, has led to a twenty-year period of nonstop mergers and acquisitions (M&A) in the U.S., according to Bruce Wasserstein, one of Wall Street's leading M&A bankers.[26] Meanwhile, the consumer growth potential in the developing world is enormous, and multinational corporations (MNCs) are rapidly capitalizing on this: for example, while a typical American consumes some 310 cans of Coca-Cola per year, the developing world consumer's average is only 32 cans.[27] The sharp contrast in potential for future growth in consumption between the OECD and the developing countries is the reason why many MNCs are investing in production and sales facilities in emerging markets. To put the present and future in perspective, ING-Barings notes:

- General Motors, the world's largest employer, now spends more per annum on its U.S. pensioners than on its employees.
- No net private-sector jobs have been created in the Common Market countries of Europe since 1974.
- Labor cost differentials are such that one could employ more than 200 Russian workers for every one Japanese worker.
- India's middle class of 350 million now exceeds the total population of Western Europe or North America.

- 12% of the world's economically active population live along the banks of China's Yangtze river.
- According to the World Bank, by the year 2000, China's economy will be larger than Western Europe's on a purchasing power parity basis. By 2005, China will surpass the U.S., and by 2010 the entire Asia-Pacific economy, including Japan, will surpass the combined economic might of Europe and North America.

In the long-run, it appears that the developing world's growth curve will be far steeper than that of the First World. While this has given rise to fear among Western economic nationalists, moves to prevent Western companies from taking advantage of the Third World comparative advantages are shortsighted. The only way to prevent the erosion of First World dominance is to adapt to and master these developments quickly, not to try to thwart them.

RISING INCOME IN THE DEVELOPING WORLD

A key component of the developing world's expansion will be its own domestic demand, fueled partly by the realization that technological industrialization is necessary to keep pace with the rest of the world. Increases in national income trigger domestic demand for goods and services, such as telephones, televisions, and cars—luxury items that are often taken for granted in the industrialized countries. Indeed, although several of the world's largest developing countries have yet to reach significant per capita GNP levels, some, such as China and India, already have far more middle- and upper-class consumers than the United States or Western Europe.

We have already seen broad efforts by corporations in industrialized countries to penetrate the markets of the developing world, a process that will accelerate throughout the twenty-first century. As national income levels grow, developing countries will be integrated into the global economy and trading system. Changes in political and social ideologies have also contributed to accelerated integration. Similarly, the development of Third World financial markets will provide an important mechanism for channeling domestic financial resources into productive, growth-inducing investments.

Contrary to much populist rhetoric in the U.S. and other industrialized countries, global economic growth is not a zero-sum game. Rising GDP in developing countries will not come at the expense of industrialized countries. Rather, it can be argued that the rapid financial and trade integration between industrialized and emerging market economies will benefit all participants. The First World will prosper from having new markets and cheaper production costs. The developing countries will gain from having access to new markets for manufactured goods and raw materials and, perhaps most important, from access to capital for productive investment. Indeed, economic expansion in the developing countries is, to a large extent, contingent on the continuation of the favorable economic environment that currently exists in the industrialized world—low inflation, modest growth, and strong stock markets. Assuming that the conditions just described will continue, the process of global economic development over the next decades will be marked by a synergy that in many ways resembles that which occurred in England and the United States early this century or, more recently, in Japan. The next wave of growth, based on today's Genius Technologies, will further propel the integration of the world's economies, altering the global geographic and financial landscape. We will see that the driving participants of this next wave of growth will be emerging market nations. Indeed, the only way the West will reserve its place on this wave is by embracing, not shunning, its alleged "challengers."

How All Roads Led to the Global Economy

THE SUDDEN EXPANSION of the developing world over the last decade is staggering: Britain, for example, took some sixty years to double its output from the dawn of the Industrial Revolution in the late eighteenth century. The United States took fifty years to double its output in the mid-nineteenth century. However, at a compounded rate of 6%, the developing world is doubling output every twelve years, with some regions like East Asia having doubled in ten years. China, the world's most populous country, has actually been doubling GDP in a remarkable *seven* years. These rates are unprecedented and are dramatically altering the distribution of power in the global economy. Many of those we consider Third World countries today will most likely attain "First World" economic status within two or three generations. This chapter answers the question, why now? In order to intelligently understand the changes and opportunities in the world today, we need to explore the evolution of the global economy from one dominated by zero-sum mercantilism into one governed by positive-sum capitalism built on the reciprocal relationships between science, technology, and the marketplace. We will touch on several reasons why the West came to dominate the world over the last few hundred years, examine the causes of the Third World's economic failures during the twentieth century, and finally identify the factors that have precipitated the developing countries' movement toward the world's economic center stage.

HOW THE FIRST WORLD BECAME FIRST

The question of how and why the West took the technological and economic lead some three hundred years ago has yet to be completely answered by anyone. However, many have provided insights into what propels a global economy, how countries have historically expanded their economies, and how they can continue to increase living standards—all of which are valuable in understanding how the First World became first.

Looking at the world as it was before 1500 C.E., one would see no sign that any one civilization would rise above the others. Many of the great scientific and practical discoveries that have allowed humanity to advance can be traced to China and the Arab world, and several indigenous groups in the Americas and Africa lived in societies as advanced as their European contemporaries.

If any civilization looked like it would advance first technologically, China was probably the surest bet prior to the Renaissance. Chinese innovations were far ahead of Western Europe's after the fall of Rome in 476 C.E. By the first and second centuries C.E., China had already made great advances in physics, mathematics, medicine, and engineering—hundreds of years prior to the West.[1]

By the fifteenth century, China was densely populated, with approximately 120 million people (compared to 55 million in Europe) spread over an area the size of Europe.[2] But despite relatively advanced transportation systems making it possible to gather, harness, and apply scientific and technological advancements in a systematic way across the land, China shunned progress. In response to frontier pressures, the Ming dynasty in the mid-fifteenth century focused on recapturing the country's glorious past, looking inward and backward, discouraging trade and entrepreneurialism, discontinuing the use of paper currency, restricting printing, and neglecting municipal drainage systems and astronomical clocks.[3] A cultural disdain for commerce and private capital, rooted in Confucian conservatism, resulted in the absence of the competitive, mercantilist spirit that was present in Europe at the time.[4] China, enormous and steeped in a rich tradition of science, chose to bask in past glories and had little incentive to innovate.[5]

There is ample evidence of a rich tradition of art, science, and technology in the Islamic world in medieval North Africa[6] and the Middle East. A tolerant Islamic society left the Byzantine empire stable and manageable until Constantinople fell to the Ottomans in 1453. Military might, particularly naval, made the Ottomans formidable adversaries in Persia, North Africa, and even southern Spain. But soon, stretched thin by imperialism and fractured by religious divisions exacerbated by a centralized despotism, the Ottomans discouraged change, fearing loss of control over the empire. Cultural and technological conservatism took hold, censoring new ideas, discouraging trade, and initiating a decline that would reach its nadir in the twentieth century.

Mesoamerican civilizations, such as the Aztecs and the Mayas in Mexico, and the Andean Inca civilization similarly flourished. But while ancient Mexico had active trading relationships, commerce was carried out by barter, since neither the Aztecs nor the Mayas had invented money. Although the Incas had a vast road system that was bigger than the Roman Empire's, the absence of the wheel precluded effective transport. Unfortunately, pre-Columbian civilizations were no match for the Spanish conquistadores' common diseases, such as chickenpox and tuberculosis, or for European technology, including guns and horses.

Although each of these cultures had a developed sociopolitical infrastructure and some had relatively sophisticated traditions of science and technology, it would be Western Europe, blessed with certain advantages that fostered a trajectory of uninterrupted and unencumbered growth, that would become the pacesetter of the world and ultimately dominate the global economy. As historian Paul Kennedy explains,

... however imposing and organized some of those ... empires appeared by comparison with Europe, they all suffered from the consequences of having a centralized authority which insisted upon a uniformity of belief and practice, not only in official state religion but also in such areas as commercial activities and weapons development. The lack of any such supreme authority in Europe and the warlike rivalries among its various kingdoms and city-states stimulated a constant search for military improvements, which interacted fruitfully with the newer technological and commercial advances that were also being thrown up in this competitive, entrepreneurial environment. Possessing fewer obstacles to change, European societies entered into a constantly upward spiral of economic growth and enhanced military effectiveness which, over time, was to carry them ahead of all other regions of the globe.[7]

Sociologist and historian Mariano Grondona argues that Protestant Western Europe had a "development-prone" culture, the essence of which was a regard for and faith in individuals, which generated an ethical system based on responsible self-interest and mutual respect, a system in which competition could thrive. In his view, a development-resistant culture (Roman Catholic societies, in his study) was distrustful of the individual, discouraged competition because it fostered envy and self-advancement at the expense of others, and saw wealth as a given attribute, rather than as something that could be created by initiative and work.[8] In his seminal work *The Protestant Work Ethic and the Spirit of Capitalism,* Max Weber noted that the Protestant Reformation, with its Calvinist emphasis on individual responsibility for self-advancement, helped liberate Europe from the medieval Christian worldview that condemned individual economic success.[9] Europeans began to think of themselves as perfecters of the world, conquerors of nature, and controllers of history: "Christianity, in absolute contrast to ancient paganism and Asia's religions (except, perhaps, Zoroastrianism), not only established a dualism of man and nature but also insisted that it is God's will that man exploit nature for his proper ends."[10] Until the Reformation, all education had had a strong religious bias, and most learning centers were formed in the confines of monasteries and other religious circles. The rise of systematized education during the Renaissance—a term coined by the French more than two centuries after it began in Italy, signifying the "rebirth" of learning—laid the foundation for the West's technological and financial power for the next few hundred years.[11]

A century of extraordinary intellectual developments—most notably the rediscovery of Euclidean geometry,[12] which led to the invention of perspective in art and to Galileo's astronomical findings—and perhaps, most important, the rise of humanism[13] all helped encourage intellectual freedom and put Western man in control of his own fate. This led to the great fountain of scientific knowledge that characterized the seventeenth century and was most embodied in Sir Isaac Newton, the Cambridge don whose principles would become the basis of physics. In what may be the three most cerebrally important years of mankind—1665, 1666, and 1667—Newton discovered scientific principles that would help define the modern world: among them, the laws of gravity, the laws of optics, and calculus.

The foundation had been laid for the systematic application of the intellectual capital of the previous two centuries. The Industrial Revolution—or "La Révolution Industrielle," the term coined by the French in the 1830s (again, being fashionably late to the party)—was characterized by the demise of the dominant agrarian way of life under the rising influence of machines, capital investment, and markets. This period has been chronicled by many, but perhaps David Landes summarized it best in his *The Unbound Prometheus* when he described the heart of the revolution as an interrelated succession of technological changes affecting economics and production, including the substitution of mechanical devices for human skills, inanimate power—in particular steam—taking the place of human and animal strength, and marked improvements in the extraction of and working in raw materials.[14] Free from the continental wars of Europe, Britain began the Industrial Revolution in the mid-1700s. The invention that started it all—although this is hotly debated by many—was probably the flying shuttle, invented by John Kay in 1733. The shuttle enabled weavers to produce cloth more quickly and in greater widths. Cloth had become a dominant staple of world trade in the seventeenth and eighteenth centuries, and by the mid-1700s England had displaced the Low Countries, particularly Flanders, as the cloth capital of the world. As the shuttle and its successors fueled the demand for yarn, new spinning equipment soon became too big to be driven by man or animal, and factories were built beside rivers, where waterwheels could provide power. By the early nineteenth century, after thousands of years of being performed at home, nearly all the spinning and weaving in the world, as measured by output, was done in factories. Indeed, from 1770 to 1820, Landes notes, textile production rose a remarkable forty-fold in England largely because of mechanization.

What grew in the West was an interconnected continental economy, "a polity of rival city-states based on an economy of bourgeois mercantile capitalism," different from and more powerful than the socioeconomic systems in the rest of the world at that time.[15] For the West, the eighteenth, nineteenth, and twentieth centuries would bring a tremendous rise in living standards. So began the symbiotic cycle of technological innovation and its proliferation, on the one hand, and capital accumulation, on the other hand, that would drive economic development.

And so, from a level playing field in 1500 C.E., the West took first place and has sustained its lead by being the primary innovator. Those who have most evidently threatened to catch up, and those, like Japan, who have succeeded, have done so by being innovative and exploiting their comparative advantage. However long three to four hundred years of leadership may seem to us, it is by no means to be taken for granted, and what we are witnessing today is the slow but steady erosion of the mile-long gap between the developed and the developing world. In the following section, we will look at how the countries of today's emerging markets—some saddled with historical baggage (for example, China and the former Soviet Union), others the victims of circumstance (the commodity exporting nations of the early twentieth century and, later, the Cold War pawns)—have been shedding the ideological manacles that have hindered their growth this century, and narrowing the gap between the West and the rest.

HOW THE REST ARE CATCHING UP

Now, on the eve of the new millennium, after centuries of lagging behind the European innovators, much of the Third World is positioned for unprecedented growth. Technologically deprived for so long, many of these countries still live in preindustrial conditions and mass poverty, but progress is now within reach. The recent history of global economic development shows that the Western-dominated world of the last few hundred years is being dramatically transformed into a world populated by several competing economic powers.

For most of the twentieth century, the developing world could not attract hard currency; without hard currency, it could not invest in technology to expand its economies and accumulate more capital; the result was economic stagnation and contraction. Following World War II, much of the developing world locked itself behind the doors of inward-looking economic policies. For some countries, a postcolonial sense of independence led to nationalistic economic policies and protectionist legislation. For others, the second half of the twentieth century began under the reign of authoritarian, largely military, regimes, whose economic policies included a government commitment to spending on large-scale, capital-intensive enterprises. And, many others became the pawns of the Soviet machine and were ruled by the philosophy of central planning.

The end of the twentieth century has seen a wave of change. Dictatorships have become unfashionable and are now the anomaly, as democracy—in one form or another—has become the norm and the basis for capital advancement and economic success. The Soviet experiment with communism is over, releasing a number of eager economies into the world market. Countries whose colonial heritage lasted until the middle of this century have passed beyond their neocolonial rebellion period and are now among the leaders of the emerging markets. These countries are catching up on the lead historically won by the West, following an accelerated version of essentially the West's development path, one characterized by the critical interplay of technology and capital accumulation.

Why has this happened now? One answer can be found in statist and collectivist economic models' failure to produce the bountiful harvests, powerful arsenals, and social justice they promised, while neoliberal economies showed their ability to generate wealth and power. To best understand this ideological victory in the war of words and images, we will first look at the way in which wartime propaganda contributed to the demise of a system—how statism in the East was undermined from the outside. We will then look at the system's inherent unsustainability—how statism, in the East and elsewhere, sowed the seeds of its own destruction.

Many who analyzed the fall of communism in the former Soviet Union as it was happening believed it was chiefly caused by political and human rights issues. People wanted certain social freedoms, and

TABLE 2.1
DEMOCRATIZATION IN THE MODERN WORLD

Year	Democratic States	Non-Democratic States	Total	% of Total
1922	29	35	64	45.3
1942	12	49	61	19.7
1962	36	75	111	32.4
1973	30	92	122	24.6
1990	59	71	130	45.4

SOURCE: Samuel Huntington, *The Third Wave* (Norman, OK: University of Oklahoma Press, 1991), p. 26.

the government's statist economic policies could not achieve living standards anywhere close to those enjoyed in the First World. Technologies such as radio and television made the citizens under Soviet rule painfully aware of what they had been missing, and eventually they rejected the oppressive communist system, which led to a breakdown of the Soviet state.

Technology was instrumental in the demise of the communist state, feeding a growing social dissatisfaction with images of either side of the Iron Curtain. The media closely documented Ronald Reagan and George Bush's twelve-year reign in the U.S., during which American military spending increased massively, from $134 billion in 1980 to nearly $299 billion in 1990.[16] The U.S. capitalist economy could afford to run up a staggering $2 trillion deficit with little immediate impact on the lives of its citizens. The Soviets tried to keep pace, even amid growing dissatisfaction over food and clothing shortages, while Communist Party propaganda continually told Soviet citizens that increased military spending was necessary to combat the growing militancy of Reaganite America.

The proliferation of mass communications—some old and new Genius Technologies such as television, radio, and telephones—helped to expose the benefits of a capitalist, free-market system to billions who had long been held hostage to ideology, economic distortions, and—in many cases—corrupt and cruel regimes. Communist

Party members had always been concerned that images of U.S. decadence would seduce their comrades and had successfully kept such images out.[17] Thanks to satellite dishes and VCRs, the luxurious American lifestyle portrayed on television helped undermine the party line by showing people what they had been missing, materially and socially.[18]

EASTERN EUROPE: COMING OUT FROM BEHIND THE IRON CURTAIN

The Cold War was in theory a conflict of ideologies, a hostile competition to see whose system could yield the most prosperity and popular support at home and who could capture a bigger slice of the world under their wing. By 1989 control of the world was fairly evenly divided, but this stalemate was broken by the failure of communism to generate wealth at home and by its consequent loss of legitimacy in the eyes of the people whose interests it supposedly served. The winners, the free market countries, rather than take prisoners or occupy land, happily exported the secret of their success, and so the twenty-seven slowly democratizing post-communist states totaling some 400 million people became the guinea pigs in a major operation to implant capitalism in an erstwhile hostile environment. The intellectual elite of the United States became committed to designing the reform programs for the Eastern bloc. Strengthening Democratic Institutions (SDI) was the ironic name of the Harvard University group sent to Russia, who on weekends could be found sporting SDI T-shirts and taking home videos of the country's first entrepreneurs: the trinket and memorabilia salesmen on Arbat Street who knew enough English to swindle the gullible hard-currency-carrying tourists. Jeffrey Sachs, a Harvard economist who had already successfully designed a stabilization program for Bolivia, wrote the economic prescription that was to make Poland the regional leader in reform, proposing "a single, stable exchange rate for the *zloty,* which will guarantee that all prices of internationally traded goods (both imports and exports) will be determined by the prices in the world market" (Simon Johnson and Marzena Kowalska, "Poland:

The Political Economy of Shock Therapy," in Stephen Haggard and Steven B. Webb, eds., *Voting for Reform* [New York: Oxford University Press, 1994], p. 194).

Eastern European countries now see membership in the European Union as crucial to ensuring the success of their new regimes. They see the customs union, the consumer markets, and, not least, the EU development funds available to members, and they realize that regional integration will guarantee their survival. They also have been eager to join NATO and the international financial institutions. Members of these clubs must be political democracies with market economies, however, and applicants have been forced to comply. They have been forced to build the institutions that support both a democratic government and a market economy and that preserve the legitimacy of both, starting with a legal and regulatory infrastructure. As Stephen Holmes explains, citing the need for state building to ensure the sustainability of reform efforts, "the legislative task facing all post-communist regimes is therefore immense, including the creation not only of contract law but also of trespass law, bankruptcy law, patent law, condominium law, environmental law, and so forth" (Stephen Holmes, "Cultural Legacies or State Collapse? Probing the Communist Dilemma," in Michael Mandelbaum, ed., *Post-Communism: Four Perspectives* [New York: Council on Foreign Relations, 1996], p. 63).

All this must be accomplished alongside efforts to satisfy many disgruntled citizenries that have seen industrial output drop more than 50% since the Soviet fall, savings eroded as currencies were devalued, and many newly privatized businesses fail in a market-oriented economy. But the signs are encouraging: most of the early Eastern Europe reformers—the Czech Republic, Hungary, and Poland—now enjoy investment-grade credit ratings. Most of the later reformers are just a fraction off investment grade. Overall, the region has rebounded from prolonged recession, and some countries, like Poland, have experienced GDP growth rates in the 6% to 8% range that rival those of the Asian Tigers.

Soviet economic ideology was further undermined when images of the success stories of East Asia, and especially postwar Japan, flooded in. Fifty years ago, Japan, Hong Kong, Taiwan, and Singapore were considered some of the poorest places on earth. Today, those countries combined hold approximately $450 billion in hard currency reserves, more than all of continental Europe. Their advances are examples for the rest of the developing world; they have found the formula to end the vicious cycle of poverty and begin the "virtuous circle" of economic success: attract capital, apply technology, grow the economy, accumulate more capital, and so on. These were not the rich, imperialist First Worlders getting fatter by exploiting the developing world, but rather previously impoverished Asian economies that were suddenly growing by leaps and bounds. Reports rolled in, via television, radio, and underground newspapers, on the astounding growth of these nations, inspiring other developing countries whose protectionist, statist, centralized policies had been failing them. The possibility of growth, if one jettisoned compromising political agendas and followed the Asian example, was very real.

A complementary reason for the demise of the statist experiment in the East and elsewhere was the inevitable economic unsustainability of what might be characterized as the "inward-looking experiment." Ironically, it had been the extent of the developing world's integration into the global economy by the time of the Great Depression that had originally led to the strictly protectionist, inward-looking economic philosophies that were to govern its economies for the next fifty years. Since the late 1850s, developing colonial countries had placed their faith in export-oriented policies, based on years of producing for export to their mother countries, in the belief that trade would stimulate economic growth and lead to growing income levels, investment in public education, and the opportunity to absorb foreign technologies, ultimately resulting in the creation of modern societies like those they observed in Western Europe and the United States. At the end of the First World War, this ideal began to erode as European imports of developing world primary products declined while Europe tried to increase its own food production.

But the Depression shattered the developing world's dreams of advancement, as global prices crashed and posed a serious threat to those economies that had relied on their export income: Chile suffered from the fall in copper prices; the coffee and sugar markets slowed down for many Caribbean and African countries; Malaysia (Malaya) and other Asian island nations were overdependent on the whims of international markets for palm oil and certain minerals; meat exports, especially from Uruguay and Argentina, suffered as Britain could no longer afford to import as it had. National incomes and levels of employment, both intimately tied to foreign trade returns, suffered. It was at this point that the state began to take a more active role in the local economies, buying up the primary products that were no longer being exported and subsidizing the creation of industrial units to produce the consumer goods that were no longer being imported. These were then protected through tariffs and import controls, and so the seeds of Import Substitution Industrialization (ISI) were sown.

Despite the end of the Depression, Europe and the United States continued their own import substitution, either producing the goods once imported from developing countries themselves, or finding that new twentieth-century technologies greatly reduced the demand for such imports. Population growth in the North Atlantic basin slowed, while the population in the developing world grew an average of 2% a year in the 1950s,[19] multiplying from 1.2 billion in 1950 to 4 billion by 1980, providing a growing domestic market for the products of state-led industrial production.[20] Many developing countries had hoped that the postwar reconstruction of Europe would bring back European demand for their primary products, but prewar international trade levels were not soon restored. Friedrich Engels's law of low income elasticity for food (the higher the income, the lower the marginal demand for food products) prevailed, and the developing world learned the difficult lesson that Adam Smith's invisible hand did not guarantee growth without adherence to David Ricardo's theory of comparative advantage—particularly for those countries with undiversified economies relying on the diminishing marginal returns of primary goods exports.

Feeling snubbed by the wealthier economies, and betrayed by their misplaced faith in liberal economics, much of the developing world—particularly Latin America—was receptive to Castro's Cuban initiative in 1959. One writer observed: "There is no doubt that the Cuban Revolution in a country long considered an archetype of a dependent economy and the resort there to socialism as the ideological basis for the achievement of political and economic autonomy produced ripples of self-examination throughout [the developing world]."[21] Cuba's outright rejection of a system the rest of the developing world was still flirting with, and its basis in Marxist-Leninist thought, provided compelling arguments to explain the economic plight of developing countries as an extension of the imperialism with which they had been all too familiar as colonies. As political independence had come to the colonies, so now would economic independence come through ISI. Capital goods industries sprang up, local savings and investment rates increased, and productivity was stimulated to feed a growing local market. Critical to the fast-track growth path developing countries had charted for themselves was the continued protection of domestic production from foreign competition—tariffs and import controls ensured that local industry would develop and economic dependence on the "core" countries would dissolve. Raul Prebisch, the Argentine economist and head of the United Nations Economic Commission for Latin America (ECLA) in 1949, was the most vociferous proponent of such policies. His message was persuasive, claiming that "the natural operation of the market works against developing countries because of a long-term decline in developing countries' terms of trade and because of Northern protectionism. What is needed is a redistribution of world resources to help the South: restructuring of trade, control of multinational corporations, and greater aid flow."[22] And by laying blame on former imperialist powers or First World exploiters, the developing world used this message as an additional rationale to commit to the ISI program.

At the heart of ISI was a devotion to statist policies, in defiance of free-market principles, whereby it was believed that industry treated in a public-sector framework would accelerate industrialization in the private sector and ultimately lead to increased living standards. Prices were not dictated by a market of buyers and sellers, but rather arbitrarily set by the governments, which also owned the means of production. As a result, true market values were unknown, social resources were ineffectively allocated, and, overall, economies were distorted. Furthermore, governments that controlled prices and industries could dispense hundreds of favors—a profitable contract here, a protective tariff there—and this corruption would lead to even greater economic distortions. Such policies were prevalent in virtually all parts of the developing world, from Latin America to Southeast Asia.

The Era of Distortions: The Excessive 1970s

At first it seemed to work. From 1950 until the late 1970s, average annual growth rates in developing countries—excluding the Soviet Union—approached 6%.[23] Real GDP per capita more than doubled.[24] Part of that was clearly the result of the major shift away from farming to manufacturing, which has an immediate GDP benefit.[25] Since the 1960s, a preference for central planning had been caused by a lack of trust in the market to relieve acute scarcity, the need to balance regional development disparities, suspicion of and the urge to curb monopoly powers, and the desire to protect the small-scale business sector from the misperceived threat of encroachment by the large-scale business sector.

But ISI was inherently unsustainable and soon ran out of steam. Protected industries were uncompetitive, and foreign investment, which had been encouraged to stimulate local industry (and had been made possible largely due to a strong dollar until 1973), soon became seen as a threat to national economic sovereignty, subverting the original aims of economic autonomy. And once again, a global economic crisis was to have serious repercussions on the economies of the developing world, despite their attempts to insulate themselves from global economic fluctuations. The oil crisis suddenly made fuel, a critical input into all developing country industries, extremely expensive, undermining growth and severely crippling terms of trade. Non-oil commodity prices collapsed to the point where, by 1986, they were at their lowest levels in recorded history in relation to the prices of manufactured goods and services, and, in some cases, lower than their Depression levels.[26] Protectionist trade policies in developing countries led to overvalued exchange rates, discouraging exports, and now developed countries were in recession and virtually halted imports. A fall in export and export-tax revenue made it difficult for the Third World governments to continue to subsidize their industrial projects, and as tax receipts were insufficient, they were forced to borrow heavily, "crowding out" private investment. Monetization of the budget led to persistent inflation. Dollars were being borrowed to fund projects that were expected to generate local currency—a huge mismatch in terms of assets and liabilities, made worse by the fact that most loans were floating-rate based. If rates moved up—as they would during the late 1970s and early 1980s—countries would owe far more than they had planned for. By 1985, the developing world owed more than $700 billion to First World banks and governments, not including the Soviet Union, which owed another $100 billion more.[27] Meanwhile, tariff-protected, uncompetitive ISI projects were not in the export sector—which would have earned hard currency—but rather were oriented toward domestic consumption. Retreating from the free market had not worked, but in the unfavorable global economic environment these countries were not yet ready to change.

THE ERA OF RECKONING: THE HARSH 1980S

Because much of the developing world was fiscally mismanaged and highly leveraged, many countries were vulnerable to external macroeconomic shocks, particularly to interest rate movements and commodity price fluctuations. Many U.S. and European banks, enjoying the stream of dollars being injected into the banking system as a result of the oil crisis, and the Japanese—with their newfound wealth—had been eager to lend at any rate. But in 1979, the U.S. was facing the threat of inflation and the Treasury decided to hike interest rates to avert an inflationary spiral. Suddenly, the interest rates faced by the borrowers more than doubled, and their debt burden multiplied accordingly.

The sudden onset of recession in 1980 and again in 1981, coupled with U.S. Federal Reserve Board chairman Paul Volcker's tightening of the money supply and the rapid rise in interest rates, increased the cost of loans and reduced world output and trade, making it more difficult for the debtor countries to earn the foreign currency needed to repay the loans.[28] Rising oil prices and interest rates plagued oil-importing developing countries with a double whammy: increased hard currency was now needed to pay for higher oil import costs *and* higher interest was owed on floating-rate loans. Liquidity problems became widespread.

Unwise enthusiastic borrowing combined with gleeful lending had led to a crisis. By 1982, Latin America transferred 4% of its annual GDP in debt service to banks abroad.[29] As countries attempted to adapt to the new financial environment, most found it impossible to service their debts without bankrupting government coffers and losing control of their economies. Faced with domestic unrest caused by the failure of these regimes to fulfill the economic promises for which political freedoms had largely been sacrificed, these countries began to reduce or suspend external payments.

FIGURE 2.1
WORLD OIL PRICES AND INTEREST RATES

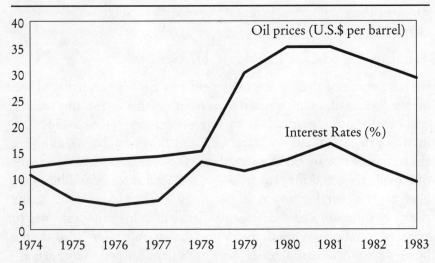

SOURCES: U.S. Department of Energy; Federal Reserve Bank of New York

Poland was one of the first developing countries to experience debt service problems in 1980–81 after borrowing heavily from international markets in the 1970s. With little choice, Poland technically defaulted on its external debt and began what would be a twelve-year restructuring process. In the spring of 1982, the Falklands War forced many British banks to cut credit lines to Argentine banks, the first sign of some problems in Latin America.[30] In August of that year, Mexico declared a moratorium on its foreign debt. The eternally hopeful international banking community saw this as a temporary liquidity crisis that would pass as interest rates normalized over time.[31]

But sensing a potential default domino effect from economically destabilized developing economies (with a keen eye on Mexico, America's next door neighbor), the U.S. government stepped in. Treasury Secretary James Baker III took an active role in handling the debt crisis, and the "Baker Plan" was a stop-gap measure allowing debtors to defer, or reschedule, short-term principal over a longer stretch of time than originally negotiated. Interest had to be paid, however, because of accounting and regulatory constraints, i.e. loans had to keep performing in bank books. For Mexico, the interest component of the debt servicing was itself insupportable; it needed additional loans to service its debt, extended by the banks under the supervision of the International Monetary Fund (IMF). To qualify for this additional financing, debtors had to sign standby agreements with the IMF promising to implement an approved program of economic stabilization and structural adjustment. This would be the beginning of the undoing of state-led, inward-looking industrialization and its replacement by the neoliberalism of IMF reform.

But the crisis was not over. By 1987, defaulters included Bolivia, Peru, Ecuador, Poland, Costa Rica, the Dominican Republic, Honduras, the Ivory Coast, Zaire, and Zambia.[32] Poland averaged 50% inflation over the period, while several Latin American countries like Brazil and Argentina had inflation of over 1,000% from 1985 to 1991.[33] This resulted in a lack of confidence in local currencies (and, more important, in the governments in charge of those currencies) and led to widespread hard-currency leaks. Smart money fled local currencies, exacerbating capital scarcity in the developing world. Capital flight grew from $20 billion in 1979 to $40 billion in 1981, and swelled to $100 billion by 1987.[34] By the mid-1980s capital investment in developing countries had collapsed: their share of global foreign direct investment (FDI) fell to 13%, from 25% in 1971.[35] The combination of hyperinflation, capital flight, and industrial overcapacities resulted in stagnant economies and even negative growth in some countries.

Once again, the Baker Plan was called upon, but the resources of small and medium-sized banks had been severely taxed by the mid-1980s. They could no longer explain to their shareholders why they were throwing new money after bad debt, and they wanted to get rid of their exposure. Creditors sold their exposure at a discount on the secondary market. As this market grew, debtor countries realized that some of their loans were worth as little as three cents on the dollar. They figured that there must be a way for them to recapture these loans, at a discount, and so retire that debt. By 1987, the large creditors realized that such a process was madness, and that it would not end until the debt claims were reduced, not just deferred. Some countries began to complain about the Baker Plan, in particular about having to take out new loans to make interest payments. As Figure 2.2 shows, the total debt owed by the developing world had increased seven-fold in just over a decade.

FIGURE 2.2

EXTERNAL DEBT OF DEVELOPING COUNTRIES (U.S.$)

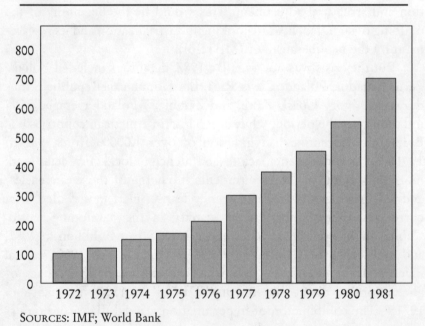

SOURCES: IMF; World Bank

INDIA: BLOSSOMING DEMOCRACY, DISTORTING BUREAUCRACY

As a result of protectionist policies and centralized planning since India's independence in 1948, the private sector was debilitated by a high level of bureaucratic control over production, investment, and trade (what economist Jagdish Bhagwati refers to as "a maze of Kafka-esque controls"). Inward-looking trade and foreign-investment policies had further undermined its efficiency: complex (and sometimes arbitrary) import-licensing controls, coupled with penalties for the unauthorized expansion of capacity, made private entrepreneurialism almost impossible. As had been the case in the Soviet Union, such controls, by curtailing private initiative, discouraged innovation and, consequently, indigenous technological developments. The failure to encourage exports under Import Substitution Industrialization (ISI) led to a decline in India's share of world exports from 2.4% in 1948 to a low of 0.4% in 1981, which undermined the country's entire industrial base (Jagdish Bhagwati, *India in Transition: Freeing the Economy* [Oxford: Clarendon Press, 1993], p. 58).

A massive public sector, meanwhile, whose domain reached beyond public utilities and infrastructure to over 240 central government enterprises, including atomic energy, iron and steel, heavy machinery, coal, railways and airlines, telecommunications, and electricity generation and distribution, was no more efficient (Bhagwati, p. 63). By 1989, the public-sector enterprises in manufacturing, mining, construction, transport, communications, banking, and insurance (including state-level enterprises) provided almost 70% of the 26 million jobs in the large-scale "organized" sector (Bhagwati, p. 64).

The inefficiency of the public sector, combined with the emasculated private sector, would lead to a fiscal and foreign exchange crisis in the 1980s. By the end of the decade, the public debt to GDP ratio was nearly 60%, almost twice as high as it had been in the beginning. The budget deficit was 9% of GDP, and the external public-sector debt to GDP ratio doubled during that decade to 21% by 1987–88. Debt service to exports tripled to 32% in seven years, and foreign exchange reserves were drained (Bhagwati, pp. 67–68). India's credit rating fell, so private borrowing was impracticable, and foreign direct investment had all but dried up. Meanwhile, post–Cold War India suffered as foreign aid was being diverted to the more politically pressing rescue of the former Soviet Union. This situation was ultimately eased by IMF loans, which, as in the case of Latin America, came with strict (and often drastic) economic reform conditions.

THE ERA OF REDEMPTION: THE BURGEONING 1990S

Most developing countries knew they were in trouble economically, but few developing-country politicians could muster the political will to take the tough fiscal decisions needed to align economies with market principles. Their huge debt overhang behaved "as a tax on a developing country's investment and growth."[36] The debt-treadmill restructurings that characterized the mid-1980s needed a fresh approach.

Enter the new U.S. Secretary of the Treasury, Nicholas Brady, long-time Wall Street pro and former chairman of the venerable investment banking firm Dillon Read & Co. On March 10, 1989, much to commercial banks' consternation, he declared that the only way to solve the debt crisis would be for them to write off a portion of their developing-country portfolios. By taking losses, Brady said, banks would be enhancing the credit quality of the debt that was left. The Brady Plan was built on the assumption that the debt would be sold on the secondary market at a discount. Thus, for the banks it was preferable to take a 40% loss on their debt now than to have to sell the debt later at an 80% loss or, as in the case of the Bolivian debt, at an 89% loss.[37] The basic problem of further indebtedness was that debtor countries had allocated enormous proportions of their GDP to the financing of their external debt and so had no resources to increase investment at home to sustain a program of development. An end to the debt crisis, the Brady Plan argued, could come only by reducing the debt burden through write-downs, allowing countries to grow again.

The Brady Plan basically consisted of having the debtors buy thirty-year zero coupon bonds whose face value equaled the matured principal. These bonds would serve as collateral on the loan, deposited with collateral agents. In the case of default on interest payments, these bonds could be accessed. Money to buy these bonds would come from the World Bank or First World governments, and the loans would be conditional on the conclusion of a standby agreement with the IMF, according to which a country would commit to a detailed structural adjustment program.[38] This orthodox, neoliberal program inevitably included heavy doses of trade liberalization, exchange rate reforms, and conservative monetary and fiscal policies. This usually entailed the privatization of many of the state-owned enterprises that had been at the heart of the nationalist policies of the 1960s and 1970s, which was meant not only to trim the excess from these economies but also to make them more appealing to foreign investors and to provide access to international capital. Redemption was in sight.[39]

By the mid-1990s, capital flows had reversed the downward spiraling trends of the 1980s. Overall, funds to the developing world had effectively doubled from 1981. Foreign reserves had increased by 800% from 1988 to 1995, the result of privatizations, returning foreign direct investment and export credit, and many sovereign flotations in the global capital markets after many absent years. The private sector's share of bond finance increased from 4% in 1989 to 47% in 1992.[40] Emerging markets' share of global stock markets doubled. In total, this improving economic health resulted in favorable credit rating movements, as Table 2.2 indicates.

SUCCESS WITHIN REACH

It is now safe to say that the old belief that capitalism is a zero-sum game has been abandoned. As one country's reforms yield the benefits of economic stability, renewed trade links, improved international credit ratings, and access to international capital (both from financial investors and MNCs), another country follows suit so as not to get left behind. "[I]mitation is not only the sincerest form of flattery; where intense competition is the rule, it is the best formula for survival. . . . in the last part of the twentieth century, rivalry among sovereign states came to involve not only contests of arms but also competition in political cohesion and economic productivity; as with armaments, the

TABLE 2.2
CHANGING FACES: DEVELOPING COUNTRY CREDIT RATINGS 1988–1998

Country	March 1988	September 1998	% Change
Poland	17.8	54.0	203%
Lebanon	7.6	31.8	318%
Argentina	24.8	41.8	69%
Chile	27.2	62.0	128%
Morocco	24.0	42.4	77%
Philippines	23.7	43.0	81%
Egypt	23.6	43.2	83%
South Africa	32.3	46.6	44%

SOURCE: Based on *Institutional Investor*'s biannual surveys of country credit, scaled from 0 to 100, with 100 being the best. The recent highest-rated country was Switzerland, which received a rating of 93.4. "Institutional Investor's 1997 Country Credit Ratings," *Institutional Investor,* September 1998, p. 134.

most successful techniques for achieving those ends were bound to spread."[41] Protectionist, nationalist ideology had largely lost its power and been replaced by a rational, neoliberal ethic—politics were beginning to follow the lead of economic change rather than the other way around. According to Robert Skidelsky, the end of the twentieth century has seen a crisis of collectivism, of which communism was only one incarnation. "Welfarism was the democratic form of collectivism, militarism the autocratic form."[42] In fact, "the struggle to correct the chronic and virtually universal imbalance between the state and the private sector—the consequence of excessive obligations undertaken by the state—[is] perhaps the most important global trend of the last quarter of the twentieth century, a trend common to Margaret Thatcher's Britain, Ronald Reagan's United States, Deng Xiaoping's revolutionary market reforms in China that began in the late 1970s, and the more modest economic liberalization begun in India in the early 1990s. Each involved an effort to restore profitability."[43] Furthermore, such reforms are prerequisites to admission to the many trade blocs that have sprouted around the world. In Latin America, the prospect of Mexico's accession to the North American Free Trade

PAWNS LEFT BEHIND: THE MIDDLE EAST

Until 1989, the superpowers, seeking to protect their perceived geo-political interests in the region, supported the military-industrial complexes of several Middle Eastern countries. The countries of the Middle East can be divided into two broad groups. The first were the Cold War pawns. The Middle East was one of many gameboards on which the bipolar competition was carried out. At different times, Iraq benefited from the military and financial assistance of both the Soviet Union and the United States, whereas Israel has enjoyed U.S. loan guarantees. The second group consisted of the oil producers, which thrived in the 1970s when the price of oil skyrocketed from $4 per barrel in 1973 to a high of $30 per barrel in 1979.

However, rapid change in the second half of the twentieth century has left the region somewhat unanchored. Key macroeconomic and geopolitical shifts, most notably the end of both the oil boom and the Cold War, have left huge financial gaps that need to be filled. Since relations between the U.S. and Russia have thawed, the Middle Eastern countries can no longer rely on unswerving support from their enemy's enemy. And increased competition from new oil-producing countries, such as former Soviet republics and Vietnam, has dramatically weakened the Middle Eastern "petro-hegemony." Economic reform in this region has been a response either to the end of Cold War aid or, for the oil-producing countries, to the fall in oil prices and oil revenues. For many of the countries whose income is derived primarily from oil, falling prices mean that they can no longer rely on the rents from petroleum extraction, or at least that the level of their annual oil income cannot be guaranteed. Faced with this reality, many of these countries have been forced to look elsewhere for capital. In order to access international capital markets, Middle Eastern countries have had to begin to radically reform their economies, both diversifying them away from oil and restructuring them to earn favorable credit ratings in the markets that they are trying to tap. (For more on the Middle East, see Peter N. Marber, "Sheikhs and Souks: Capital Market Formation in the Middle East," *Journal of International Affairs* (Summer 1995) 39, no. 1, pp. 75–101.)

Agreement (NAFTA) provided an extra incentive for reform, along with the move toward regional free trade through MERCOSUR. As mentioned earlier, Eastern European countries long for admission to the EU. These and other trading blocs are enormously attractive to investors.

All over the world, governments have trimmed their budget deficits by divesting themselves of state-owned industries. Privatization has both relieved the state of obligations to loss-making industries and also brought in the money needed to help it clean its economic house. By 1994, of the approximately 7,000 enterprises privatized worldwide, some 2,000 were in developing countries.[44] Privatized industries are interesting vehicles for MNCs and foreign investors, as we will see in the next chapters. But a shift to private ownership also brings an increase in investment, an adjustment of price levels to reflect their market value, and an increase in productivity as managers are forced to watch their bottom lines, as opposed to the former state management, which had access to the national mint.

Despite these success stories, it is not simply a matter of consulting the IMF doctor for a prescription. There is more to pulling out of economic stagnation than a simple set of policies: unqualified political commitment is required as well. "You can't just say 'liberalize trade' and expect thereby to create competition. It would take quite a leap of imagination to believe that in many parts of Africa the grip of a noncompetitive private sector on certain kinds of productive activities could be unlocked simply by liberalizing trade."[45] In Nigeria, the multilateral financial institutions had twice recommended market reform, but it was only when Ibrahim Babangida came into power in 1985 that economic reforms became politically viable. Exchange rate reforms, privatization, and the elimination of marketing boards were finally introduced, but even so, the continued lack of an independent central bank, a tradition of clientelist politics, the lack of democratic accountability, and an unresolved sense of postcolonialism have all hindered success.[46]

But such impediments are not insurmountable. If the incentives are sufficiently strong, there is overwhelming evidence in parts of Africa, Asia, the former Soviet Union, and Latin America to suggest that countries can overcome domestic opposition to changing what might be for some a very comfortable status quo. The benefits are simply immeasurable. After all, "transplants of modern institutions take quite readily even in very traditional soil (such as, the Meiji Restoration), and [. . .] 'cultural resistances to change' often turn out to be state-created vested interests. All the great economists, from Adam Smith to Keynes and Hayek, have emphasized the heuristic value of ideas."[47]

As a graduate student in the mid-1980s, I met few professors who thought the developing world was all that noteworthy. These countries were seen as peripheral players, mired in debt and nationalism, that were being used in the geostrategic chess game between the U.S. and the Soviet Union. Not many scholars at the time were predicting the imminent reunification of Germany, the breakup of the U.S.S.R., market reforms in China, or the end of apartheid in South Africa—all massive societal changes that were just around the corner. While the changes in some of these countries may have appeared on the radar screens of Pentagon officials, they certainly were absent from the strategic expansion plans of OECD multinationals. How quickly the contemporary world changes.

After centuries of economic and often military domination by the West, the Third World finally has begun accelerating its economic modernization. Having abandoned decades of inward-looking policies of statist and collectivist governments, developing countries now embrace the neoliberal economics that has been historically associated with the West. Once called "undeveloped," later called "underdeveloped," later still known as "least developed," and finally, more optimistically, as "developing," these countries have turned a definite corner: they are now emerging markets. No longer are they looked upon as the laggards; now the name "emerging" reflects their potential. The results of economic reform have alerted international strategic and financial investors to these new and profitable possibilities that await overseas. For OECD multinational corporations, the five billion citizens living in the developing world are no longer the earth's wretched but its salt: both as new cheaper producers and as new customers that will propel First World economies upward in the twenty-first century.

SUCCESS IN THE FAR EAST—AND ELSEWHERE

Rather than experiment with the inward-looking development strategies employed in other developing parts of the world, the Asian Tigers instituted outward-looking, market-oriented economic policies, underscored by an emphasis on education and health care (Nicholas D. Kristof, "Why Africa Can Thrive Like Asia," Week in Review, *New York Times,* May 25, 1997, pp. 1, 4). While many regions grappled with ideologies, the Asian Tigers gave economic pragmatism precedence over politics. Taiwan, South Korea, Hong Kong, and Singapore, the rapid modernizers of the postwar era, along with Japan, represent less than 1% of the world's land mass and less than 4% of the world's population, yet the region's share of world output has increased from 17% in 1980 to 25% in 1996, while foreign exchange holdings have grown from 10% to 50%. The overall growth rate in East Asia for the past decade (excluding Japan) has been 8.5%, four times that of the West (Andrew Tanzer, "The Pacific Century," *Forbes,* July 15, 1996). The third quarter of 1997 has seen some upsets in these otherwise reliable markets, hiccups that began with the overvalued currencies of Malaysia, Thailand, Indonesia, and South Korea, and reached the New York and London Stock Exchanges overnight.

But however much shares may have fallen, this most recent slump was arguably a healthy development. Since the last stock market crash, the number of global investors has multiplied, inflating markets with cash previously placed in (mostly government) debt instruments. Analysts have ascribed the recent turmoil to market correction, the result of almost unbounded optimism in share performance, ironically partly due to the swiftness of the stockmarkets' recovery after the 1987 crash. In addition, many in East Asia had become complacent about their "miraculous" pedigrees and were due for a reminder of their own mortality. Fiscal austerity and slower growth will be inevitable while these economies readjust to devalued currencies, and, as was the case after the 1995 Mexican peso crisis, increased disclosure of facts and figures will be demanded by investors from now on. Furthermore, a reexamination and possible restructuring of the concentrated business institutions might be in order.

While Asia has long been considered the paradigm of emerging market growth potential, there is much to indicate that this growth miracle can be replicated in other parts of the world. In Latin America, for example, Chile has experienced 5+% per annum growth for nearly a decade (and 7.7% in 1997). Its legendary pension system is being studied by many developing and industrialized countries (including the United States). Having crushed inflation to OECD levels, Brazil is now the eighth largest economy in the world, exporting everything from toothpaste to cars. In Argentina, a constitutionally U.S. dollar–pegged currency and mass privatization under President Carlos Menem have resulted in a mushrooming economy. And even Mexico is experiencing growth shortly after its unfortunate Christmas 1994 peso devaluation. The country's massive shift away from oil toward diversified manufacturing in the late 1980s, coupled with the weaker peso, has helped Mexico generate a 5% growth rate and billions in hard currency from increased trade.

Possibly the greatest growth potential can be found in Africa, where the industrial base is relatively underdeveloped. As birth rates drop and literacy rates rise, human capital is finally being harnessed throughout the continent. Uganda, for example, has emerged from years of stagnation and grew at 10% in 1997. Zambia is amid large-scale privatization and reported 1997 growth at 6.4%. Angola reported 12.5% in 1996. Lesotho is undergoing severe economic reform designed to achieve a target expansion rate of 10.2%. Malawi is following the privatization trend in Africa and expanding quickly, making it the fourth African "tiger" (Kristof, p. 1).

CHAPTER 3

New Technologies Refine and Redefine the Global Economy

WHY TODAY'S ECONOMIC ENGINES ARE UNIQUE

Today the world stands, once again, on the brink of monumental social and economic change generated by technological innovations. In the last two hundred years, Genius Technologies such as steam power, railroads, and electricity have acted as global economic engines. However, what makes today's cutting-edge technologies so extraordinary is that their sheer pervasiveness directly accelerates and accentuates the integration of the global economy in ways never seen before. Genius Technologies are creating a marketplace that is more efficiently exploiting comparative advantage than ever before and building capital markets that stretch worldwide. The late-twentieth-century wave also differs from previous globalization waves, such as those of the nineteenth century, in that the older cycles were driven mainly by falling transportation costs that stimulated international integration by moving more goods across borders faster. Today, not only is global trade accelerating, but cheap and efficient communications networks are allowing companies to locate different parts of their production process in foreign countries while maintaining real-time contact with head offices. These information technologies simultaneously alter all sectors of agriculture, manufacturing, and services and, in doing so, integrate the developing world into the global economy faster than any theorist could imagine. Not only can these technologies be applied to all sectors of the economy (which was also the case with electricity), but they can affect every function within a particular company. Moreover, unlike steam or electricity, today's technologies can be both inputs and final products. In short, today's dominant technologies are capable of revolutionizing the production and distribution in all industries and sectors, while at the same time offering a vast range of new products and services.

Today's Genius Technologies are redefining how corporations manage large operations, as well as how investors invest capital. For possibly the first time in history, commerce and finance truly know no boundaries, and capitalism itself is being forever altered more profoundly than it ever was by the railroad or television. More than half of all GDP in rich economies now comes from knowledge-based industries, including information technology, pharmaceuticals, and education. We are witnessing an unprecedented trend toward globalizing production and financial markets. This process intensifies competition and accelerates the diffusion of technology through foreign direct investment (FDI). So while previous Genius Technologies acted as global economic engines, today's are self-lubricating engines, stimulating the creation of new technologies that, in turn, strengthen and reinforce globalization trends.

TODAY'S NUMBER ONE GENIUS TECHNOLOGY: INFORMATION

Among the many great technological advances in the late twentieth century, without a doubt the most significant innovations have come from what has been dubbed Information Technology. IT consists basically of telecommunications (including phones, networks, satellites, et al.) and computing (hardware and software).

Most First Worlders are familiar with the consumer applications of the IT revolution: digital and cellular telephones, facsimile machines, personal computers (whose productivity is maximized when used within networks), electronic mail, and the Internet and its information link, the World Wide Web. On a more technical level, it is the technologies behind these innovations that represent the true revolution—the development and applications of fiber optics, microprocessors, satellites, and networks. What the applications of these technologies allow businesses to do is itself worthy of a book or perhaps volumes; it is that revolutionary. But in simple terms, IT allows people to gather more information faster than ever before, to process and analyze that information faster and in ways never dreamed of, and to make decisions and implement actions faster—and in more places—than ever before. This has dramatic consequences for all aspects of manufacturing and services and, in effect, completely alters the world's productivity paradigm. Interesting comparative economic advantages that could not before be profitably exploited suddenly become possible. IT allows credit card companies to offer their services in two hundred countries, grocers in London to buy fruits and vegetables daily from Harare, Detroit car companies to manufacture pick-up trucks in São Paulo and sell them throughout sub-Saharan Africa, and Milanese designers to assemble suits in Mexico City and sell them in New York. Of equal importance, IT allows a pension fund in Green Bay or a life insurance company in Yokohama to invest in Kiev and Djakarta instantaneously. In total, IT has given birth to the world's superhighway of global comparative advantage and financial markets.

The applications of IT are revolutionary, but the essence of the information technology revolution is the depth and extent of its application—it touches every business, every industry, every sector. There are many other applications of IT that have profound effects: in the realm of organic science, IT creates biotechnology, which makes possible everything from agriculture on previously infertile soil to heart transplants. Overall, IT and its applications are allowing more people on the earth to participate in a more globalized economy than ever before. And in doing so, greater economic wealth is being created than at any other time in history. Table 3.1 presents an overview of the major IT sectors, although information in this sector is often outdated before it goes to print.

The economic and technological waves have been confirmed by the ultimate capitalist arbiter: the stock market. There used to be a saying in America that as General Motors goes, so goes the nation.

TABLE 3.1
THE CURRENT RAGE

Sector	Subset Companies	Product/ Services	Applications	Market Capitalization ($ billion) (Dec. 1998)
Telecommunications				
	AT&T	Phone lines	Global phone networks	$145.7
	Lucent	Networks/satellites	International information networks	$144.7
	Motorola	Wireless	Portable cellular phones	$40.8
Computing				
	Intel	Microprocessors	Speed and memory of computers	$215.7
	IBM	Personal and mini-computers	Computing	$176.6
	Sun	Workstations	Servers	$32.2
	Microsoft	Programming, software	Spreadsheets, word processing programs, and Internet browsers	$342.6
	Cisco	Network equipment	Dial-up access servers	$146.0

SOURCE: Bloomberg News, January 1999

How quaint that seems today. Anyone born after 1975 would probably not know that old GM was ever the king of American companies, just as most of us don't know that U.S. Steel (now called CSX) was America's first billion-dollar corporation, making it the most valuable company in the United States in 1901.[1] Wall Street is a world of changing expectations, and the expectations are expressed in stock prices. Based on market capitalization today, the world is keenly watching the IT sector, whose bellwether companies have displaced the powerhouses of the past, as Table 3.2 shows.

That the companies of the IT sector have become stock market leaders today is testimony to the power and prevalence of Information Technology. As individuals and businesses around the world apply IT to their daily activities, the value of IT companies continues to increase. Investors stake their faith in the continued, widespread use of IT, rightly seeing these increasingly useful (and financially powerful) companies as huge investment opportunities. As testimony to IT's status as Number One Genius Technology, we should note that in the same ten-year spans (1989–99), both Microsoft and Intel—the leaders of the new wave—increased their worth some forty and thirty-two times, respectively, while General Motors and Ford (yesteryear's leaders) have had only two- and four-fold increases in terms of market

TABLE 3.2

PASSING THE BATON, MARKET CAPITALIZATION OF PAST AND PRESENT LEADING U.S. CORPORATIONS

	1979 ($ billion)	1989 ($ billion)	1999 ($ billion)
General Motors	14.5	27.2	46.9
Ford	9.2	18.2	71.6
Intel	1.3 million	6.7	215.7
Microsoft	N/A	8.6	347.6

SOURCES: FactSet; Bloomberg News

Note: 1999 figures reflect market capitalization in January.

TABLE 3.3
SELECTED OCCUPATIONS IN THE U.S.
FORECAST % CHANGE 1994–2005

Bookkeepers	−10%
Machine-tool workers	−16%
Telephone and switchboard operators	−17%
Textile workers	−18%
Farmers	−20%
Bank tellers	−22%
Typists	−26%
Communications-equipment installers/repairs	−27%
Computer system analysts/programmers	+90%

SOURCE: U.S. Bureau of Statistics

capitalization. In doing so, the stock market valued the two techno-giants at $557 billion compared to $118 billion for the two old auto-giants at year-end 1998. In total, the info-sector—which includes telecommunications and computing—now has market capitalization of well over $1 trillion, or nearly 20% of the entire U.S. stock market. For further confirmation of the impact of Genius Technology on financial markets, note that one hundred years ago, at the peak of the Age of Rail, railroads also accounted for approximately 20% of stock market capitalization. These trends—the rise of IT and the decline of many low-skill, manual labor sectors of the economy—are being mirrored in the job market.

The technological innovations of the past—railroads, steam power, electricity—were revolutionary because they sped up production and shrank distance. But the benefits of such technologies could be reaped only by certain businesses. Information Technology can help *every* business produce and create better, faster, cheaper, and bigger than before. And because IT is applicable to every business, IT alters paradigms of production throughout the world, transforming the process of production, from product design, sourcing raw materials, transport, manufacturing, and delivery, to marketing. In turn, it accelerates the integration of the economies of industrialized and developing countries.

Adding new technologies to the world and, in turn, folding new countries into the global economy suggest an image of new patches being sewn together in an ever-expanding economic quilt. I used to think so. In reality, the global economy is more like a kaleidoscope in which new pieces of glass, representing the new technologies and countries being integrated, are being added to create novel patterns and colors at every turn. And yet, today's dazzling technologies are inherently ephemeral, fleeting patterns that will be radically altered as the kaleidoscope turns in a never-ending process that has come to symbolize the continuing triumph of technology and markets. Moreover, this kaleidoscopic process has only just begun.

Most previous economic expansions have been driven by a technology that was developed in symbiosis with other technologies. The railroad revolution, for example, was clearly linked to steel production, as was the automobile revolution. One primary difference of IT is the way it acts as a self-lubricating engine. But IT is different from any other technology because of the way it integrates sectors and economies, resulting in an explosion of global trade and an exchange of ideas and capital. The high-speed proliferation of IT and its applications has radically altered the economic stratification of the world. The core of IT and its applications is telecommunications, which is its "nervous system," and computing, which has been called "the brain of the integrated economy."[2]

TELECOMMUNICATIONS

Falling telecommunications costs and the increased capital of the industry have made international communications less expensive and more efficient than ever before. Before the mass sale and use of computers, IT was primarily a telecommunications sector. And like IT on the whole, telecommunications, by enabling international production and global trade through the transformation of international communications, has a tremendous capacity to stimulate economic and social change. It has become increasingly easy and cheap to communicate with people all over the world, leading to an unprecedented increase in the global exchange of ideas and flow of information. The significance of a thriving telecom sector is best analyzed by Metcalfe's Law (named after Bob Metcalfe, the inventor of the Ethernet, the world's dominant local area network): the "value" of a network—defined as its utility to a population—is roughly proportional to the number of users squared.[3] One person with one telephone is useless. Two people each with a phone is the beginning of a network. As international telephone density increases—and it is expected to increase by 10% to 15% annually, driven by both technology and capital—networks expand and so do their economic value.[4] Meanwhile, the rest of the economy enjoys the productivity and integration benefits from the application of telecommunications improvements. That is why most analysts view the telecom sector as one of the most powerful and valuable forces behind growth in the world today.

Demand for telephones in industrialized countries has increased exponentially over time, resulting in the very high per capita telephone density we have today. High-income countries have an average of 49.14 main telephone lines per 100 inhabitants.[5] Phone density in the United States alone has increased by 40% over the last ten years.[6] First World countries spend an average of $120.40 per annum on telecom investments per inhabitant.[7] Some 40 million phones are sold annually in the U.S., and Internet connections in the U.S. grew by 100% in 1996 alone. Today there are 12 Internet connections for every 1,000 people, which can be made on one of 365 computers per 1,000 people.[8] There are also 47.2 million cellular phone subscribers in the U.S., compared with 11 million subscribers in 1992.[9] Worldwide, one new phone subscriber in six will choose a cellular phone as people in developing countries opt to keep pace with the technological revolution instead of waiting for traditional hard wiring.[10]

Today, especially in the U.S., phone companies have reached market saturation, competing with each other for customers by offering dime-per-minute and flat-fee phone rates to the numbers their customers dial most frequently. The number of TV commercials for long distance services is an indicator of how hard phone companies are trying to maximize profit and of how many of their customers are making frequent international phone calls. Offering fax lines, Internet connections, and cellular phone and paging services, phone companies are profiting from the many ways in which they can connect their customers to the world.

In addition to increased demand and penetration, the net result of these developments is a dramatic decrease in cost. IT has lowered the price of a three-minute phone call from New York to London from $250 in 1930, to $12 in 1970, to less than $1 today.[11]

As markets approach saturation in the First World, there is greater potential in the emerging markets of Africa, Asia, Latin America, and the former Soviet Union, as Figure 3.1 illustrates. There are only, on average, 0.8 main lines per 100 inhabitants in low-income countries,[12] with a large main line imbalance between urban and rural areas, as urban businesses are usually the first in developing countries to obtain access to new technology. Even worse, the existing phone lines are not capable of successfully connecting 40% to 65% of all calls

FIGURE 3.1
TELEPHONE DENSITY

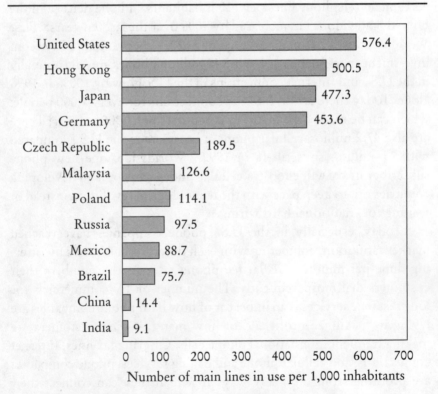

Country	Number of main lines in use per 1,000 inhabitants
United States	576.4
Hong Kong	500.5
Japan	477.3
Germany	453.6
Czech Republic	189.5
Malaysia	126.6
Poland	114.1
Russia	97.5
Mexico	88.7
Brazil	75.7
China	14.4
India	9.1

SOURCES: Comsat Corp.; Economist Intelligence Unit

made.[13] To put things into perspective, half of the world's population has yet to make a phone call.

For emerging markets to be able to compete globally, they need adequate telecommunications technology and infrastructure. Because of its critical importance in accelerating business growth, the telecom sector is often the first sector to be privatized in the developing world: telecom accounts for some 50% of all revenues generated from recent infrastructure privatizations in the 1990s, according to the World Bank. Keeping Metcalfe's Law in mind, one can only imagine the economic possibilities when 3 billion individuals get connected to the world's information superhighway.

A developing market's telecom sector invites foreign investment, facilitates international production and manufacturing, and, on a more basic level, offers a great opportunity for earning foreign currency. Clearly, there is opportunity for financial gain by all parties involved in the growing market of developing countries' telecom infrastructure and consumption. And as emerging markets grow, people in these markets realize that they need to be plugged in and on-line, generating consumer demand for more technological services in developing countries. The booming IT sector in emerging markets is the beginning of a process of empowerment that will continue to integrate emerging markets and maximize their competitive comparative advantage. By reducing the cost of international communication, IT has helped to globalize production and financial markets, in addition to helping local developing market economies thrive within their own borders.

Fiber-optic networks have revolutionized international communications, making information transfer cheap, easy, and quick. In addition, these networks carry much more communication and information traffic than traditional copper-wire cables. In 1960, transatlantic telephone lines could deliver only 138 conversations simultaneously.[14] Now a typical fiber-optic bundle can carry 1.5 million conversations.[15] Although the cost of installation is the same, fiber-optic wires are 80% cheaper to maintain than a wired network—and maintenance accounts for one-quarter of network operating costs. This explains why phone companies around the world are replacing copper wiring with fiber optics. In fact, so many fiber-optic networks are being laid so quickly that as of 1997 half of them placed beneath the Atlantic Ocean had not been used.[16]

In February 1997 the World Trade Organization arranged an agreement between sixty-nine countries to open domestic telecommunications markets to international competition. This landmark agreement will expedite the development of the telecommunications infrastructure in developing countries. As the cost of international telephone calls plummets, demand for a functional telecom infrastructure will rise, bringing global carriers into emerging markets. This free marketization under the WTO agreement of telecom services will accelerate the flow of information across borders, a process that will further integrate the developing world.

COMPUTING

When ENIAC, the first mainframe computer, was used at the University of Pennsylvania in 1946, it occupied a two-car garage and crashed every seven minutes.[17] The average personal computer (PC) used in most homes today has hundreds of times the power of ENIAC contained in a pea-sized chip.[18] When NASA sent the first spaceship up in 1961, it had less power than the computer I used to write this book. The computer revolution officially began when Intel introduced the microprocessor in 1971, but it was not truly underway until the IBM PC was launched in 1982. Until the advent of the PC, computers were

TABLE 3.4

**CUMULATIVE GAINS FROM TELECOMMUNICATIONS
LIBERALIZATION, 1997–2001 ($ BILLION)***

Europe	$288
East Asia and the Pacific	$211
Japan	$201
Latin America	$120
South Asia	$56
Rest of the world	$170
Total	$1,046

SOURCE: Institute for International Economics

* Excludes countries such as the U.S. and Britain, which already have competitive markets.

obscure machines, an understanding of which was possessed by a few programming geeks who spoke an incomprehensible language. But from 1982 to today, the number of PCs used by businesses has increased dramatically, with U.S. financial firms alone investing $100 billion in IT in 1995.[19] The growing importance of computers in our lives is indicated by the fact that as of this writing, one-third of all homes in America have a PC. The proportion of PCs sold for home use in developed markets has risen to 50% today, from 20% in 1985.[20] And the capabilities of computers have increased at an astounding rate. As measured in MIPS (millions of instructions per second), computing power quintupled in only six years, from 112,000 in 1986 to 553,231 in 1992, and will have risen another twenty-fold by the time this book is published.[21] According to Moore's Law, as postulated by Intel founder Gordon Moore, microprocessing speed doubles every eighteen months. In twenty-five years, for example, computers will be more than 100,000 times faster than they are today. As computer power increases, the amount of time it takes for a computer to complete a task decreases, increasing overall productivity. The astounding rate at which the IT boom has occurred is nothing short of phenomenal.

As with telecommunications, computing costs are falling so quickly that it borders on the ridiculous. Computer prices have been dropping by more than 30% each year. Some estimates suggest that computer power today costs only one-hundredth of one percent of what it did some twenty-five years ago. This is historically significant: never before has a Genius Technology dropped in price so fast and its productivity increased so rapidly. In the case of steam power and railroads, it took fifty to sixty years before their price fell by 50% from their original costs. To put it in perspective, *The Economist* notes that if automobiles were invented in 1970 and dropped in price accordingly, while increasing features, a typical car today would cost less than five dollars and drive 250,000 miles on one gallon of gas.

The fact that computing power is becoming affordable so quickly for many developing countries makes it a more revolutionary technology than electricity or the railroads. It took so much time and money to transfer the previous Genius Technology to the developing world that their beneficial effects could often not be felt quickly enough to allow them to compete effectively. Cheap, accessible, and portable,

IT's impact on the developing world has been more immediate and more profound than that of any other previous Genius Technologies.

THE POTENT COCKTAIL: TELECOMMUNICATIONS + COMPUTING = INTERNET

When the U.S. government in 1969 developed ARPANET, a test vehicle through computer networks linking many universities and research centers, it never could have envisioned the potential that would be unleashed for global communications and economics. The development of ARPANET, the "grandfather" of the Internet, was a laborious process: an Internet protocol technology needed to be developed to define how electronic messages were packaged, addressed, and sent over the network. TCP/IP (Transmission Control Protocol/ Internet Protocol) was invented in 1977, allowing users to link various branches of other complex networks directly to the ARPANET, and it soon became known as the Internet.[22]

Today the Internet is made up of more than 100,000 interconnected networks, including commercial, academic, and government networks, in over one hundred countries. Each local network is connected to one or more other local networks (usually over high-speed digital telephone lines), thus giving birth to the global exchanges of data, news, ideas, and capital. The Internet initially gained a devout following because of its electronic mail capabilities through the World Wide Web, an Internet function that links documents locally and remotely. The Web, which was developed at the European Center for Nuclear Research in 1989 to share research information on nuclear physics, became the center of Internet activity because of its easy "point and click" access that allows users to retrieve information from the largest collection of on-line information in the world. Herein lies the inherent utility of the Internet in conjunction with the Web: unprecedented, unrivaled, inexpensive, real-time access to a wealth of information on any and all topics, pooled from global resources. This world of information can be accessed instantly on the Internet, for less money and in less time than it would take to buy a subway token and travel to a library, where one could only hope to find one-tenth of the information that is available on-line.

Because of its ease of use and low expense, Web and Internet activity has grown at an exponential rate, from 500 Web sites in 1994 to an estimated 200,000 by 2000.[23] According to Forrester Research in Cambridge, Mass., the value of Internet commerce is expected to grow from just $600 million in 1996 to more than $66 billion to 2000.[24] As financial information is increasingly available to all, capital soon follows, flying around the world with the click of a mouse.

Many feel the commercial potential for computing and the Internet is almost unquantifiable, and for good reason. The Internet's virtually free and global-reaching communication will transform the way almost all business is transacted. As in the past there will be winners and losers as the new paradigm replaces the old.[25] Winners have already emerged in the stock market: almost every Internet variant, from service provider (e.g., America Online (AOL) with $166+ billion market capitalization as of April 1999) to on-line retailer (e.g., Amazon.com, $28+ billion as of April 1999), seems to trade at price-earnings multiples of which old Genius Technology companies (e.g., auto manufacturers, utilities) can only dream. Much of this price inflation may be irrational exuberance for *anything* computer- or Internet-related, similar to the rage for railroad stocks in the late nineteenth century. As in previous Genius Technology waves, many weak companies will undoubtedly go bust amid greater competition. Yet some of today's high-tech players will survive the current hype and become tomorrow's blue chips. Don't be surprised if in the future we hear chants, "As AOL goes, so goes the global economy."

IT and Transportation

Advances in and the proliferation of technology, as applied to auto, rail, hydro, and air transportation, have made movement across borders easy and cheap. IT, in the form of computerized tracking devices, electronic cooling systems, and electropneumatic braking systems, allows for intermodal transport that ensures the safe and speedy delivery of goods thereby accelerating globalization trends.

The dramatic change in the speed and execution of international travel and transport is reflected statistically. In the U.S. alone, passenger traffic has tripled since 1970, mirrored by a 50% increase in miles traveled per capita.[26] In 1993, 12.4 billion tons of goods worth more than $63 trillion were transported over 3.7 trillion miles. Air cargo traffic has seen the largest increase, up 434% over a twenty-five-year period. Perhaps the most important indicator of the impact of these developments on international business is that 70% of all travel in and out of the U.S. was made for business and work-related reasons.[27]

These developments in IT and transportation, enabling a company in Houston to manufacture toys in China and sell them in Paris, have affected the global production paradigm: a business can save money by exporting production or assembly to a country that can do it more cheaply. That country then enjoys increased employment and economic enfranchisement and becomes an exporter, which, in turn, integrates it more fully into the global economy.

IT IN MOTION

The cycle of innovation, capital gains, profit, and investment in research and development leading to new innovations pushes America's IT sector further and further ahead, at the same time stimulating other businesses to use IT to their advantage. Most analysts cite technology as the driving force behind their increased sales and profits. IT allows companies to escape from traditional macroeconomic business cycles by anticipating and responding to consumer trends, making it economical to tailor goods to the needs of individual customers and minimizing profit loss by managing stock more appropriately.

To see IT in motion, let's examine a sector we all know a little about: supermarkets. Before computing, managing a grocery store was an incredibly time-consuming, labor-intensive business. Operating a supermarket is largely about managing information and capital: what to buy and when to buy it. This is generally dictated less by the grocery owner's taste than by his customers' purchasing patterns, making his an exercise in inventory management. In the old days, taking inventory was something performed manually. Often a grocer would have to close down early and would require the assistance of many employees to count stock, and this was necessary if he wanted to place orders in time to replenish goods. The last thing a grocer wants is empty shelves. The old tedious process of hand-counting large quantities of merchandise has been replaced by high-tech scanning systems that allow stores to simultaneously log both inventory and price information into a database connected to the cash registers. As items are checked out of the store they are scanned, and supermarkets know immediately how much they have sold and how much profit has been generated. A more complex system then sends messages to suppliers so that refill orders can be placed without even needing to make a phone call. At the end of the day the store manager has very little to worry about—he already knows how much he has in stock, how much has been ordered to replace sold stock, and how much money he's made. His capital is not tied up in dead (or maybe spoiling) inventory; his rent is not being wasted on unused real estate (for warehousing slow-selling products); he does not need to close the store for inventory; he does not need to hire extra people for warehousing and inventory. In short, all aspects of the grocery have been altered by IT, and this is reflected in ever-lowering prices. Supermarkets operate on some of the thinnest gross margins of any industry, somewhere between 3% and 7%.

IT's impact on retailing is very visible. Across the country "mom and pop" shops, as well as small and medium regional retailers, are being put out of business by the so-called superstores such as Toys R Us, Barnes & Noble, and Staples, as well as online sellers such as Amazon.com—companies that use IT and inventory management to reduce prices dramatically. Wal-Mart, the largest retail chain in America, records every sale in every store in a "giant data warehouse."[28] This electronic system allows Wal-Mart to track the speed and volume of merchandise sales, and enables the company to replenish stock in one store with products that may not be selling in another. This is how IT allows businesses to streamline management to eliminate loss and maximize profits. As a result, only the biggest companies that can invest in IT, manage inventory well, and keep prices low will be able to survive in the future. In fact, we are beginning to see Internet retailers that sell "virtual" inventory—stocks of merchandise that are warehoused with manufacturers until orders come in. When the orders arrive, they are actually shipped directly from the manufacturer to the buyer, with the retailer merely collecting a small margin for selling the goods.

IT has also increased productivity in many manufacturing sectors. One can extrapolate the impact on any business in which multiple inputs and processes need to be efficiently managed. To understand IT's impact, look at the manufacturing process within the IT sector itself. Dell Computers, whose earnings grew at three times those of the personal computer industry's overall rate in 1996, is a shining example of how production and sales have been altered by a confluence of IT.[29] The philosophy behind Dell, which is the reason why the company has been so successful, is posted on its Web site: "Dell was founded in 1984 with a bold plan: bring the right computers directly to our customers at the lowest possible price ... Each computer is built to your specifications ... Dell's direct business approach eliminates reseller markup and brings you leadership products at lower prices."[30] Dell's credo also allows it to remain on the cutting edge of technological innovations: because their computers are custom made and the company retains no inventory, Dell can design each computer with the newest, best technology as soon as it becomes available at no extra cost to the company or the customer. Dell maximizes IT in every possible way. Just look at the way it does business—via phone orders and orders placed to the on-line store at its Web site. Two technologies, one that is increasingly improved and made cheaper, another that is new and booming, enable Dell to thrive as a company of the future, today.

As more and more companies realize the utility of Information Technology, companies are making tremendous investments in IT (see Figure 3.2). For example, General Electric has decided to convert its entire supply chain from paper to the Internet. Getting the entire company up and running on-line is a costly venture, one from which Dell and other computer suppliers will likely profit nicely. But the company's investment will quickly pay off. GE expects that its shift to the Internet will save it hundreds of millions of dollars each year.[31] The key to staying one step ahead of your competitor is knowledge—knowledge of your market, your customers, and what your competitor has planned next. IT allows companies to tap into that knowledge, using it to their advantage to cut losses sooner or, in the best-case scenario, to avoid losses altogether. All in all, IT allows for the recharting of the macroeconomic cycle. Businesses maximize their profits and minimize their losses by using IT to their advantage.

FIGURE 3.2
INCREASED RELIANCE ON IT

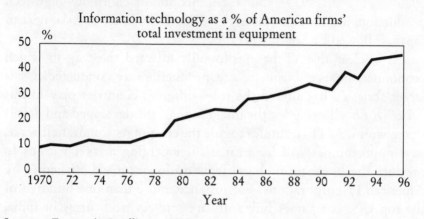

Information technology as a % of American firms' total investment in equipment

SOURCE: Economist Intelligence Unit

Another benefit of IT is the way in which it allows corporations to expand their operations by moving them abroad. Internationalizing production slashes communications costs that otherwise make international integration impossible, enabling companies to keep in constant contact with their overseas producers and customer base, minimizing errors, and specifying production to fit orders. Meanwhile, such international production stimulates the economies of countries where production is being carried out, generating more money for those countries' economies, more jobs, and higher, postagrarian salaries for workers. Employees can then take their income and pump it back into their developing local economy, either through individual consumption or savings, in turn reinvesting back into the economy through financial markets. As waves of development are accelerated by new technologies, emerging market economies bolster their own manufacturing capabilities as older processes are vacated by First World nations. These industrialized countries, in turn, begin focusing on developing and applying new Genius Technologies, which themselves will ultimately find their way abroad in the same way, where they can be more cheaply produced, speeding up cycles of technological innovation. This is exactly how Malaysia, Taiwan, and South Korea have become some of the largest exporters of computer wares. High-tech exports from emerging market nations more than doubled in thirteen years, from 12% of total world exports of high-tech items in 1980 to 28% in 1993.[32] China, another site of enormous high-tech production, has the third fastest growing PC market in Asia, next to Japan, followed by South Korea.[33]

It is clear that IT has profoundly affected the way in which economics, finance, business, and production are conducted. On a larger scale, IT has altered the roles different countries play in this cyber world, allowing for the integration of the developed and developing world. As IT continues to ride the crest of its Kondratieff wave, new opportunities will be created for emerging market nations to produce the lower-technology items no longer made efficiently by American IT corporations. For instance, more than one hundred of the top U.S. companies buy software services from firms in India, where programmers are typically paid less than a quarter of the American rate. This has helped boost India's computer software exports, which more than doubled between 1990 and 1993 while allowing U.S. firms to invest in innovation.[34]

With more and more of the world getting connected, the need to travel diminishes. If you can communicate with anyone, anywhere, by phone, fax, or electronic mail, cheaply and expediently, you often do not need to travel to see them in person. Multinational corporations have taken advantage of this and established production overseas, controlling trade and inventory electronically. IT has erased distance and made borders superfluous, producing an unprecedented influx of First World companies into developing countries.

IT's IMPACT ON GLOBAL FINANCE AND THE DEVELOPING WORLD

Information is vitally important to finance. Investing is largely a process of amassing information, analyzing it, and making investments. This is particularly true for fiduciaries—mutual funds, banks, insurance companies, and pension funds, all of which ultimately manage other people's money. For these financial gatekeepers, information breeds confidence, and confidence supports investment. Given the relative paucity of available information in previous decades, it is easy

MARRYING IT AND THE DEVELOPING WORLD: COMSAT CORPORATION

As MNCs venture out into the developing world, their single most effective weapon is information technology—the ability to closely monitor an overseas operation with on-line, instantaneous data. In some respects, without it, expansion would not happen.

One of the pioneers in connecting MNCs to their home offices is COMSAT Corporation, a Maryland-based company that provides global telecommunications and information services by fixed and mobile (satellite) technology. In short, COMSAT provides voice, video, and data through its global satellite networks.

A full 50% of COMSAT's business today is serving the needs of MNCs and local businesses in the developing world, contributing to what Treasurer Paul Pizzani calls "teledensity," or the growth of telephone lines hooked to personal computers. Pizzani notes that the United States is very connected, with 174 phone lines per 1,000 PCs. Germany is close behind with 70 per 1,000, but most developing countries are much less connected: Brazil has 15 per 1,000, India eight, and Indonesia only three. Pizzani is already witnessing a dramatic increase in the local networks COMSAT is helping to build in the developing world. Some of COMSAT's largest clients include Sony do Brazil, commodity giant Cargill, Procter and Gamble, and MasterCard.

MasterCard is an interesting example of how COMSAT uses IT to tie the First and developing worlds together. Let's say a MasterCard credit card is being used in Bangalore, India. The information is dialed into a MasterCard country network server in Mumbai. In turn, the request for credit authorization from India is beamed to the United States and to MasterCard's credit verification in St. Louis, where an authorization can quickly be bounced back to India, resulting in a credit approval at the local Bangalore shop. This is all done in a matter of seconds.

COMSAT notes that its emerging market network sales are increasing at 40% a year and will total some $500 million by 2000. This will be accelerated, according to Pizzani, by the WTO global telecom agreement.

to understand why few invested in the developing world until the last decade or so.

The impact of IT on finance over the past fifteen years has been staggering. In the early 1980s, very few developing economies had reliable phone systems. Much communication was done via Telex, a modern version of the telegraph. If a New York bank wanted timely information from an Argentine or Malaysian stock market, it was out of luck. If a developing-world president was assassinated on a Friday, one might not hear about it until Sunday in the newspapers.

Today, all this has changed. Advances in IT provide people with instantaneous access to all sorts of information: political, social, and economic. If there is a coup d'état in Africa, the world knows about it instantaneously, as CNN beams it into our living rooms. Digital links and satellites allow us to gather data from a hundred stock markets instantaneously; it allows thousands of companies to operate with multinational facilities worldwide. With IT, business and information are never more than a phone call away. And it is IT that has allowed the global trade and currency markets to flourish. In fact, trading in foreign exchange now totals more than $1 trillion a day, many times more than the value of physical goods moving across borders. With information on prices, products, and profit opportunities readily available, IT has made markets more transparent, allowing buyers and sellers to compare prices more easily. At the same time, telecom advances have brought down transaction costs by slashing communications costs between far-flung parts of the globe and by allowing direct contact between buyers and sellers.[35]

GLOBAL REORGANIZATION

IT has begun the process of integrating emerging market nations into the global economy. As American IT powerhouses such as Microsoft and Intel grow, the capital they accumulate is directed toward research into and the development of new technologies. These companies leave in their wake room for emerging markets to manufacture the less technologically complex products that they have abandoned in favor of more complex items. Emerging markets can manufacture these products quickly and more cheaply than American companies could

THE BUSINESS OF BUSINESS INFORMATION

Providing financial information is big business. Reuters, the 150-year-old British news firm, has nearly 300,000 of its financial terminals sprinkled across the world (Mark Laudler, "Traders Want Some Space, Too," *New York Times*, February 2, 1997, p. 1). And the rising upstart in this field, Bloomberg L.P., which began only in 1981, has experienced a doubling of its terminals from 1993 to 1997. Michael Bloomberg, the company's visionary founder, has virtually pioneered the IT financial sector not only by providing great series of data and news, but having systems that perform sophisticated analytic functions that were previously unavailable. For example, the Bloomberg provides historical pricing on thousands of global securities—stocks, bonds, commodities, and currencies. Not only do subscribers have the prices, but they can compare how they have moved over time in relation to other asset prices. The ability to regress data to create if/then scenarios has provided financial professionals with the most powerful tool since the calculator. Coupled with personal computers, the capabilities of financial professionals today make them look like F-14 fighter pilots compared to the hang gliders of the 1970s and early 1980s. It should come as no surprise that companies in the financial sector alone spent a whopping $29 billion on network hardware for their firms in 1996 ("Linking Up," *The Economist*, April 15, 1997). As a result, these financial pilots are taking investors to places that in the past they had only read about in exotic travel journals.

when the technology was new, and so they can exploit a comparative advantage that enables them to compete in global trade on the global market.

As noted in Chapter 2, altering economic paradigms has led to ideological and political shifts in the world. The virtually instantaneous transmission of information globally—made possible by the application of IT to telecommunications, the Internet, and audiovisual multimedia—to and from anywhere on the planet now reveals how people everywhere live: amid injustice and poverty for many, and with freedom and wealth for others. The technological achievements that have blessed the First World are now being incorporated into all aspects of human life on the planet. Intrinsically bound into the process is the business community's increasing reliance on such technologies to boost production efficiencies and broaden markets. This is radically altering economics in our lifetime, pushing the notions of free trade and comparative advantage to their maximum incarnations.

How Multinationals Are Helping the Poor Get Richer and the Rich Stay Rich

THE CUMULATIVE EFFECT of the proliferation of Genius Technologies and the abandonment of economically insular policies by the Third World is a more integrated, sophisticated, and differentiated global marketplace than ever before. Never in history have so many people on earth been bound together by capitalism, and the opportunities to produce and sell in the developing world, as well as to financially invest there, are unprecedented. In this chapter, we will analyze how strategic operators from the First World (as well as some Third Worlders) are profiting from these new economic opportunities in a mutually reinforcing manner.

MNCS: THE VANGUARD OF BORDERLESS CAPITALISM

In the last three decades, the possibility of producing and selling abroad has given rise to the multinational corporation (MNC). To understand the global impact of the MNC, First Worlders need only examine the origins of the products that fill their shopping carts: fruits grown in Chile, jeans made in Sri Lanka, and computers assembled in Taiwan—materializations of the ideas of Smith and Ricardo. Through MNCs everyone's life is commercially touched by the developing world, and the trend should only accelerate. Meanwhile, if we look at what lines the shelves of Third World stores, we see cans of Coca Cola, bottles of Bayer aspirin, and packages of Nabisco cookies—all made by First World MNCs that are tapping into the increasing purchasing power of a growing number of emerging market consumers.

The rise of the MNC represents the same capitalist stroke of genius that Henry Ford pioneered decades ago in the United States when he decided to pay his workers a relatively high $5 per day: the creation of new and global Third World "laborer-consumers" who earn enough eventually to buy the goods they currently produce for export. MNC production-for-export ventures abroad today are ensuring future sales abroad tomorrow.

The root of First World MNCs' aggressive expansion into developing countries is cold, hard economic necessity: they are driven by profit and nothing else. MNCs look to the Third World to lower input costs, to maintain or increase margins on existing business, and to expand sales into untapped consumer markets. In theory, rich countries always become victims of their own success, as the rewards of prosperous, productive societies are high living standards and wages that drive up input costs. The wealthy economies of today's First World are populated by a growing number of older people and a shrinking number of youths. This age distribution affects spending patterns, particularly by reducing domestic demand for consumer goods. When this happens, MNCs are forced to look abroad to find new markets for sales growth. While baby boomers in the United States and Germany move toward social security, half of the population in many emerging markets is under thirty. As these young nations become more industrialized, their disposable income—and thus their consumption—increases. MNCs know this. In fact, they often work to create demand in markets that have little current purchasing power but great purchasing potential. Tea drinkers in India may not know yet that they are part of the Pepsi Generation, but they soon will. For MNCs, the developing world is the global oyster waiting to be opened.

That the MNCs of wealthy countries will inevitably expand into the developing world for profit opportunities is not a new idea. Adam Smith in 1776, Ricardo in 1817, and Malthus in 1820 emphasized capital export as necessary for the survival of capitalism. They foresaw that the costs of production would outstrip the rate of consumption and profits would decline and, even two hundred years ago, that an MNC today would have to move beyond First World borders to find ways to overcome diminishing returns in their own markets.

All of these thinkers understood diminishing returns on capital. But it was perhaps the Marxists who articulated the theory best. While Marx himself in 1894 commented on how capital needed to move around the world, it was Lenin who, in 1917, wrote about the profit motivations behind export capital in his seminal *Imperialism: The Highest Stage of Capitalism:*

> An enormous superabundance of capital has accumulated in the advanced countries.... As long as capitalism remains what it is, surplus capital will never be utilized for the purpose of raising the standard of living of the masses in a given country, for this would mean a decline in profits for the capitalists; it will be used for the export of capital abroad to the backward countries. In these backward countries profits are usually high, for capital is scarce, the price of land is relatively low, wages are low, raw materials are cheap.... The necessity for exporting capital arises from the fact that in a few countries capitalism has become "overripe" and ... capital cannot find "profitable" investment.[1]

In short, it is the limits of capitalism in one society that allow capitalism to be limitless around the world. Ricardo put it more kindly: "It is quite important to the happiness of mankind, that our enjoyments should be increased by the better distribution of labor, by each country producing those commodities for which by its situation, its climate, and its other natural or artificial advantages, it is adapted, and by their exchanging them for the commodities of other countries, as that they should be augmented by a rise in the rate of profits."[2] Ultimately, he argued, consumption through comparative advantage could be increased through trade with other countries by driving costs down, allowing consumers to spend a larger portion of their income on other goods.

First World countries find themselves exporting those things in which they have a comparative advantage and importing those in which they do not. Because of huge increases in living standards and wages, OECD countries no longer have a relative advantage in manufacturing and other labor-intensive industries. They have, however, developed comparative advantage in the high-technology and service sectors, both of which have been optimized by the applications of several Genius Technologies. At the same time, emerging market nations—now freeing themselves from market-distorting policies like Import Substitution Industrialization—have discovered their own comparative advantages, making them viable manufacturing bases for MNCs. This allows emerging markets to generate and attract capital, and reinvest it back into their own economies. The process, in turn, builds a new class of workers who earn disposable income that can be spent on newly available consumer products, or saved and rechanneled into burgeoning emerging market economies.

The advent of new Genius Technologies at this point in history, which has propelled many First World service and high-technology sectors, has left economic voids now being filled opportunistically by the Third World's increasing capacity to manufacture and apply older technologies in the production of things such as cars and refrigerators. This process began in recent decades and has created monumental shifts in the organization of global production of goods and services. Some developing countries, such as the Asian Tigers, are moving into their third and fourth decades of fast-paced economic growth and capital accumulation. Some, like Hong Kong and Singapore, have jumped into the First World echelon of GDP per capita. They, too, have begun to experience the limits of success, finding themselves no longer able to competitively produce low-wage manufactured goods, such as textiles—as they once did. Now these countries are moving toward more capital-intensive production—like automobiles and computer components—while moving certain manufacturing components to their less developed neighbors.

One of the first modern economists to see this "food chain" trend was Kaname Akamatsu, a scholar who studied Japan's development between the two world wars and in the postwar period. Akamatsu suggested that developing economies begin by producing simple products that are labor-intensive, and then move on to producing more sophisticated products that require more capital and more technology. This process, when graphed, resembles a "wild geese flying pattern"— the name Akamatsu gave to the trend:

> The wild geese flying pattern ... includes three subpatterns. The first basic pattern is the sequence of import–domestic production–export. The second pattern is the sequence from consumer goods to capital goods and from crude and simple articles to complex and refined articles. The third pattern is the alignment from advanced nations to backward nations according to their stage of growth.[3]

Akamatsu's theory neatly ties together three concepts: how technology is proliferated, how advanced countries continue to innovate and forge ahead, and how "backward" countries move forward along the food chain.

During the postwar period certain East Asian countries provided a good example of Akamatsu's Flying Geese pattern, first shifting exports from primary goods (raw materials) to light manufactured products (such as textiles) and then to more complex goods (electronics). According to the World Bank, the more advanced countries made way for these East Asian gains by giving up market share—the United States in virtually all manufactured products and Japan and the newly industrialized economies in lower-end manufactures.[4]

For example, South Korea is a country in which three decades of rapid GDP expansion (averaging a remarkable 10% per annum from 1962 to 1992) and accumulation of capital, in conjunction with the dramatic liberalization of its economic policy, led to skyrocketing wage hikes. The previously low wage rates had made South Korea attractive for labor-intensive goods like sneakers and gloves. Although productivity had increased, wages had been kept low through government intervention. However, reforms in 1987 allowed real wages to reflect real productivity in a huge single leap. Since 1988 wages have increased four-fold, and certain goods from South Korea have risen in price and left the country uncompetitive in low-skill, labor-intensive production. Purchasers are now looking to other markets—like China, Vietnam, and Laos—for those goods. As a result, South Korea faces the painful challenge of shifting its production to those more capital intensive domains in which the labor advantage is not so critical, something Americans and Europeans have been dealing with for nearly two decades.

THE IMPORTANCE OF TRADE

Capitalism and globalism are natural partners because capitalism flourishes in a tariff-free, differentiated world economy. Capitalism thrives on production and consumption differences between countries, as Ricardo's comparative advantage approach suggested. The more pronounced the differences, the greater the impetus to globalize. In their search to reduce costs and increase profits, MNCs have harnessed new technologies that have allowed trade to increase dramatically since World War II and to evolve in new ways. Much of global trade now lies in *intermediate* goods—things manufactured for use in producing other goods—often between different arms of a single MNC in order to save money and increase profits.

The modern trade in intermediate goods is made possible by the ability of producers, in Paul Krugman's words, to "slice up the value chain, breaking a production process into many geographically separate steps."[5] Information technology facilitates instant information transfer around the globe. Innovations in transportation also make this process possible. For instance, the development of the long-distance jet airliner in 1958 and the wide-bodied jet in 1967 made air freight practical and changed the face of trade.[6] In 1993, 29% of U.S. exports departed and 21% of U.S. imports arrived by air.[7] As Krugman and Cooper remind us, many items such as cut flowers and fresh fruit are now tradable despite great distances: "Air freight also permits the international organization of production slicing, and combines it with just-in-time [manufacturing]. Goods can leave Singapore today and arrive anywhere in the United States tomorrow."[8] This process, according to Krugman, has led to the emergence of "supertraders" such as the Asian Tigers, and to the rise in large exports of manufactured

TABLE 4.1
UNDERSTANDING PRODUCTION

Type	Definition	Examples	Represents highest percentage of GDP for:
Raw materials	Goods that are not processed or manufactured	Oil, rubber, minerals	Africa, Central Asia, Middle East, and several Latin American countries
Intermediate goods	Goods that are manufactured for use in production of another product	Car parts, semiconductors for computers	Parts of Asia and former Soviet Union countries
Final goods	A product that is sold to its final user	Automobiles, computers, T-shirts, electrical appliances	First World countries, parts of Asia, Central and Eastern European countries

goods from low-wage emerging economies. The net result is truly globalized manufacturing that can take advantage of the most productive mix of inputs and labor. Indeed, the automobile you drive probably is made of parts manufactured in ten different countries and partially assembled in three, all of which reduces production costs and, ultimately, lowers the purchase price you pay.

Differentiation of the world economy and the slicing up of production both stimulate and are stimulated by international trade. It is a mutually reinforcing process whereby countries can have access to cheaper goods than they are capable of producing domestically and are, thus, able to consume more. Although promoted by technology, growth in free trade has also been encouraged by mechanisms such as GATT and NAFTA, not to mention regional trade organizations.

Ninety percent of tariffs on industrial products imported in 1947 by the industrialized nations are now gone.[9] These reductions in trade barriers have played a crucial role in facilitating increased trade, particularly in the area of intermediate goods. The developing countries themselves have, in many cases, unilaterally reduced tariffs and created tariff-free zones in order to promote the production of intermediate goods within their borders. The MNCs have been presented with new opportunities for cutting costs and increasing profits.

The convergence of all the trends discussed above has resulted in the increased importance of the role that developing countries play in the world economy, as well as the increased interdependence of all economies: developing countries' share in world exports of manufactures jumped from 10% in 1980 to an estimated 22% (in 1994)[10]; overall, exports from emerging markets increased 217% from 1985 to 1996.[11] This is merely a glimpse into how developing countries are being integrated into the global economy, creating benefits for both the First World (in the form of cheaper goods and higher profits) and the Third World (in the form of job creation, capital accumulation, and higher living standards).

THE BIG TEN EMERGING MARKETS

In 1993, U.S. Commerce Secretary Ronald H. Brown asked his Under Secretary Jeffrey Garten to help him determine the ten Big Emerging Markets (BEMs), countries that would present the greatest opportunities for American exports. Although trade with traditional partners (Europe and Japan) was still healthy, Brown realized that mature OECD economies lacked the export potential of the growing BEMs and that growing world trade would best be served by further integration of industrialized and developing nations.

The ten countries identified were Argentina, Brazil, China, India, Indonesia, Mexico, Poland, South Africa, South Korea, and Turkey. Garten's BEMs share several characteristics, including large populations, recent economic reforms (with more expected in the future), major political importance to their respective regions, and the ability to act as economic "drivers" by generating further economic expansion in neighboring markets ("The Big Emerging Markets: Changing American Interests in the Global Economy." Remarks by Jeffrey E. Garten, Under Secretary of Commerce for International Trade, before the Foreign Policy Association, New York City, January 20, 1994).

Brown and Garten anticipated that exports to the BEMs would grow to $1 trillion by 2000. By 2010, BEMs would be importing more from the U.S. than the European Union and Japan combined. Brown established an Advocacy Center to ensure that U.S. companies competing for projects in BEMs have the resources and support of various government agencies, including the State Department, the Export-Import Bank, and ambassadors to the BEMs. Affectionately referred to by Garten as "the war room," the Advocacy Center by 1994 had closed $45 billion in deals for U.S. companies, half of them with BEMs.

The specifics of the BEM policy include actions that would allow BEMs open access to our markets, which would in turn facilitate their growth. Brown and Garten encouraged BEMs to implement economic reform and motivated U.S. companies to share technology with them. Ultimately, the Department of Commerce would outline a strategy for dealing with each BEM in a way appropriate to that country's economic situation and political relationship with the U.S. Garten realized that engagement with the Big Emerging Markets would go beyond commercial policy and would involve economic, social, and political debates that would alter American policy and America's role in the world (see Jeffrey E. Garten, *The Big Ten: The Big Emerging Markets and How They Will Change Our Lives* [New York: Basic Books, 1997]).

MNCS RACE TO REDUCE COSTS AND INCREASE PROFITS

Multinationals are one of the many catalysts of increased globalization. To put their global economic importance in perspective, MNCs produce roughly one-third of world GDP and would collectively rank as the fourth largest country in terms of fixed asset investment.[12]

Make no mistake, MNCs are putting their money where their mouths are: foreign direct investment (FDI)—capital, plant, and

FIGURE 4.1

MULTINATIONALS: THE FOURTH BIGGEST COUNTRY

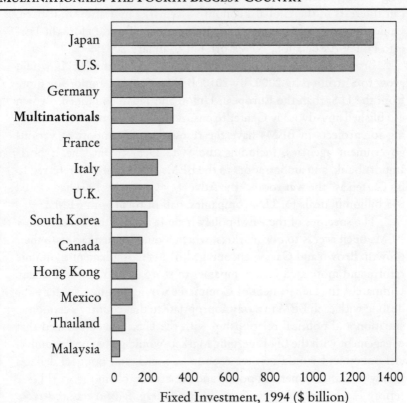

Fixed Investment, 1994 ($ billion)

SOURCE: ING-Barings Securities

equipment going abroad—swelled from approximately $20.5 billion in 1987 to an estimated $100 billion in 1997, according to the World Bank. Investments in manufacturing in developing nations totaled $56 billion in 1995 and was estimated to grow to nearly $90 billion for 1997.[13] The power of the MNC is increasing around the world.

Many factors draw MNCs to emerging markets, and labor is one of the most highly debated and sensitive areas when examining MNCs' overseas production. Few public figures in the First World openly promote the export of low-skill jobs to developing countries. Outcries come from the left, from liberals such as Ralph Nader, who protest the use of cheap labor on humanitarian grounds, and from the right, from nationalistic capitalists such as Ross Perot and Pat Buchanan, who hate to lose any job to another country. Unfortunately, both camps miss the point. Cheap labor is the primary comparative advantage possessed by the developing world, one whose use wealthy nations should not condemn on moral or economic grounds, as many tried to do during the NAFTA debates. Critics fail to remember that, one hundred years ago, the U.S. was built on sweatshop labor that was cheaper than labor in Continental Europe or Britain. American labor conditions in the 1890s were no better (and were probably worse) than they are in the developing world today.

As several academics have controversially argued, to deny these countries the opportunity to exploit their own comparative advantage—cheap labor—makes First World protests seem hypocritical, self-righteous, and economically shortsighted. For developing countries, it is an essential first step toward economic modernization and development. Krugman has noted that, for many children in developing countries, sweatshop labor is a positive alternative to the other dismal options that await them, such as malnutrition, poverty, and starvation, or perhaps being sold for slave labor or into prostitution. "If that is the alternative, it is not so easy to say that children should not be working in factories," Krugman has said.[14] The utilization of cheap labor allows developing countries to exploit their comparative advantage, which jump-starts the process of economic development. Over time, as has happened with Hong Kong and Singapore, countries become richer and transcend the need to exploit cheap labor, developing a comparative advantage in another sector. Only then can countries afford to institute protective labor laws. Before a country can entertain such policies, it must achieve a minimum level of economic success where it no longer has to worry about child starvation, for instance. Therefore, to criticize a company's decision to employ cheap labor, or to chastise a government for allowing these practices to take place, is naive and shortsighted. By using cheap labor to attract investment and generate capital, developing countries will begin a process of industrialization, the rewards of which will more than compensate for the early sacrifice of cheap labor. For the

First World, it enables MNCs to thrive amid increased global competition.[15]

The wage differentials are significant between advanced and less developed countries. As of 1997, Germany boasts the highest labor costs, at more than $30 an hour, substantially higher than America or Japan, at $16 and $19 an hour respectively. By contrast, hourly labor costs are only $5.60 in South Korea, $2.40 in Mexico, and less than $1 in Indonesia. Some countries in the Western Hemisphere, like Haiti, offer labor for as low as 68 cents an hour. Based on aggregate lifetime expenses associated with employing an industrialized worker (wages, health and retirement benefits, and work environment costs), one European bank estimates that an MNC could effectively employ hundreds of Russian workers for every Japanese employee.[16]

However, it is important to remember that low wages reflect lower productivity by individual workers. From this perspective, pay per unit produced is less divergent among countries than nominal wage scales. For instance, one U.S. worker may receive $16 per hour to sew blue jeans. In that hour he may produce eight pairs of jeans. A worker in a developing economy may receive $2 per hour and produce only one pair of jeans. In both cases the worker is paid $2 per unit produced. So labor costs per unit of output in developing countries are closer to U.S. levels than they appear. The trick for MNCs is to find the optimal mix: a worker who is paid $4 an hour who can produce three pairs of jeans—at a cost of $1.33 per unit. The overall labor/productivity mix of several OECD and emerging market nations for fabricated metal production is compared in Table 4.2.

As Table 4.2 shows, low-cost labor helps in places like China and Indonesia, but note that poor productivity makes labor in the Philippines no bargain—the U.S. and Switzerland are, net, more competitive in this sector. In general, however, it becomes clear that low-skill work like metal fabrication needs to go to the developing world because of its huge comparative advantage in cost of labor. Other variables will also come into play: quality of goods produced, transportation, and storage costs—factors that may make one country more or less competitive in one kind of production versus another.

Remember, too, that wages tend to rise over time in line with productivity increases and currency appreciation when labor markets

TABLE 4.2

COMPARATIVE PRODUCTIVITY, 1995
FABRICATED METAL PRODUCTION

	Hourly Wages for Manufacturing Work (in $)	Hourly Labor Productivity (in $)	Productivity per $ of Labor (in $)
China	0.11	0.56	5.09
Indonesia	0.25	1.08	4.32
Hungary	1.89	5.64	3.55
Mexico	2.48	8.39	3.38
Malaysia	1.55	4.06	2.62
Taiwan	4.86	12.63	2.60
Czech Republic	1.59	3.88	2.44
Chile	1.98	4.03	2.04
Japan	19.32	37.58	1.95
Switzerland	23.05	41.64	1.81
United States	16.82	28.14	1.67
South Korea	5.66	8.31	1.47
Philippines	0.79	1.15	1.46
South Africa	5.77	8.29	1.44
Germany	23.53	33.39	1.42

SOURCE: *World Competitiveness Report 1995* (Geneva: International Institute for Management Development, 1995), p. 617.

become tight. One study of four Asian countries (South Korea, Thailand, Malaysia, and the Philippines) examined factory wages and productivity and found that, although 1990 factory wages and other compensation in these four developing countries amounted to only 14% to 32% of U.S. pay, unit labor costs were 71% of U.S. levels in South Korea, 86% in Thailand, and actually above U.S. levels in Malaysia and the Philippines. Interestingly enough, back in 1970, unit labor costs in these four countries were less than half U.S. levels. In the intervening 20 years, a combination of currency appreciation and increases in real wages fostered by productivity gains closed the gap.[17] The future for labor looks increasingly bright in developing economies. According to World Bank projections, the global work-force is expected to grow by approximately 600 million between now and 2010, but only 6 million of this workforce will come from high-income OECD countries. While Asia will remain a key area, the Middle East and Africa are rapidly emerging as significant global labor markets. Asia is expected to contribute less than half of the growth over the next fifteen years. Sub-Saharan Africa, on the other hand, which represents less than 10% of today's labor force, will account for almost 30% of the growth. And though the Middle East and North Africa account for less than 4% of the workforce today, these regions are expected to contribute more than 10% of the growth over the next fifteen years.[18]

Wages are only one component of total labor costs. Labor costs in the First World also include medical and dental coverage, various insurance policies (life, disability, etc.), retirement and pension schemes, and occupational safety requirements for workers. MNCs can reduce these expenses by moving production to the developing world.

The net effects of integrating the developing world seem to be beneficial for all participants. Government policies in countries that embrace global trends by aggressively engaging the international marketplace have enabled a doubling of the world's workforce over the past thirty years and a doubling of the productivity of the average worker.[19] In an effort to stimulate economic and labor growth, as well as to attract technology and capital to accelerate modernization, many emerging market governments are luring overseas investors with direct incentives. Tax savings are common bait: free-trade zones, tax-free holidays, attractive treatments for joint ventures, and lenient rules for the repatriation of dividends. But often governments offer other enticements, including reduced red tape regarding energy use, environmental regulations, and other potential costs to the MNC.

China has been among the most aggressive developing countries in luring foreign direct investment, as well as the most successful: in 1996 it attracted more than $40 billion in FDI, or approximately one-half the world's total. A key incentive has been the establishment of twelve Special Economic Zones (SEZs), largely in the east, which have offered investors unique packages of tax breaks, including reduced land fees, reduced import and export duties, and priority treatment in obtaining basic infrastructure services. Government incentives designed to increase automobile production in China, coupled with the prospect of 1.2 billion new customers, have brought Ford and Daimler into the country. Cheap leases have also been used to attract financial firms to both Shenzen's Futian district and Pudong in Shanghai in hopes of attracting investors. A potential investor involved in China's fledgling high-tech and export-oriented industries could expect even more incentives. Going forward, it is expected that the government will use similar incentives to lure investment in China's less developed interior provinces.

Other Asian countries have followed suit. India has six specified free-trade zones (FTZs) and export-processing zones (EPZs), offering tax exemptions and other subsidies that have attracted Unilever, among others. The Indian government has targeted the garment industry for export growth and is attracting small-scale joint ventures by exempting them from selected parts of the labor legislation originally designed to prevent the exploitation of textile workers.[20] EPZs and FTZs now can be found throughout the Asian islands, including the Philippines, Malaysia, and Indonesia.

While latecomers to the capitalist game, many Central European and former Soviet nations are quick learners. In the Czech Republic, the commercial code guarantees identical treatment for foreign and domestic investors. Companies are allowed to enter joint ventures in nearly all sectors of industry or to establish wholly foreign-owned enterprises. They have also established five free-trade zones offering a VAT tax exemption on intermediate goods. Neighboring Poland has offered ten-year corporate tax relief and a further 50% reduction in tax for the following ten years. The Poles also offer relief on customs duties for imported plant and equipment in certain economic development zones. In Russia, Boris Yeltsin waived the oil-export tax for three years and eased the country's 23% excise tax for most foreign investors.[21]

Around the world we find more of the same. In Africa, Nigeria offers investment tax relief for a company that has incurred an expenditure on electricity, water, tarred road, or telephone for the purpose of trade when the company is located at least twenty kilometers away

DO THIRD WORLD COUNTRIES STEAL
FIRST WORLD JOBS?

The benefits and drawbacks of globalizing production, in most cases to cheaper bases in the Third World, are hotly debated. There are exaggerated fears that multinational expansion will come at the expense of First World jobs (take, for instance, the recent spate of books with titles such as *The End of Work*). But the answer can be determined rather simply: who buys more from whom?

Import-export statistics should give a clear indication as to who is winning. According to recent trends, it appears that the First World is exporting far more to the developing world than it imports. Since the beginning of this decade, exports from the G7 to the developing world have shifted from approximately a $38 billion deficit in 1990 to an estimated $92.1 billion surplus by 1997, according to ING-Barings. In this analysis, the benefits to date seem to indicate that the First World possesses a slight advantage. But it is because the developing world is growing at approximately 6%—or double the First World rate—that it can even afford to support the G7 surplus, which suggests these countries, too, are winning.

Clearly, the G7 is benefiting from resuscitated developing economies. Growth in these countries fuels expanded domestic consumption and investment, which, in turn, leads to greater imports of capital goods. This is good business for the First World, as it has shipped billions more in capital goods to the developing world than it has imported from it. Things look particularly bright in the U.S., as the Department of Commerce has estimated trade growth between 8% and 10% per year for the next few years (*U.S. Global Trade Outlook: 1995–2000* [Washington D.C.: Department of Commerce, 1995]).

While exports from the G7 look good, what about job trends and unemployment? In the U.S. the picture is clear. While unemployment rose for much of the 1970s and early 1980s (largely due to oil-shock-induced recessions), it has steadily declined over the last decade. As of this writing, U.S. unemployment stands at 4.8%, the lowest it has been since 1973. Also, more than two and a half million jobs have been created each year since NAFTA came into force (Sidney Weintraub, "In the Debate About NAFTA, Just the Facts Please," *Wall Street Journal,*

June 20, 1997, p. A19). The U.S. has been the leading industrialized economy to restructure its labor force to compete in the global marketplace. Comparative advantage rules in corporate America, and the downsizing, merger, and acquisition trends of the last decade are beginning to bear fruit. Growth areas such as computing, aircraft manufacturing, and the service sector are creating jobs with attractive salaries. Contrary to what Generation-Xers would have us believe, not all jobs available are "McJobs"—low-paying, burger-flipping, minimum-wage work. At Boeing, for example, many starting manufacturing salaries now approach $15 per hour—or nearly triple the U.S. minimum wage. For the time being, it appears that Smith and Ricardo were correct: free trade and comparative advantage produce win-win results for all participants.

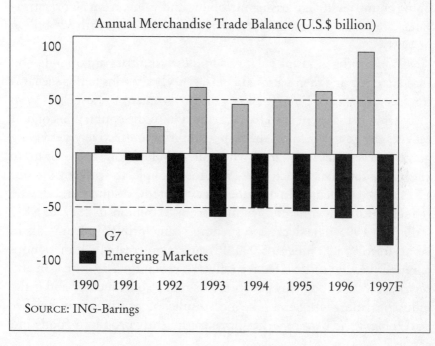

Annual Merchandise Trade Balance (U.S.$ billion)

SOURCE: ING-Barings

from such infrastructure. In Latin America, Brazil is hoping to become the Detroit of MERCOSUR, luring substantial investment from global carmakers, including Fiat, GM, and Ford, by offering reduced import duties on vehicles and parts to companies manufacturing within the country. The products manufactured in Brazil are sold throughout Latin America and are also exported to the industrialized world. In total, the developing countries have wisely decided to publicize comparative advantages and are competing fiercely for every dollar of foreign direct investment.

MNCS: A PRIVATIZING COUNTRY'S BEST CUSTOMER

As governments begin to dismantle the industrial holdings created through statist policies, great opportunities arise for MNCs to buy into new marketplaces through privatization. Privatizations in developing countries are increasing in volume and value, from 50 privatizations worth $2.5 billion in 1988 to 750 privatizations worth $24 billion in 1994.[22]

While indigenous populations in these countries are offended by foreigners buying their national assets, everybody wins in this scenario for several reasons. First, it allows the government to raise cash from asset sales, bringing needed hard currency into the country. Second, it relieves the government of the responsibility for effectively delivering goods and services to citizens, when this could be done better or more cheaply in the private sector. In 1992, for example, the privatization of FEPSA, the Argentine national railway system, resulted in a drastic reduction of government spending, from $1 billion in 1987 to $150 million in 1993. The decline in spending came primarily from cuts in labor, from 95,000 jobs to 5,000. Privatization created a leaner, more competitive, and more effective railway system for Argentina. In any sector, privatization helps governments reduce bureaucracy and make industries more efficient. The net results of privatization: smaller government and better market-priced, efficiently produced goods and services.

For MNCs, the ability to buy large monopolistic companies in these markets offers many attractions. Learning how a sector operates—who are the customers, how goods and services are produced and delivered to them—takes enormous amounts of time and money. Buying a telephone system or a steel company—even if it is not the most efficient operation—jump-starts MNC expansion. In this vein, privatized companies are viewed as turnaround situations with huge sales potential. The MNC brings three crucial elements to the table: cash to buy the company (as well as for future investments), first-rate professional management, and world-class technology. Often, all three—money, management, and technology—are part of successful bid packages for privatizations.

The facilities MNCs buy are often the least important assets. It is common for MNCs to completely raze old, dilapidated facilities (many of which governments can no longer afford to maintain). Sometimes an MNC will still operate under the privatized company's name. This way the MNC can ease its way into its new market, in some cases luring customers by offering an improved-quality product under the original name. Eventually, the MNC usually replaces the company's name with its own, thus completing the process of integration into the developing country market.

Developing world governments are selling state-owned companies in record numbers. Privatizations in developing countries accounted for 85% of all privatizations from 1988 to 1993, yielding $271 billion in revenue.[23] The impact on developing country economies is so huge that the average share of national GDP attributable to the private sector for four countries in Eastern Europe has increased from 20% to more than 50% over a three-year period. Foreign investors have been involved in 29% of these transactions, and a total of $33.1 billion in foreign exchange was generated by sales representing approximately 34% of total revenues from privatization.[24] In Eastern Europe and Central Asia 57% of all privatizations involved foreign investors.[25] Regarding foreigners involved in privatizations, competing MNCs often line up at the auction block: AT&T and Deutsche Telekom (telephone companies), Philip Morris, BAT, and RJR (tobacco), Unilever, Gerber, Parmalat, and Kraft (food), Heineken and Miller (beer), and Owens-Illinois and Pilkington (glass). These MNCs are gaining footholds and experience in tough markets which, in turn, give them greater know-how in handling new privatization opportunities.

MNCS AND EMERGING CONSUMER MARKETS

Just as MNCs turned to the international arena to improve profit margins through reduced production costs, they are now looking to the emerging markets to improve profits by selling to their expanding consumer base. While in the past First World markets offered MNCs stable sales, the potential to sell to the 4.6 billion in the developing world is key to MNCs' future financial success. The developing world offers excellent demographic trends and the prospect of dramatically increasing consumption. Once perceived as an underclass too poor to buy anything, the billions in developing countries are now seen by MNCs as future shoppers. Their pent-up desire for consumption and rising amounts of discretionary cash will fuel this market.

Moreover, just as markets for labor in the OECD countries have become increasingly expensive due to capital accumulation, markets for traditional consumer goods have become increasingly saturated. It is an economic fact that as people get richer their rate of consumption in relation to income decreases. While First Worlders are making more money, they are spending a smaller percentage of it on consumer goods, as a person can eat and drink only so much, according to Engel's Law. At current GDP per capita levels in the OECD, few First World markets can consume much more volume than they currently do. Under these circumstances, MNCs must strategically gear their efforts toward stealing customers from competitors in highly competitive, saturated markets—what companies call capturing "greater market share." Many of these markets are controlled by two or three major players (Coke and Pepsi, Brillo and SOS, Ben & Jerry's and Häagen-Dazs, Miller and Budweiser) with high brand recognition. These firms must compete for current customers either on a price basis or through product differentiation. Consequently, advertising and packaging become much greater cost components relative to the actual goods themselves. Indeed, a can of beer costs less than ten cents to produce, while typical advertising for that beer may add another ten cents to the purchase price. This is an expensive process, making it more difficult to make a high profit margin on each unit sold—living proof of diminishing returns. While the prospects of persuading Chinese farmers to buy instant coffee may be dim, Maxwell House has even greater difficulty increasing its market share in the U.S., Japan, or Europe—areas where there have been few new customers for its product. In general, developing countries' expenditures for these consumer goods are growing faster than the First World's expenditures.

As economies grow, the marginal amount spent on staples such as food and beverages will decline in relation to income. Therefore, although the growth in consumption for China is impressive when compared to the unchanged consumption in Japan and the sluggish growth in the United States, what is even more remarkable is South Korea's decline. While South Korea's demand for consumer goods levels off, the country should also see huge growth in the consumption of durable goods, which is appropriate for this increasingly wealthy country. The forecast for Russia, a country still experimenting with a free market system, indicates that major spending will be allocated for housing, consumer goods, and transport. Overall, as an economy becomes more industrialized and its citizens wealthier, spending patterns will shift toward luxury items. Furthermore, economies with older populations will invest more money on health care and less on consumer goods such as food and entertainment. Future projections are that the fastest-growing markets for all consumer expenditures

TABLE 4.3

GROWTH IN CONSUMER GOODS EXPENDITURES (AVERAGE ANNUAL % INCREASE)

	1980–92	1995–2000 (est.)	2000–2005 (est.)
China	2.8	4.9	4.7
Japan	1.5	1.5	1.5
South Africa	2.1	3.1	3.3
Russia	N/A	4.4	3.6
South Korea	5.9	3.9	3.3

SOURCE: John Whitley, *Consumer Spending Forecasts for the World's Largest Economies* (London: Economist Intelligence Unit, 1995).

per capita will be in Eastern Europe and the former Soviet Union (with an average growth of 4.7%), Latin America (where growth will average 3.2%), and Asia (where growth will average 3.8%).[26] It is no wonder that many MNCs are fighting to create and maintain market share in these countries.

In examining the impact of increased wage growth and increased consumption patterns, it is interesting to note that in many countries patterns of consumption follow patterns of production. Just as countries move from production of consumer products to consumer durables, they also move from increased consumption of food, drink, and tobacco to increased consumption of household goods and finally to increased consumption of consumer durables such as refrigerators and washing machines.

When countries produce higher-value-added products, wages increase and lead to more disposable income. Looking at the countries of Western Europe, we see that thanks to increases in technological innovation they experienced remarkable productivity increases between 1870 and 1979 after centuries of minimal growth. As a result, GDPs have risen dramatically for these countries in the past 120 years. The growth rates of developed countries indicate what the process of industrial development and technological change will be on wages and the standard of living. What is attractive about these emerging markets is not that the dollar figures are higher than in the developed world, but that because the growth rates of consumption in certain sectors are higher, the future growth potential of consumer markets is greater than in the First World.

Real GNP growth in China averaged 13% in 1992 and 1993. According to one report, this GNP growth produced a surge in consumer spending, with increases of 7–8% a year. The outlook for China is for 7–8% per year after a peak of 13–14%. Food, drink, and tobacco account for approximately 50% of total consumer spending in China and, together with clothing, footwear, and other domestic goods and services, represent some 80% of total spending. Clearly, ownership of durables is currently low and spending in this area should rise during the next decade. In another example, India now has a middle class of over 300 million people, thanks to annual GDP growth rates of 5+% on average.[27] In Poland, private consumption grew 7% in 1996 and is expected to grow 5.25% per year, fueling overall economic growth.[28] This rise in consumption is accompanied by falling unemployment, indicating that job creation and rising employment are linked to spending power.

The soft drink market is a classic study in purchasing patterns, especially because consumption of food items such as soda and candy increase in proportion to increasing disposable income. The international soft drink market is growing at twice the rate of America's. Per capita soft drink consumption in developing economies is currently high and yet has much room for expansion. This is one of the reasons that MNCs will invest in these markets even if initial dollar-value profits are higher in advanced First World countries. Although the country with the highest per capita soft drink consumption rate is Mexico (333 cans per year), followed by the U.S. (306 cans) and Australia (274), the international average is only 114 cans.[29] Emerging markets such as South Africa (146), Hungary (111), and Thailand (54) demonstrate considerable consumption, while countries such as Russia (5), China (3), and India (2) show tremendous room for sales growth.[30] Potential revenue drives MNC expansion: Coca-Cola sells 62% of its volume internationally, and this percentage is expected to grow to some 80% by 2010.[31] This is why Wall Street has bid up Coke's stock price to nearly forty-five times current earnings, up from just twenty-five at the beginning of the 1990s: the company has transcended its role as a dominant player in the "mature" First World, becoming a leading force in the growing overseas beverage market.

Similar consumption patterns occur with beer. According to Anheuser-Busch, average annual beer intake by Americans is 90 liters per person. In Mexico consumption averages 47 liters, but is expected to grow 5% per year, proportional to increases in income, whereas only 1% growth is expected in the U.S. This was the incentive for Anheuser-Busch's joint venture with Mexican beer producer Modelo in 1993. Chinese beer consumption is only 9 liters, leading Anheuser-Busch to invest in a joint venture with Tsingtao, China's largest domestic brand, and to produce and market Budweiser beer in China. By coming at the market from both sides, Anheuser-Busch will sell to consumers who have a developing taste for the local brand, as well as to consumers who are attracted to the well-known American label.[32]

Pent-up consumption goes beyond food and beverages, and spills over to other goods and services. Look at phone density: the U.S. averages 534 telephone lines per 1,000 people. Hong Kong, with 530 per 1,000 people, has higher phone density than Britain or Germany. At the other end of the spectrum, India has only 13 lines per 1,000 people.[33] For a telecom MNC such as AT&T or Deutsche Telecom, these untapped markets have the potential for decades of rapid expansion.

As countries work their way up the food chain and achieve certain income levels, various sectors of the economy expand. In some respects, as Table 4.4 shows, the process describes the life cycle of consumption.

In the infancy stage, demand for staple consumer goods will be high and will be accompanied by a demand for infrastructure such as energy and telecommunications. In anticipation of such demand Motorola opened a beeper manufacturing plant in Mexico that will produce solely for export to markets in Latin America and the Pacific Rim.[34] At the Adolescent stage, with GDPs per capita in the $2,000–$4,000 range, demand for durables or "white goods" like Whirlpool washing machines and Maytag refrigerators will be high. At $5,000 and higher, banking—along with other financial services—becomes important to Young Adult economies. MNCs like Citicorp and American Express will find great sales potential in these economies. As countries move to Middle Age status, with GDP between $8,000 and $15,000 demand for automobiles and entertainment (Hollywood movies, Sony Walkmans, video games) accelerates. As countries

TABLE 4.4
THE LIFE CYCLE OF CONSUMPTION

Economic Stage	Annual GDP per Capita	Growth Sectors	Examples
Infancy	$500–2,000	food, beverages	China, India
Adolescence	$2,000–4,000	durables, retailing	Mexico, Russia
Young Adult	$4,000–8,000	financial services	South Africa
Middle Age	$8,000–$15,000	cars, entertainment	South Korea
Senior Citizen	$15,000+	health care, computing	U.S., Japan

advance further above $15,000 to Senior Citizen status, demand for health care, travel, and many other services increases. In countries experiencing huge growth in infrastructure, energy consumption and personal expenditure on housing will increase dramatically. In Russia, it is expected that annual expenditures on housing and energy will increase by $20 billion, to $70.2 billion by 2005. In China they will double, from $6.4 billion to $12.4 billion by 2005.[35]

One merely needs to compare demographic trends in developed and developing countries to understand the sales potential and motivations for MNCs. In the First World, birth rates have been declining for decades and family size has been shrinking.

Furthermore, people in the First World are living progressively longer and retiring earlier, and workforces are growing more slowly, if at all. The cumulative results of these demographic trends are striking. By the year 2030, there will be only two workers to support each pensioner in the United States.[36] Fewer workers means fewer wage earners with disposable income entering the economy. The graying of

TABLE 4.5
GLOBAL DEMOGRAPHIC TRENDS

	Industrialized World	Developing Countries
1997 population (millions)	1,175	4,666
Annual population increase	0.1	1.8
2010 population	1,212	5,682
2025 population	1,226	6,810
Births, per 1,000	11	27
Deaths, per 1,000	10	9
Population under 15 (in %)	20	35
Population over 65 (in %)	14	5
Male retirement age	64	59
Workers to pension beneficiaries	2.5:1	4:1
Pension spending (% GDP)	9.2	3.2

SOURCE: Population Reference Bureau

First World nations means that their consumption and savings patterns are shifting. As a large part of the population ages and retires, savings levels will decrease, contributing to slower economic growth. This spells trouble for MNCs.

In sharp contrast, the developing world's population is relatively young and growing, and prone toward increased spending—a dream for MNCs. For example, while 25% of the United States population is currently over fifty years old, less than 4% of the Mexican population are senior citizens and more than 50% of the population is under age thirty.[37] In comparison, an average of 15% of the populations of the United Kingdom, Germany, and France are over age sixty-five. In Asia, Japan looks ancient compared to some of its Pacific neighbors: in Japan only 17% of the population is under age fifteen, but in the Philippines it is a remarkable 40%.[38] Older populations are an enormous burden, as support ratios grow and pension spending consumes an increasing portion of GDP, inhibiting economic growth. It is easy to see which of these populations will offer higher potential consumer growth in the upcoming years. Moreover, what makes these demographics so compelling is that as emerging market countries become integrated into the global economy, it is the segment of the population between the ages of fifteen and forty that will benefit the most because they consume the most. This is the population bulge that has children and buys groceries, clothing, and other household items.

One industry that seems to epitomize the dual-edged cut of global capitalism is the automobile sector, a direct beneficiary of cheaper production costs and growing consumer markets.

The advantage of cheap labor in the auto sector has been well documented. Routinely we read about assembly plants moving from Michigan to Chihuahua, and even from Yokohama to Shenzhen. While car production has become considerably more automated over time, human labor is still a large component of costs, making wage reductions an economic imperative. For example, Audi recently shifted production of certain engines of its A4 model from Germany a few hundred miles into Hungary, where labor costs were approximately 15% of domestic wages. The net result was a $2,800 (or 8%) drop in sticker price from 1996 to 1997, which led to a more than 25% increase in U.S. sales over the same period.

FROM EMPTY NESTS TO BABY BOOMS

Few industries rely more on demographic trends than the baby food sector. It is no wonder that companies such as Gerber, Nestlé, and H. J. Heinz are some of the first to enter the developing countries. These household names know firsthand that First World birth rates dramatically lag behind those in the developing world. This is seen particularly clearly in Europe, where the market for jarred baby food is stagnant and even declining in some countries like Italy ("Nutricia pays DM820 for Milupa," *Financial Times*, August 25, 1995, p. 19).

Gerber has seen the handwriting on the wall. Despite having a 60% share of the U.S. market, the company has built an aggressive international expansion plan around the developing world. Currently, the firm claims only 17% of world market share. In designing its market strategy, Gerber examines demographic trends, including annual births, increasing per capita income, urbanization, and the number of women going into the workforce. Using these criteria, Gerber identified potential markets in Latin America, Central Europe, the Middle East, Asia, and the Pacific Rim.

As a result of its strategic planning, Gerber, in a joint venture, now has 100% of the Mexican jarred market and holds an 85% share of the Puerto Rican market, which has the highest per capita baby food consumption in the world. In Poland, Gerber bought the privatized Alima company and plans to supply that country (with more than 40 million people and currently the fastest-growing economy in Europe) as well as to produce for export to France, Hungary, and the Czech Republic. Latin America and the Caribbean have huge revenue potential, with 12.4 million births annually. Asia was deemed an attractive market because of its size and birth trends (for example, Thailand, where fertility rates are high), but also because more women are moving into the workplace. Since disposable income in Asia is also increasing and the new middle class can afford to purchase jarred baby food, Gerber has noted in recent annual reports that it is targeting opportunities in Taiwan, South Korea, the Philippines, Malaysia, and Singapore.

While most emerging markets begin as production bases, in some cases local demand for goods produced in emerging markets creates a new market. As MNCs move production abroad, money is generated for the local economy that will financially enfranchise a burgeoning middle class. Once this class is born, demand for durable goods becomes the next link in the consumption chain, and some emerging markets are growing into increasingly powerful consumer bases whose demand for durable goods commands the attention of MNCs. The potential for car sales is huge: while in the U.S. there are two people for every car (and 2.5 in Europe), there are 11 people per car in South Africa and Brazil, and 675 people per car in China.[39] And emerging markets' growing importance should not be underestimated.

According to the Department of Commerce's *1995 U.S. Global Trade Outlook*, U.S. auto shipments to OECD nations totalled $4.4 billion, against a remarkable $5.1 billion to the emerging markets. Moreover, many developing countries are experiencing double-digit growth estimates in new car registration, including Bulgaria (up 22%), Indonesia (18.4%), India (12.3%), and Vietnam (11.5%), which far outpaces new car registrations in First World countries such as Austria (−1.4%), Japan (−.07), France (−.04), and the U.K. (−0.3).[40] Overall, Latin America is the fastest-growing automobile market, with sales expected to reach 3.8 million units per year by 2000.[41] Significant growth markets also exist in India, where the government's open door policy on domestic motor industry investment has attracted several major auto companies and whose production is expected to grow by 600,000 units per year until 2000[42]; the Philippines, where auto sales are expected to grow 41% from 1997 to 2000; Thailand, the world's second largest pick-up truck market after the U.S.[43]; and China, where the government hopes to triple auto production to 8 million vehicles per year by 2003.[44] The auto market in developing countries has so much potential for revenue that car companies are beginning to design cars especially for emerging markets.

Beyond earning great fortunes for auto companies, emerging market car production and sales will profoundly impact the future socioeconomic destinies of these countries. Car "culture" spawns a certain kind of economy. Just as lifestyles were radically changed as countries evolved from agrarian to industrialized, a country that

THE POWER OF PLASTIC

Many service industries are taking notice of the growth potential in emerging markets, particularly as information technology makes it increasingly possible for financial, insurance, and consulting firms to profit in these markets. One prime example is the development of the credit card industry in Asia. Combined MasterCard and Visa charge volume in the Asia-Pacific region reached $163.9 billion in 1994, nearly double the $84.2 billion in 1992 billings. Nor is the boom showing any signs of slowing down. In the first quarter of 1995, MasterCard volume hit $25.6 billion, a 43% gain from the previous year, and Visa volume totaled $21.5 billion, up 18%. These growth rates have led experts to predict that the Asia-Pacific region will catapult ahead of the United States in bank card volume shortly after the turn of the century.

Asia's middle class, which is driving personal consumption and, hence, card spending, is expected to swell from 200 million currently to about 500 million people by the turn of the century ("A Dragon by the Tail," *Credit Card Management,* July 1995, pp. 34, 45). Not only is the credit card industry itself growing in leaps and bounds, but its growth levels indicate how consumption has also been increasing in this region. Also, the countries in the Asia-Pacific region with the highest charge card growth rates are not Japan or Australia, but rather the Philippines and India.

becomes increasingly automotive will look and feel very different from one that opts, for example, for greater reliance on rail transport. Economies are largely the product of the dwelling, spending, and saving habits of their consumers, who are, in turn, significantly influenced by available forms of transportation. Highly developed public rail systems, for example, might foster greater urbanization, concentrating commerce in the big cities (similar to Western Europe's) while dense national highways (as in the U.S.) encourage automobile use, which leads to suburbanization. By extension, dominant transportation modes will dictate demand for the raw materials associated with them: reliance on railways may ultimately reduce the demand for steel, rubber, and petroleum, while increasing the demand for other forms of manufactured goods, energy, and services particular to rail systems.

In this respect, developing country governments obviously control much of their economic future. How a country privatizes transportation infrastructure, for example, will impact not only how goods are distributed, but also future demographic trends, leisure time availability, consumption patterns, and sector growth. Indeed, the future economic identities of these markets will be shaped by current governmental decisions. Governments' budgetary priorities will change as more money is invested in private and national roads, a self-reinforcing process to encourage car usage, as we witnessed in the U.S., which has now become a national mandate in China.[45] The dichotomy between city and rural life will disappear as people can more quickly and efficiently travel between these two spheres. Sprinkled between cities and rural villages will be suburbs and towns with their own inevitable business districts. Cities will no longer need to be the only location of industrialized civilization: suburban office and commercial parks may blossom, supermarkets and shopping malls will take root. With the mass use of cars comes the need for gas stations, and MNCs such as Shell and Texaco are making themselves very visible on the newly built roads and highways in developing countries. Don't underestimate the power of the automobile; for billions around the world, the car symbolizes an economic and social freedom for which they have yearned and that is now within reach.

The opportunities mentioned above only skim the surface of the possibilities that await MNCs and other investors in the developing world. Lower production costs are generating record capital flows of foreign direct investment into emerging markets, providing unprecedented manufacturing capacities. The results of these flows are cheaper goods in the First World and greater employment and GDP expansion in the developing world. Undersaturation, coupled with pent-up demand for Western consumer goods, should guarantee increased sales for MNCs well into the next century. Whether one looks at cookies, clothes, computers, or, eventually, CAT scans, the future markets lie in the developing world.

In many ways, this demand goes beyond the economic sense of balance sheets and income statements; it touches the very psyche of every developing country have-not who optimistically believes he or she will become a have. For that opportunity, billions of people are working cheaply for MNCs and saving for a long-sought-after lifestyle filled with material goods. This unparalleled production/selling maelstrom will act as important capitalist fodder for great investment opportunities to come.

AMERICA'S ULTIMATE EXPORT: AMERICA

When traveling to the developing world, one cannot help but see the affinity Third Worlders have for things Western, particularly goods associated with America. Whether one is traveling through urban centers like Moscow or through the pampas in Argentina, McDonald's Big Macs, Reebok sneakers, Pepsi, and Camel cigarettes seem to have universal appeal. These goods are not just things to be worn, eaten, or drunk; they symbolize freedom, wealth, and leisure—the culture and life the First World casually enjoys, what author Benjamin Barber calls "McWorld."

The wearing of Levi's jeans, for example, translates to a positive sign of economic growth, indicating that consumers can now afford to buy the emblems of Western life they have been deprived of for so long. By and large, people in the developing world will choose Western (especially American) brand name products because they are believed to be inherently better than domestic brands. People in developing countries think that if Americans drink Budweiser beer it must be of the highest quality, and they will, therefore, purchase it because with ownership of a Western item comes a taste of the American way of life.

MNCs know this and are devising their strategies accordingly. Outside the U.S., Marlboro is a brand name on clothes and other consumer items. Crowded Planet Hollywood cafes line the trendy sections of Third World cities such as Djakarta and Johannesburg, and T-shirts bearing Nike and Harley–Davidson are hawked everywhere. American music can be heard all around the world, blaring from Sony Walkmans. MTV has more viewers in developing countries than in the U.S. (Bernard Wysocki Jr., "The Global Mall: In Developing Nations, Many Youths Splurge, Mainly on U.S. Goods," *Wall Street Journal,* June 26, 1997, pp. A1, A11). Movie theaters showing American blockbusters like *Jurassic Park* and failures like *Waterworld* are packed with moviegoers who prefer even the schlockiest Hollywood imports to domestic cinema.

Developing world consumers aren't just buying a product—they're buying an experience, what Barber calls "the ideology of fun." Consumers believe that if they can afford Western goods, they are experiencing the lifestyle that Westerners have enjoyed. People drink Coke and eat at Pizza Hut because they want to experience what it feels like to be an American: young, free, sexy, adventurous, enjoying life in a wealthy economy. And in the end they all get what they want: consumers in developing countries have money to buy the goods they crave, and MNCs turn profits by catering to their demands. Whether or not this will cause the decline of indigenous cultures, or whether consumers are being brainwashed by MNC advertising, is not the issue at hand. What matters for our purposes is that the cycle of industrialization and capital accumulation has reached the next level: Third World consumers finally have enough disposable income for Western products, and MNCs are ready, willing, and able to supply that demand.

CHAPTER 5

Financial Modernization and the Changing Complexion of Capital

ECONOMIC SUCCESS IS TIED TO FINANCIAL SUCCESS

While most observers comment on the conspicuous signs of economic advancement in developing countries—such as new luxury hotels, MNC factory building, and massive infrastructure expansion—an equally important though quiet revolution is taking place: financial modernization. The interrelationships between economic growth, capital accumulation, and financial markets are critical to the Third World; in fact, the nature of these links is a huge factor in making "developing" countries develop. The installation of plants and equipment by MNCs results in job creation and, eventually, increased savings. Ultimately such savings accumulate, creating the basis for domestic capital and money markets. Financial marketization is further accelerated by cross-border capital flows, with direct investment traditionally being the first source of foreign capital. However, hard currency credit also is extended to developing countries (or companies) by foreign commercial banks, through corporate export loans (made to Third World purchasers by First World sellers of heavy goods like airplanes or turbines), or by supranational lenders such as the IMF or various OECD government export-import banks. Outright grants and foreign aid are also made available to select, poor countries by First World governments, whether through philanthropy or with ulterior political motives, although these amounts have declined since the Cold War's end.

The more critical capital sources, however, are true financial market flows that are channeled through securities—stocks or bonds. This is where the story gets interesting. While the Third World advances by building domestic savings and local markets, overripe capitalism is forcing the First World to look for greater yields beyond its borders, promoting record foreign capital flows to developing nations. With much of the less developed country (LDC) debt overhang gone, industrialized countries now are taking these economies seriously and investing more—in terms of both volume and variety of instruments—than ever before.

The importance of financial markets to economic growth has been a hotly debated topic for theorists over the last hundred-odd years. English social commentator Walter Bagehot, whose family owned a prominent bank in the late nineteenth century, was among the first to comment on the value provided by financial institutions to Great Britain's industrial development.[1] In his 1911 work *The Theory of Economic Development,* Joseph Schumpeter maintained that banks played a vital role in financing innovation, effectively greasing the "creative destruction" process. Because banking today is only a small part of the larger global capital market, the concept should be now expanded to include all forms of finance: one need only ask some Silicon Valley startups where they would be without venture capital or a thriving IPO (Initial Public Offering) market in the United States. The Third World is now beginning to understand what the First World has known for a long time: capital markets are a prerequisite and a continuing lubricant for economic expansion.

RELATIVELY LOW BUT GROWING LEVELS OF MARKETIZATION

A common feature of all developing countries is that their financial markets are relatively small compared to their growing economies. Many Wall Street professionals and academics like to analyze this

FIGURE 5.1
ROBUST ECONOMIES AND UNDERDEVELOPED FINANCIAL MARKETS OFFER GREAT POTENTIAL

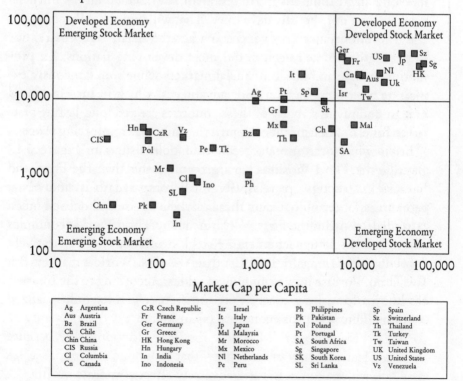

Financial Development vs. Economic Development
Market Cap/Head vs. GDP/Head, 1996E

Ag	Argentina	CzR	Czech Republic	Isr	Israel	Ph	Philippines	Sp	Spain
Aus	Austria	Fr	France	It	Italy	Pk	Pakistan	Sz	Switzerland
Bz	Brazil	Ger	Germany	Jp	Japan	Pol	Poland	Th	Thailand
Ch	Chile	Gr	Greece	Mal	Malaysia	Pt	Portugal	Tk	Turkey
Chin	China	HK	Hong Kong	Mr	Morocco	SA	South Africa	Tw	Taiwan
CIS	Russia	Hn	Hungary	Mx	Mexico	Sg	Singapore	UK	United Kingdom
Cl	Columbia	In	India	Nl	Netherlands	SK	South Korea	US	United States
Cn	Canada	Ino	Indonesia	Pe	Peru	SL	Sri Lanka	Vz	Venezuela

SOURCE: ING-Baring Securities

relationship in determining whether these markets have long-term appeal. As Figure 5.1 notes, most developed countries boast stock market capitalization (total number of shares outstanding multiplied by price) that equals or surpasses per annum GDP. Current stock market capitalization in the U.S., for example, is approximately $30,000 per capita while GDP per capita is around $28,000—in other words, the financial market is roughly 105% of the economy. In some industrialized countries like Japan, the market capitalization/GDP ratio is even higher, but most G7 countries hover around 100%. Yet some of the recent Asian Tiger financial markets have grown to OECD levels or even higher: Singapore, Hong Kong, and Taiwan—countries that by all measures are truly First World—surpass all G7 members except Japan.

Developing countries typically have market capitalization of roughly 20% to 50% of GDP. In some heavily populated countries like China and India it slips to less than 10%, which means financial markets have not yet fully developed. That will undoubtedly change: it was only twenty to thirty years ago when the Asian Tigers had ratios in the 20% to 50% range, as did most developing nations. By promoting savings and liquid financial markets while simultaneously exploiting their comparative labor advantages, which in turn increased income and savings, many of these countries created long-lasting platforms for economic growth through this mutually reinforcing process. (This is why some investors can read dollar signs in Figure 5.1.) Because the Third World is now growing faster than the First, and because its markets are relatively small compared to its individual economies, one would expect these markets to rise and deepen much faster than those in the First World. As many Third World economies surge, one would expect emerging stock markets to have a relatively *higher* price-earnings ratio (P/E) than the First World's market. But such is not the case in the emerging markets. According to the International Finance Corporation (IFC), the average P/E for industrialized stock markets is approximately 26 (as of March 1999) versus only 18 for the developing world. I believe the P/E is low probably because investors fear—rightly or wrongly—that economic reform processes may fail, which would, in turn, adversely affect corporate profits.

Clearly, financial market size is an important gauge of economic achievement and potential in the developing (as well as the industrialized) world. But perhaps more important is the *liquidity* of the stock markets; in other words, the amount of trading and turnover of shares. A recent study by Ross Levine and Sara Zervos using data on forty-nine countries from 1976 to 1993 further contributes to the notion that economic development and financial marketization are tightly linked. Their analysis suggests that liquidity—as measured by stock trading—is positively and significantly correlated with current and future rates of economic expansion, capital accumulation, and productivity growth. Why does liquidity matter? Zervos and Levine believe that most investors—domestic and international—tend to be skittish of illiquid investments. From my own trading experience, I would agree. Developing countries typically offer long-term opportunities, yet investors conceptually loathe the idea of *committing* their money for long periods of time, even though many do so voluntarily. A liquid stock market, therefore, allows investors to buy and sell shares easily, while still providing local firms with much needed long-term capital through equity. Zervos and Levine note that companies in liquid stock markets are often regulated by bodies that require timely disclosure of financial information, a factor that often makes local banks more inclined to lend to those listed companies. As a result, these economists have found that the ratio of local bank loans to GDP has also risen in line with local stock market turnover. The economic results of greater stock market liquidity are striking: for example, had Mexico's *bolsa* been as liquid as Malaysia's stock market in 1976, its GDP would have risen by an additional 0.4% per annum for the seventeen-year period to 1993.[2]

Having traded in more than fifty developing country markets, I have witnessed the huge psychological benefits that come from great liquidity. High-turnover markets often produce a "culture of money" that permeates all aspects of society. One needs only to visit a Hong Kong or a São Paulo to understand this; there seem to be cash registers ringing everywhere (literally and figuratively), and everyone seems stock market conscious. The more liquid a market, the more willing people are to participate, which begets even greater liquidity. This process is typically reinforced by a healthy macroeconomic picture, one that also entices people to save more and invest in financial

TABLE 5.1
EMERGING STOCK MARKETS

	Value Traded U.S.$ million	Market Cap U.S.$ million	Liquidity %
1985	45,156	171,263	26.37%
1986	82,968	283,308	29.29%
1987	164,846	319,322	51.62%
1988	413,616	500,409	82.66%
1989	1,170,928	755,210	155.05%
1990	899,920	613,621	146.66%
1991	616,030	908,406	67.81%
1992	631,277	1,000,014	63.13%
1993	1,106,387	1,699,811	65.09%
1994	1,667,171	1,925,999	86.56%
1995	1,046,546	1,939,919	53.95%
1996	1,529,971	2,293,437	66.71%
1997	2,701,711	2,229,508	121.18%

SOURCE: IFC

markets, all of which creates a more confident atmosphere for both local and foreign investors—a capitalist "buzz" that one can instantaneously sense when stepping off a plane in one of these countries.[3]

THE CUP RUNNETH OVER

Just as MNCs have been driven to the developing world because of overripe capitalism, so have financial investors. Whereas MNCs make direct investments in hard assets like factories and buildings, foreign investors largely buy financial assets such as stocks or bonds. In the past, most OECD investors had little or no access to developing countries' financial markets. The first reason why is simple: few such markets existed. Remember that large parts of the Third World lived under statist policies, and governments owned most companies. Prior to 1980, few countries outside the OECD even had stock markets, and today it is estimated that half the world's countries still lack them. Second, many Third World governments made it very difficult for foreigners to invest in their economies. Hurdles for foreign investors to overcome would include currency restrictions, cumbersome dividend remittance, limits on foreign ownership, illiquid shares, and poor and minimal minority rights, among others. Foreign investors were also plagued by practical issues: poor or nonexistent securities laws (as well as ill-defined property laws in general) and difficult and expensive ways to buy shares and perfect security interests. More important, poor company information and disclosure shook investor confidence.

Another obstacle for foreign investors to overcome has been First World political agendas. First World governments have often legally forbidden their investors from doing business in countries considered "enemies of the nation" or whose politics were in conflict with their own, which has been embodied in the U.S. with the enactment of the Johnson Act of 1940.[4] Up until 1991, U.S. investment in most of the Soviet Union and communist bloc countries was prohibited. Cuba is still blacklisted by the U.S., and Americans are forbidden from doing business with North Korea, Libya, Iraq, and Iran, political trouble-makers that the U.S. government has wanted to squeeze economically. Some countries, including Serbia and, until 1993, South Africa, have been punished with economic sanctions because of international con-demnation of human rights violations. As a result of these obstacles, the First World made very little portfolio investment in the Third World through the early 1980s. However, over the last two decades developing countries have made enormous strides at reorienting their economies and opening financial markets. As Figure 5.2 shows, the result has been a radical change in the complexion of capital flows to the emerging markets.

Through the 1980s foreign bank lending—whether from official lenders like the World Bank and the Paris Club or from commercial banks—was the dominant form of international finance. In 1981, the year before Mexico's liquidity crisis, roughly 73 cents out of every dollar from First World investors came via foreign bank loans. This kind of finance has obvious limits—typically short terms and floating rates—and it does little to foster local marketization or investor par-ticipation, hindering the development of the money culture described earlier. In sharp contrast, note how in 1980 very little actual money went into financial assets. Less than $3 billion of capital was invested in emerging market stocks and bonds.

What a difference a decade makes. By the mid-1990s the aggregate

FIGURE 5.2

CHANGES IN ANNUAL CAPITAL FLOW COMPOSITION TO
DEVELOPING COUNTRIES

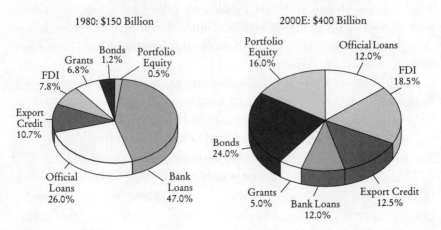

1980: $150 Billion   2000E: $400 Billion

SOURCES: World Bank; Bloomberg News; Economist Intelligence Unit; author's estimates

amount of First World capital invested in the developing world more than doubled. But more important, the complexion of capital flow has changed for the better. Foreign direct investment is actually growing in absolute and relative terms, the result of MNC expansion. This alone bodes well for the developing world's future as modern economic infrastructure is being built on its soil. Even more encouraging is the explosion of stock and bond investments. It is estimated that $100 billion was raised by emerging market countries and companies through bonds in 1997, some of which were scheduled to stretch a remarkable *one hundred years* in maturity.[5] Portfolio equity now totals some $50 billion per annum and should continue to grow even more over time.

Why does the investment cup runneth over at this time? Several times I have noted that the investment process is largely rooted in confidence. What breeds confidence? For First Worlders contemplating the emerging markets, it has been the ideological changes and the swift rise of capitalism in the developing world discussed earlier. Macroeconomic policy reforms—cutting deficits, controlling inflation, and privatization—have resulted in monetary and fiscal stability.

This new stability has been reinforced by financial market reforms, all of which have piqued investor interest. Moreover, technology has provided investors with more information than ever before, as well as the ability to process and analyze it to make more informed and sounder investment decisions. Finally, investors have gained confidence by seeing the growing size and liquidity of local financial markets, which helps turn the virtuous circle of reform to move faster and faster.

    This is not to say that such confidence cannot be deflated quickly in the short run. One need only to remember Mexico's peso crisis in 1994 or the Asian financial emergencies in 1997 to understand that key local reforms can stall or be abandoned, and market transparency can be compromised, which undermines investor confidence. The flood of foreign funds can be reduced to a trickle in days, and foreign outflows

FIGURE 5.3
THE VIRTUOUS CIRCLE OF FINANCIAL REFORM

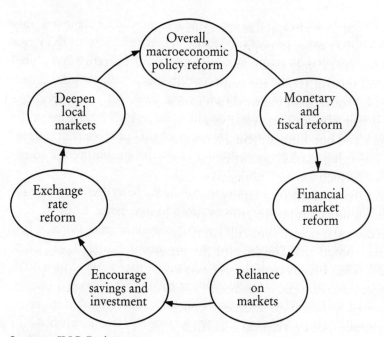

SOURCE: ING-Barings

often undermine local confidence, leading to capital flight. But despite the periodic setbacks in individual countries, continued reforms and increasing disclosure should minimize future crises of confidence, and given healthy economic fundamentals, the trend toward greater overall financial flows from the First World to the Third World should continue.

In some respects, reliance on financial markets to price capital represents the last stage of the developing world's reform process. The faster developing-country companies can be weaned away from direct or indirect financial assistance from their governments, the faster those companies can begin to compete at world-class levels. The ability to rely on markets for expansion or acquisition requires financial discipline by borrowing companies, and results in share prices, interest rates, and other variables being determined by the market itself, not arbitrarily imposed by statist-minded governments.

WAVES OF GLOBAL MONEY

The formation of a truly global capital market could be achieved only at a moment in history such as this, a time when more people than ever live under capitalist systems bound together inexorably by global production and instantaneous telecommunications. While cross-border capital flows have existed since the dawn of commerce, the amount that has whirled around the globe since 1980 has eclipsed the aggregate of all previous historic flows. And this process is accelerating, the direct result of more and more countries becoming economically enfranchised.

Economist and market strategist Michael Howell views the late-twentieth-century global investment flows in five distinct but slightly overlapping waves.[6] The First Wave took place in the mid-1980s, when First World investors began pouring money into the large, liquid stock markets of New York, London, and Tokyo. In those years almost 60% of new cross-border equity money went into these markets, but by 1993 this had declined to less than 40%. One of the most important explanations for this change is the cornerstone of modern portfolio management: diversification, the technical term for not putting all of one's eggs into one basket. The principle of diversification is to invest in assets that are not highly correlated with each other. With a portfolio of fifteen or twenty assets, for example, some decline while others rise, smoothing out the overall return. This simple principle effectively governs the *trillions* of dollars that are managed by pension funds, endowments, mutual funds, and other fiduciaries around the world.

During this First Wave most OECD institutional investors had little exposure outside their own borders. When it came time to venture out into foreign lands, other First World countries were the first beneficiaries. Remember, this was before the Brady Plan, and few investors were seriously looking at the developing world. The debt overhang and statist ideologies—along with a modest dose of xenophobia—kept foreign investor flows away from the Third World. However, even this first attempt at global asset allocation to other First World markets by the notoriously stodgy fiduciary community would lead to important lessons for international investing. The Second Wave, which ran from the late 1980s through the early 1990s, was dominated by MNCs who were experiencing falling profits in the wealthy West. The stock market crashes of 1987, subsequent recessions, changing demographics, and overripe capitalism forced companies outward. With the Brady Plan seeming to work and macroeconomic reform in progress, the developing world seemed to be getting its act together. The MNCs became attracted to the rising incomes and young populations. According to ING-Barings, over that period the combined value of cross-border corporate finance and mergers and acquisitions (M&As) represented three and a half times the value of cross-border flows into stock markets: international M&As rose from $39.2 billion to $156.2 billion from 1986 to 1994, while new stock market flows grew from approximately $11 billion to $58.1 billion over the same period.[7]

The Third Wave of cross-border capital surged into emerging stock markets beginning in late 1989 (just as the first Brady Plan for Mexico was being completed) and is still raging today. From 1989 to 1994, roughly 30% of all new foreign portfolio investment dollars found their way into developing country stock markets in Asia and Latin America. As noted earlier, much of that capital could be linked back to the structural reforms undertaken by many countries,

FIGURE 5.4

TRENDS IN EMERGING MARKET FOREIGN DIRECT INVESTMENT

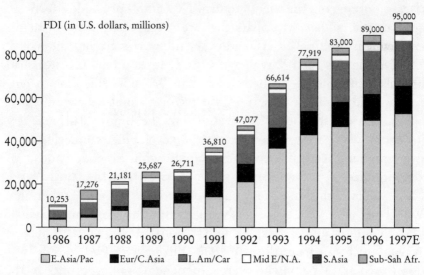

SOURCES: World Bank; Bloomberg News

including the mass privatization that created stock markets and companies for sale. However, there were other theoretical and practical reasons that led foreigners into these regions as well.

As noted in the First Wave, OECD investors were gaining experience in global diversification. A more sophisticated version of diversification uses the Efficiency Frontier, a model that analyzes the best risk/return blend of two or more assets. As the theory goes, there might be a mix that can actually reduce risk and increase return based on the assets' price movements. Like errant knights, most portfolio managers seek the Holy Grail of highest return at the lowest risk. The Efficiency Frontier was put to the test in early 1993 when the IFC, the private-sector investment arm of the World Bank, teamed up with the financial firm Barra to analyze whether emerging market stocks would be useful in a traditional portfolio of OECD stocks. Figure 5.5 illustrates the dramatic results.

For the period 1986–1993, the IFC/Barra study found that the return for a 100% OECD stock portfolio averaged approximately 7%

FIGURE 5.5

ADDING EMERGING MARKET STOCKS TO FIRST WORLD PORTFOLIOS

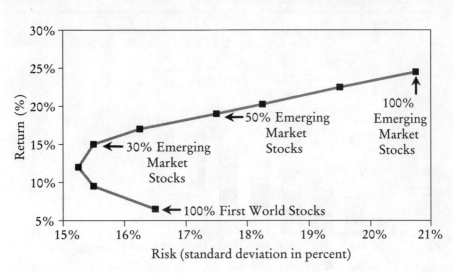

Source: IFC, Barra

per annum with a risk factor of 16.75%. A portfolio of emerging market stocks, over the same time period, would have generated a return of nearly 25% per annum but with a risk factor of 21%. But when overlaying the Efficiency Frontier, the IFC/Barra study showed that, if the traditional portfolio was weighted to include 30% emerging market stocks, returns would have jumped to 12% while the risk factor actually *dropped* to 15.25%. A modern financial Holy Grail had been found.[8] Armed with this analytic tool, U.S. institutional investors began plowing money into emerging market equities in record numbers.[9] And while the optimal mix of traditional/emerging stocks will tend to change over time, the investment concept remains sound. This is reinforced by statistical correlation analysis which illustrates that the emerging market universe has few links to other major financial markets, as Table 5.2 shows.

Correlation analysis provides insight into how often and to what extent certain markets move together. Markets that rise and fall together 100% of the time in the same magnitude would have a correlation coefficient of 1. Coefficients above 0.7 typically mean high

132   FROM THIRD WORLD TO WORLD CLASS

TABLE 5.2
IFCI PRICE INDEX CORRELATIONS
(U.S.$; DECEMBER 1992–DECEMBER 1997)

	S&P 500	UK FT 100	Japan, Nikkei	IFCI Composite
S&P 500	1			
UK FT 100	.54	1		
Japan, Nikkei	.23	.29	1	
IFCI Composite	.41	.44	.22	1
Argentina	.48	.44	.26	.67
Brazil	.30	.17	.22	.58
Chile	.28	.20	.15	.52
China	.16	.19	−.15	.43
Czech Republic	.09	.25	−.15	.33
Hungary	.31	.30	.19	.45
India	.11	.14	.03	.39
Korea	.07	.14	.39	.42
Mexico	.36	.38	.17	.73
Poland	.15	.21	.25	.46
South Africa	.13	.27	.22	.54
Zimbabwe	.03	−.13	.17	.28

SOURCE: IFC

correlation and below 0.4, low correlation. In general, emerging markets have registered approximately a 0.3 coefficient with First World markets, indicating that over time these markets are not that related.

Statistics aside, the theory also makes common sense: the markets of India or Morocco are not strongly linked to the markets of Japan or Germany. More important, *intra-emerging market* correlations also have been statistically weak. One of my favorite classroom sayings is "the only thing Poland, the Philippines, and Peru have in common is that they begin with the letter P." Their economies and markets have little connection. As Table 5.3 reveals, diversification can theoretically—and practically—work investment wonders.

Around 1994 a Fourth Wave began, which expanded to include

TABLE 5.3

CORRELATIONS OF EMERGING STOCK MARKETS (U.S.$; DECEMBER 1992–DECEMBER 1998)

	IFCI Composite	Argentina	Brazil	Chile	China	Czech Republic	Hungary	India	Korea	Mexico	Poland	South Africa	Zimbabwe
IFCI Composite	1												
Argentina	.67	1											
Brazil	.58	.36	1										
Chile	.52	.46	.38	1									
China	.43	.27	.09	.15	1								
Czech Republic	.33	.09	.26	.05	.46	1							
Hungary	.46	.36	.55	.31	.12	.31	1						
India	.39	.12	.33	.51	.25	.30	.39	1					
Korea	.43	.25	.19	.43	.25	.04	.06	.25	1				
Mexico	.73	.69	.49	.34	.18	.17	.49	.20	.19	1			
Poland	.46	.30	.37	.17	.24	.47	.43	.22	.19	.35	1		
South Africa	.55	.33	.07	.25	.36	.07	.08	-.01	.39	.29	.20	1	
Zimbabwe	.29	.17	.13	.19	.22	-.01	.07	.28	.34	.11	.29	.04	1

SOURCE: IFC

regions such as the former Soviet Union, China, India, and parts of Africa—many countries that had been off limits for reasons previously described. From a small *negative* capital position—due largely to disinvestment in South Africa—flows to these regions had grown by nearly one third by 1996.[10] MNCs continue to target such regions. Financial investors have only begun to tap these markets, and there are indications that more will follow. In 1997, for example, Russia was included in the IFC's Investable Index for emerging stock markets, which should result in billions of index funds scrambling to get exposure. Howell, too, believes the Fourth Wave is still cresting and that another one is emerging—perhaps the most important wave of all.[11]

As capital has accumulated locally in many developing world countries over the last two decades, "regional money" has now emerged as one of the most important sources of cross-border capital flow. These funds include portfolio as well as strategic investments. What makes this Fifth Wave special is that these flows occur *between developing or newly industrialized countries,* bypassing the First World altogether. We now witness Chilean pension funds investing in Argentine stocks, Hong Kong companies buying privatizing entities in Vietnam, and numerous other examples of intraregional cross-border flows. I have even heard that some Brazilian and South Korean banks had been large traders in Russian debt prior to the country's

TABLE 5.4

GROWTH IN HARD CURRENCY RESERVES (U.S.$ BILLION)

Country	1980	1998
China	2.5	143.7
Brazil	5.7	43.9
Thailand	1.5	27.8
South Korea	2.9	48.8
Mexico	2.9	30.7
Poland	128 million	26.1
Chile	3.1	14.9
Turkey	1.1	21.6
Czech Republic	1.8	12.4

SOURCE: International Monetary Fund, *The Economist*

meltdown in August 1998. Thanks to such growth in capital flows to developing countries, their hard currency reserves have swollen over the last few years.

High local savings rates in the developing world are channeling capital not only into the local market but also into neighboring economies that offer higher returns or diversification benefits. Most of the more prominent emerging market economies now boast savings rates considerably higher than those in the First World. Challenging the critics who complain of Third World labor exploitation, it appears that the workers in these countries are getting paid not just subsistent wages, but enough to create some of the world's highest savings rates.

FIGURE 5.6
SAVINGS RATIOS AS A % OF HOUSEHOLD INCOME

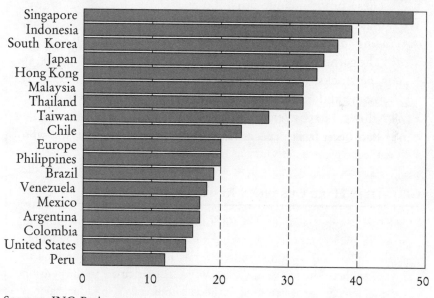

SOURCE: ING-Barings

These five cumulative capital waves over the last two decades, combined with the economic overhauls undertaken by many emerging market countries, have meant vastly more efficient links between global savers and capital users. These links have been reinforced by technologies that make such capital flows painless and instantaneous.

A PESO SAVED IS A PESO EARNED: CHILE'S PENSION PLAN

Chile is the tiger of Latin America, having experienced 5+% per annum growth for more than a decade, and it is on the fast track to becoming the next member of NAFTA. Beyond adopting an export philosophy and curbing government expenditure, Chile has focused on savings as the key to widespread citizen participation in the country's economic success.

The country's now famous pension program, "a defined contribution system in which mandatory deductions from each worker's salary go into individual, privately managed accounts, with the assets invested in stocks and bonds," has become the model for aging populations from the U.K. to Singapore (Peter Passell, "How Chile Farms Out Nest Eggs," *New York Times*, March 21, 1997, Section D, p. 1). Implemented by Augusto Pinochet in 1981 to replace a costly, unsuccessful pay-as-you-go system, Chile's pension plan requires that workers contribute 13% of their wages into individual retirement accounts. These accounts are managed by one of twenty Administradoras de Fondo de Pensiones (AFPs), who invest 40% of assets in government-backed debt, 24% in interest-bearing bank deposits, and 35% in Chilean stocks, and who were recently given authority to invest abroad (Passell, p. 1).

The retirement funds have returned an average of 12% over the past twelve years, allowing workers to earn an annual pension equivalent to 70% of their final salary. Once a worker retires he can withdraw from his savings account freely or purchase annuities. The government provides 100% support for those who have not saved enough under the pension plan and for those whose funds have not earned enough to cover the cost. Some 60% of Chile's workers participate in the pension scheme, which has contributed to the astounding 29% national savings rate, enabling Chile to become the fastest-growing economy outside Asia.

Perhaps the greatest benefit of the pension scheme is the culture of savings that it has nurtured among Chileans. Chile has become a role model for developing countries, demonstrating how government policy, supported by enthusiastic citizens who profit from savings, can strengthen the economy. This process has laid the groundwork for consistent industrialization that, coupled with Chile's active trade, has made the country globally competitive.

Many countries are taking notice. In the United States, the Social Security system is fast becoming burdened by an aging population. By 2025 there will be only two workers to support each retiree. Many economists have recommended that the U.S., and other wealthy, graying economies, follow the Chilean example to ensure that pensioners are provided for, and possibly to jump-start these mature economies.

As they grow and adopt First World market practices, foreign markets feel less foreign each day. As investors become more seasoned at international investing, one can expect capital to begin flowing to some of the most remote markets in the world. As we head into the next millennium, we should not be surprised to see the portfolios of widows and pensioners invested in places as obscure as Mongolia.

CREATING THE GLOBAL CULTURE OF MONEY

In the early 1980s, the First World was mired in utter inertia and anxiety over its lack of exposure, however limited to the developing world, and that is what makes today's global awareness so intriguing. With hindsight, the Brady Plan acted as the single most important financial catalyst to rebuilding sovereign lending and formatting liquid, foreign investor–friendly stock markets in the developing world. Modern financial trading in developing countries probably would not have emerged if the situation had once not been so desperate.

Overborrowing in the 1970s left many developing nations macroeconomically unbalanced, but the products of debt restructuring provided fodder for trading that would nourish the emerging debt markets in the late 1980s. Volatile commodity prices and rising interest rates in the 1970s and 1980s led to a complete halt of fresh cash in the developing world by the mid-1980s, and these primary markets for sovereign credit (the single hottest area in commercial bank lending only a few years earlier) practically evaporated. In Latin America,

BANKER TO THE DEVELOPING WORLD: CITICORP

Just as Sir Walter Scott once remarked that the sun never sets on the British empire, so similar words could be echoed by CEO John Reed of Citicorp, whose Citibank franchise has been masterfully marketed throughout the world. With very high savings rates and strong GDP growth, developing countries are natural markets for Citibank. Therefore, it comes as no surprise that Citi, with 1,333 branches and offices in 98 countries, generates 68% of its corporate banking revenue and 44% of its consumer banking business in emerging markets (*Citicorp Annual Report*, 1996).

Citi has always had global aspirations, with a presence in China since 1902 and in Mexico since 1929. Under the stewardship of former CEO Walter Wriston, Citi was an active syndicator of loans to developing country governments in the 1970s. In defense of this risky lending, Wriston became famous for saying that "governments don't go bankrupt." And while no country has filed for Chapter 7 or 11, many argue Citi itself came close in the late 1980s. As the bank with the most "LDC debt" exposure—nearly $12 billion, more than primary bank capital at the time—Citi might have been technically insolvent if it had been forced to write off these loans. It is no wonder that the bank became a leading institution in Brady Plan restructurings. While many banks exchanged old loans for secured Brady Bonds, Citi shrewdly pursued riskier debt-for-equity options under such plans, recording billions in recoveries and capital gains by swapping its debt for stakes in privatized phone companies, industrial concerns, and utilities. When the Brady cycle was over, Citi's profits from the emerging markets made many of the U.S. and European banks (who had fled the developing world during the debt crisis) look spineless and shortsighted. With hindsight, Wriston now looks like a genius and a visionary. Reed has moved the bank in a different, safer direction, toward selling traditional banking services in the developing world in the 1990s. Selling picks and shovels to prospectors, Reed believes, is the bank's business—not prospecting itself.

Citibank's corporate banking strategy in the post-Wriston era is to enter a new market in the early stages of development and begin business there with cash management, local currency, and trade finance—largely to serve the needs of clients like Coca-Cola or Nabisco, which are expanding operations. Tailoring their services to the sophisticated financial needs of MNCs, Citibank will then move on to project finance, securities custody, and eventually bond underwriting (often for governments) and asset-backed securitization.

The key to Citibank's international success is brand building. Much as you are guaranteed to get the same hamburger at McDonald's whether you're in China or Poland, Citibank offers its customers consistent, first-rate financial services throughout the world. As developing country economies become more integrated with each other and with the developed world, Citibank has realized that offering customers an instant link to today's global money, coupled with confidence that customers will receive the same high-quality financial services around the world, will give it a competitive edge. Customers seem satisfied: total revenue for consumer and corporate banking in developing countries was $270 million in 1980 and $534 million in 1985; revenue from consumer banking in emerging markets was up to $3.6 billion in 1996, while revenue from corporate banking had reached $3.4 billion in 1996.

Reed's personal vision of Citibank as the premier provider of financial services to corporations and citizens worldwide is fast becoming a reality, especially since Citibank has very few competitors. U.S. banks like Chase Manhattan and Bank of America are trying to consolidate their positions domestically through mergers, and European banks are grappling with their fate amid the politics of the upcoming economic union. In Asia, Japanese and Korean banks wrestle with structural problems in their respective economies. Yet Citibank marches on in the developing world, building market share in places on few radar screens. True to its motto, the Citi never sleeps.

there were no new bond offerings by governments from 1982 until 1989, a seven-year drought. As previously mentioned, approximately 50% of the hard currency going from the industrial world to developing countries was from commercial banks, with less than 3% in stocks and bonds.

How could markets and a money culture be born from a stock of bum loans, a pool of assets that caused some of the greatest anxiety in international banking history? Necessity dictated that a market evolve from these old, troubled credits. When the primary markets began drying up in the early 1980s, a secondary market began to thrive. In the 1970s and 1980s, First World domestic commercial bank lending had begun to decline as creditworthy companies went directly to the capital markets in a process known as financial disintermediation. To compensate for sluggish loan growth, commercial banks needed to lend more to Third World countries, whose governments had few sources of capital locally and insufficient global presence for bond access. So banks began lending aggressively to such governments, which would often pay two to four times the interest spread of a U.S. corporate bond. While some may believe that this type of lending would be extended only by the largest banks in New York, London, or Frankfurt, it was actually being done, in some cases, by the smallest regional banks in the U.S. and Europe. When a Citibank or Deutsche Bank would organize a $1 billion loan to the United Mexican States or the Kingdom of Morocco, the loan would often be sold to large syndicates of banks. Citibank might underwrite 20% of the issue itself (and maybe syndicate it down further), while selling the other 80% in four pieces to an English bank, a Swiss bank, a French bank, and a Japanese bank. In turn, those foreign banks might then sell down their $200 million position to twenty-five to fifty smaller banks in their respective local markets. Thus, the seeds of a market were sown. Small-town banks in Cleveland, Ohio, and Milwaukee, Wisconsin— banks that traditionally had been in the mortgage and credit card business—suddenly had exposure to the National Bank of Yugoslavia and the Central Bank of the Philippines without ever leaving their county, let alone country.

When several developing countries such as Poland, Mexico, and Argentina announced repayment problems in the early 1980s, many of these small banks headed for the hills. Realizing that such lending for them was foolish, many began to sell down their loans. Not prepared to take losses, early sellers first had to swap exposure. For example, a German bank may have felt comfortable with Polish credits because it shared a border with the country, but uncomfortable with the Philippines, which was thousands of miles away. The reverse might have been felt by a Japanese bank that was more comfortable with the Philippines than with Poland. Small intermediary shops evolved that

CAPITALISM RUN AMOK?
PYRAMID SCHEMES IN TRANSITIONAL ECONOMIES

Some developing countries will suffer in the new winner-take-all world of market economics. As some economies shed statism and become market oriented, attempts to earn quick fortunes through capitalism can often end in tragedy. Often the optimism and gullibility prevalent in such economies create an opportunity for crafty, scheming entrepreneurs to become wildly successful at other people's expense. Such has been the case throughout Eastern and Central Europe, recently (and most harshly) in Albania, where thousands of people have fallen prey to the lure of financial Ponzi or "pyramid schemes."

Under such scams citizens are enticed by promoters to invest in a fund that will pay high rates of interest. By attracting new investors, promoters pay out to the first few investors the stated rate. Satisfied investors spread the word, and after months such schemes lure thousands—sometimes millions—of naive investors. To keep up with the exorbitant interest rates owed, more and more investors must be found. Eventually such funds run out of investors and, as the fund begins to take in less than it owes, the pyramid collapses. All those investing near the end are left holding worthless promises.

The MMM scandal in Russia in 1994 victimized an estimated 30% of the population as millions of people were desperate for a taste of capitalism's sweet rewards. Sergei Mavrodi, MMM's president, fleeced investors through a scheme in which investors bid up his share prices in Russia's new stock exchange. Promising investors 1,000% returns, Mavrodi took MMM's stock from $1 to $1,100 in less than a year only to have it plummet when he was arrested for tax evasion. Many saw this incident as an unfortunate footnote in Russia's capitalist development, but others, especially those who lost money in the scam, are still nursing their wounds.

In early 1997, Albania, the poorest country in Europe, was almost bankrupted by a billion-dollar pyramid scheme that had spread throughout the nation, swindling thousands out of their meager savings. Emerging from fifty years under a Stalinist regime, Albania has been struggling with the transition to democracy, burdened by a stagnant economy and 20% unemployment. When presented with the opportunity to become rich practically overnight, Albanians could not resist. Virtually every Albanian family was enticed by the false promises of this pyramid scheme, selling houses and cows to come up with enough money to invest in the fund.

One of the principal architects of Albania's largest scam was Rrapuch Xharferri, a former army officer known for his conspicuous displays of wealth, including his sponsorship of a Miss Albania pageant. Xharferri was eventually jailed, but only after several months of visible operations leaving questions open as to whether the government tolerated, or maybe even encouraged, these scams. Some suggest that the government turned a blind eye to the schemes out of fear that a backlash would occur amid Albania's national elections in the fall of 1996.

In October 1996, the IMF expressed concern over Albania's frenzied informal market and urged intervention to end the schemes. Finally, on January 25, 1997, the government seized more than $255 million held in banks by Xharferri and other pyramid operators.

traveled the world to uncover which banks wanted out of which country. Eventually they began to match banks together to create a "secondary" marketplace for the debt. Small as they were, with little-known names like Eurinam, Finamex, Giadefi, and Turan, these independent firms began brokering billions in Third World portfolios between the largest banks in the world.[12] Eventually a cash market evolved, capitalized in part by flight moneys from in-country investors who understood the risk/return nature of these assets. Some governments used auction schemes to buy back some of the debt, which established a cash price. Many of the first dedicated funds to buy these discounted loans came from Wall Street's "vulture" market, the distressed players in high-yield "junk bonds." Michael Milken, the infamous mastermind of the defunct but legendary firm Drexel Burnham Lambert, was one of the market's first players. He established his DBL Americas Development Fund in 1987 to take advantage of Latin American debt which, in the case of Peru, had traded down to three cents on the dollar.

As more dedicated funds began to take advantage of this busted bank loan market, Wall Street began building huge divisions to support

MALAYSIA'S FIDELITY: PERMODALAN NASIONAL BERHAD

Despite its recent economic growing pains, Malaysia is one of the world's great developing country success stories, averaging more than 10% annualized growth since the 1960s. Much of this expansion can be attributed to the government's comprehensive macroeconomic strategies, such as the Second Industrial Masterplan (1996–2005), which frame official policies for sustaining growth and economic development. However, the strong Malaysian economy has been bolstered, in large part, by Malaysians' investments in government-backed unit trusts, such as Permodalan Nasional Berhad (PNB). In establishing PNB and similar trusts—which function like mutual funds in the U.S.—the government has recognized that Malaysia's economic infrastructure would be more resilient if it is financed by its own people (versus flighty foreign capital), while ensuring Malaysian citizens' participation in and understanding of the world of finance and investing.

In 1970 the government implemented its first official blueprint for Malaysian socioeconomic development. The primary objective of the New Economic Policy (NEP) was to promote national unity in Malaysia's multiracial society through the eradication of poverty and the elimination of racial stratification in the economy. Malaysia's population is composed of 60% Bumiputeras (indigenous Malaysians), 30% Chinese immigrants who came to Malaysia in the 1930s, and 9% Indian immigrants, and the immigrants have had a more successful economic and financial record than the indigenous Bumis. In particular, the NEP sought to increase the participation of the Bumiputera community in the corporate sector. This grass-roots approach to economic infrastructure development was a powerful gesture designed to educate the Bumis on the importance of saving and investing. The ultimate goal of the NEP was to have 30% of the share capital of companies owned by Bumis, 40% by other Malaysian communities, and 30% by foreign investors by 1990. As a result, in 1978, PNB, Malaysia's state-owned investment agency, was incorporated as a wholly owned subsidiary of Yayasan Pelaburan Bumiputera (YPB), a government-owned entity that receives and administers funds created by Parliament. On inception, a portfolio worth $431 million was created for PNB through the transfer of shares from forty trust and government agencies. In 1979, Amanah Saham Nasional Berhad (ASNB) was established as a wholly owned subsidiary company of PNB to function as an investment scheme. ASNB now has 4.2 million investors (Abdul Razak Chik, "Pushing Forward," *Malaysian Business*, July 16, 1996, p. 6).

In 1989, Amanah Saham Bumiputera Scheme (ASB) was launched, introducing the Akaun Remaja (youth account), which invites investment from Bumis between the ages of twelve and eighteen. Presently PNB investors include children, housewives, and the growing class of Bumiputera entrepreneurs who, encouraged by the culture of savings enabled by PNB's schemes, have become active members in the Malaysian corporate community. In 1996 the Amanah Saham Wawasan 2020 Scheme (ASW 2020) was launched with the intention, for the first time, of attracting investors from all Malaysian races, particularly those aged twelve to twenty-nine, to help boost the national savings rate (Vijayan Menon, "770,000 Invest in Wawasan Fund," *New Straits Times*, November 16, 1996, p. 1). Investors can make their investments at their local post office.

PNB has $12 billion in investment funds and investments worth $11 billion in 220 companies, 159 of which are listed companies ("Release Equities to Capable Bumi Companies, PNB Urged," *New Straits Times*, May 30, 1996, p. 24). PNB's activities include investment holding, property management, management consulting, and equity financing. Some PNB funds are invested in overseas markets such as the U.S., the U.K., Japan, and Germany, as well as in Malaysia's largest conglomerate, Sime Darby, and the four largest listed bank groups: Maybank, UMBC, Kwong Yik Bank, and Oriental Bank. What is unique about PNB is that investors are not just shareholders, they are also managers of their shareholdings. This empowers Bumi investors, giving them a sense of autonomy over their finances. They have input into corporate decisions and are able to see the direct results and returns on their investments, which encourages them to continue saving and investing. Investments in PNB and its subsidiaries have helped to boost the Malaysian savings rate to 38.8% of GNP in 1996, and it is expected to reach 41.2% in 1997 (Economist Intelligence Unit forecast, June 1997).

PNB and other Malaysian unit trust companies comprise only 7.5% of the Kuala Lumpur Stock Exchange, whereas unit trust companies in other developing countries typically comprise 30% of the stock market. However, the government remains optimistic that unit trusts will reach 40% of market capitalization by 2020 (Jailani Harun, "Unit Trust Share of Mart Cap to Grow," *Business Times,* February 17, 1997, p. 1).

Like Chile's lauded pension plan, Malaysia's unit trust funds have helped create a pervasive culture of savings. PNB symbolizes the success that can come from the policies designed to enfranchise all segments of society, making capitalism a way of life for all citizens.

the growing market in developing country assets, which had been renamed "emerging markets" from previous monikers such as "LDC debt," "value impaired countries," "restructured countries," or "Third World." Even the self-regulating trade organization called the LDC Debt Traders Association, realizing how the markets had mushroomed beyond troubled credits, renamed itself the Emerging Markets Traders Association (EMTA) in 1990. The small band of institutions that began trading sovereign bank loans have now come to dominate the multibillion dollar business of emerging markets, providing integrated sales, market making, research, and capital raising services for the major countries of Asia, Africa, the Middle East, the former Soviet Union, and Latin America. In doing so, they are drawing in investors from all reaches of the planet, from the largest pension funds to the smallest retail savers, creating a global culture of money.

CHAPTER 6

How First World and Third World Investors Are Profiting in Emerging Markets

WE HAVE SEEN how the developing countries are profiting from First World capital flows. The question to be answered in this chapter is: how are investors reaping rewards from emerging markets? And, what are the risks? First, remember that a failure to accumulate capital is the chief reason developing countries have lagged economically. At this writing, the First World's financial markets are estimated at approximately $17 trillion in equity and $25 trillion in debt, versus the Third World's tiny $2 trillion in equity and $1.5 trillion in debt. To continue the virtuous circle of reform and stoke historic growth, the Third World must rely on capital flows from industrialized countries. The haves are now investing in the have-nots, and the have-nots must pay a premium for that capital because First World investors expect a higher compensation for shifting their money to developing countries, whether in debt or equity form.

Is this higher-risk premium justified? As a trader, I would hedge by answering, it depends. Often the underlying commercial risks in emerging markets are comparable to or better than those in the First World; economies are growing fast and that creates cash for dividends and debt payments. However, the political risks—reforms that may stall, new elections that might beget wayward policies, coups or civil wars that may erupt—always seem to weigh on investors' minds, and I believe this is why developing countries are forced to pay a premium for First World capital. It is this fundamental tension between great premium opportunities versus the possibility of political instability that creates both high returns and inefficiencies for skilled investors in the emerging markets. Such situations, theoretically, do not exist in First World markets because political risks—risks of nationalization, expropriation, currency inconvertibility, civil war, radical changes in property laws—are deemed to be virtually nonexistent.

In addition to higher returns, First Worlders can achieve greater diversification from developing countries, which lowers overall portfolio risk. Furthermore, sophisticated players also have chances frequently to extract interesting returns from inefficient markets, though efficiency develops organically over time as markets grow larger with greater capitalization. Often one hears of "arbitrage," "market neutral," or "relative value" trades that seep out from the developing world's embryonic financial markets. While none are truly risk free, many Third World investment situations do *overcompensate* investors for the market risk; these are windows of opportunity that would never remain open in the First World for more than a few moments.

For investors prepared to assume and analyze the risks inherent in the developing world, some of which are large and legitimate, others merely perceived and relatively small, enormous possibilities await, ranging from long-shot opportunities rarely seen in the OECD to low-risk arbitrage situations, and including everything in between.

THE GREATEST RISK?

Do emerging financial markets resemble those in the First World? Like developing economies themselves, emerging markets lie in the chrysalis between a caterpillar and a butterfly, a unique transitional period. Financial textbooks describing developed markets assert that all assets have intrinsic values, that financial markets are relatively efficient, and that price and value will differ only randomly.[1] However,

BRINGING EMERGING MARKETS TO MAIN STREET: TEMPLETON'S MARC MOBIUS

Perhaps no single fund manager has had more success in mainstreaming emerging market investing than Dr. J. Marc Mobius, chief strategist for several developing country products for mutual fund giant Franklin-Templeton. From his Gulfstream jet (in which he flies some three hundred days a year), the shaven-headed Mobius is a modern-day explorer of stock markets, an Indiana Jones of Wall Street. His Templeton Emerging Markets Fund (EMF) was the first of its kind to be listed on the New York Stock Exchange (in 1987), providing one-stop shopping for investors wanting exposure in the developing world.

EMF has been marketed to the most and the least sophisticated investors in the U.S. and around the world. Mobius entices them with a carefully worded prospectus that explains growth opportunities throughout the developing world. On the EMF web site, potential investors are informed that they are probably unaware that "Korea . . . is a leader in industries such as apparel, television/electronics, and telecommunications" and that Zimbabwe "is a competitive player in mining." Mobius attempts to demystify emerging markets to Mr. and Mrs. Smith in Omaha—as well as to Mr. and Mrs. Tanaka in Osaka— sharing with them facts about emerging market investment opportunities that "most serious investors know" and plenty, he claims, do not. EMF boasts of Mobius's extensive emerging market experience (he has been investing since 1980) to assuage investors' fears of the acknowledged risks that come with this territory. Mobius hypes the undervalued, bargain stock opportunities that exist in the developing world and makes emerging market investments seem as normal and rewarding as buying stock in GM.

One must pay tribute to Mobius's marketing genius. While EMF's annualized rate of return has netted only 1.5% more than the U.S. stock market since March 1987, the fund's popularity has grown exponentially. At the end of its first year, EMF's fund size approached $87 million; by the beginning of 1997, it had passed $11 billion.

Under the auspices of Mobius, often called the "dean of emerging markets," the fund as of mid-1997 was invested in thirty-seven emerging markets ("Templeton Emerging Markets Fund Team Passes U.S.$10

Billion Level," *Business Wire,* November 4, 1996). The fund's largest
exposure is in Brazil (13.87%), Hong Kong (11.33%), and Mexico
(8.4%), and it invests in some obscure stock markets in Bangladesh,
Oman, and Namibia (Templeton Emerging Markets Fund web site,
April 30, 1997). Templeton says its EMF investors come from 120
countries (CDA/Spectrum 13 (f) Filing Report). EMF's success has
spawned many other similar developing country products from household mutual fund companies like Fidelity, Scudder Stevens & Clark,
and Merrill Lynch. Indeed, some funds allow monthly purchases in
amounts as small as $25. By year-end 1995, emerging market mutual
funds in the U.S. were worth an estimated $18 billion, and by May 1997
they were growing at a rate of 10.5%. One can only imagine the dinner
conversations in Omaha about how well Mr. Smith's "exotic" stocks are
doing.

these rules may not be applicable to every one of the dozens of
heterogeneous developing markets from all corners of the globe. The
last decade has shown that the difference between price and value in
the emerging markets is not random, but fairly *systematic.* What has
typically affected emerging market prices over time—for both debt
and equity—has been *liquidity.* Looking over the developing marketplace, one often finds that not all strong economies necessarily
offer the best investment opportunities and that some of the best
investments come from weaker economies. What determines price is
often not relative value but the ebb and flow of capital. Understanding
emerging market finance, therefore, means understanding liquidity.[2]
   To understand liquidity, one must keep in mind two dimensions:
one, the existing cash available in a local marketplace, and, two, new
capital flows, whether internally or externally generated. Across most
asset classes in the developing world, prices have been far more influenced by who is buying and selling than by price-earnings ratios or
sovereign ratings. While it is invaluable to understand whether or not a
country's macroeconomic policies will generate sustained growth, ultimately cash flow is king. As a trading friend of mine often asks:
Would you rather buy a stock with a low P/E or a stock that's going up
in price? He has often noted that regardless of price, "If you don't have

the money, you can't buy the shares," and that "when the last investor has thrown in his last dollar, the market must be at a peak."[3] Sometimes in the emerging markets, one must forget about political science or economics; one must go with the flow and run with the bulls or flee from the bears.

LIQUIDITY AND THE ART OF EMERGING MARKET PRICE FORMATION

Studying emerging market price formation means analyzing the supply and demand mechanism in developing countries. If it's liquidity we're after, let's think of it in plumbing terms. For example, if a bathtub's drain is plugged, a running faucet will raise the water level. Conversely, if the faucet is closed but the drain open, the water level will fall. If the faucet is running and the drain is open, the level will depend on how fast water is flowing in and out.

However, what if the bathtub itself could actually stretch and contract in size? In that case, understanding water levels becomes a bit more complicated. One needs to monitor water coming in, water going out, and the changing size of the bathtub. This is analogous to the cyclical financial patterns that are fairly common in the developing world. Price (water level) is dependent on cash inflows (water from the faucet) or outflows (water down the drain), while keeping track of the amount of stocks and bonds outstanding (the size of the bathtub). All mature markets are subject to similar patterns, but emerging market liquidity cycles tend be more frequent and rapid. Therefore, while the fundamental analysis of politics and economics is important in developing countries, to be successful at emerging market investing one should ultimately analyze such phenomena with the following in mind:

- *Existing Ownership.* Who currently owns stocks or bonds? What percentage is held by locals and by foreigners? What are the holders' motivations for buying and selling? Are they going to be adding or decreasing exposure in the future? Is the local savings rate increasing or decreasing? All these factors will affect liquidity.

- *Self-generated Inflows.* What new money is coming into the market? Perhaps trade surpluses, monetary adjustments, or lower bank reserve or stock margin requirements will add liquidity to a marketplace that, ultimately, will help boost share prices.
- *Foreign Financial Flows.* Are there changes in local laws making it more favorable for foreigners to invest? How is the economic health of the First World? Where are First World interest rates? How high are its own stock markets? All of these factors can influence whether a local market will gain or lose foreign money, ultimately affecting price.
- *New Issuance of Stocks or Bonds.* Are companies issuing or buying back stocks and bonds? Remember, the size of the bathtub also determines price.

The bathtub theory of liquidity applies to both debt and equity. While fundamental factors impact price, always keep in mind who is buying what assets and why. Not all debt and equity markets behave the same way. In fact, the only common factor among emerging financial markets is their differences, differences that arise from the distinct histories of each country and region. As we shall see, there are two main categories of financial investing—debt and equity. Within those, however, there are very distinct categories with different risk/reward profiles. The savvy investor pinpoints those differences, assuming only the risks deemed worthwhile relative to an expected return. Let's examine those differences.

THE DEBT MARKETS: HARD CURRENCY VERSUS LOCAL CURRENCY OBLIGATIONS

Given the size and history of developing countries' indebtedness and foreign borrowings, any discussion of emerging markets should begin with debt opportunities.[4] Note that not all debt is created equal; there are instruments denominated in local currency and others denominated in *hard currency* (largely U.S. dollars but may include some half-dozen other First World currencies such as Japanese yen or German deutschemarks), with different considerations for both issuers and investors. For example, let's say Mexico is ready to borrow $100 million for one year. The country can borrow either in U.S. dollars from the market at 10% per annum, or in pesos from the market at 20%. At first blush, the answer seems simple: borrow in dollars, it's cheaper. But there are many things to consider. First, one should ask why interest rates are higher in Mexico. The simple answer is that inflation is higher in Mexico (approximately 10% more), and the theory of Interest Rate Parity dictates that the Mexican peso most likely should decline against the dollar over the year at the inflation differential, in this case, 10%. Theoretically, therefore, the borrowing costs for Mexico should be the same.[5] However, this is not the whole story.

Mexico's ability to repay pesos is completely in its own hands; it has the sovereign ability to increase taxes (the primary source of government revenue) and to print pesos. Now, whether those pesos are worth anything is another matter. But repayment physically can be made by virtue of Mexico's sovereignty. However, when Mexico borrows in U.S. dollars, the only way it can meet its dollar obligations is to generate hard currency from either exports or new foreign investment (from both MNCs and financial investors) it cannot guarantee; it is completely *market-oriented*. If Mexico is having a tough time attracting FDI and exporting, and has few overseas investors interested in its financial markets, the country may not be able to generate hard currency and repay dollar-denominated debt. Therefore, investors who buy Mexican dollar-denominated bonds are assessing risk differently than Mexican peso bond investors. They are focusing not on whether they will be repaid, but rather on what the foreign exchange rate will be in one year and whether Mexico will allow free conversion from pesos to hard currency.[6] This underscores the primary differences in risk between hard currency and local currency sovereign debt.

As the macroeconomic risks in developing countries have stabilized, the markets for both hard currency and local debt have mushroomed dramatically since the mid-1980s, a reflection of greater marketization in the Third World. In addition, according to EMTA,

Figure 6.1

A Changed and Changing Debt Marketplace

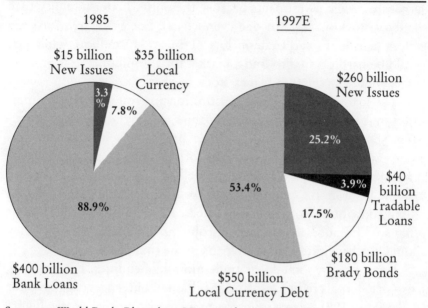

SOURCES: World Bank; Bloomberg News; author's estimates

the volume of debt traded for all emerging markets rose from some $100 billion in 1990 to more than $4 trillion by 1997.[7] As Figure 6.1 illustrates, the market has also broadened out considerably in Tradable Loans, Brady Bonds, New Issues, and Local Currency instruments.

TRADABLE LOANS

The stock of troubled private commercial loans fueled the rebirth of the sovereign debt markets in the late 1980s. At one point more than 90% of the tradable emerging debt universe was composed of such hard-currency (largely U.S. dollar–denominated) tradable loans; today they total no more than 15%. While some $300 billion has been converted to Brady Bonds, there still remain some nonperforming loans from places such as Cuba and Sudan trading at steep discounts with some prospect or expectation of a Brady deal. There are loans that have been classically restructured and trade for their high yields to maturity. These loans are held for capital appreciation, and are often surrogate equity investments because they offer better liquidity than the local stock markets (if one even exists). For example, Moroccan government loans can trade in lots of $5 to $10 million, while one would be hard pressed to find a market for $2 million of a Moroccan equity locally in the Casablanca stock market.

The loan market is largely institutional investor territory dominated by banks and insurance companies, with retail investors effectively shut out. As a result, until the Brady game was played, this sector was plagued by fluctuations of liquidity, with prices being determined by who was buying and selling, much like a commodity market. Rumors on country buybacks or large international banks selling contributed to fluctuating prices. As mentioned earlier, banks often sold because of accounting problems or a realization that they should not have extended such loans in the first place.

Interestingly, some loans trade more like equities. For example, Russian external credit—nearly $25 billion of old Soviet debt assumed by Russia in 1991—have rollercoastered in price for years (see Figure 6.2). While in default in the early 1990s, these loans were priced with accrued interest at less than twenty cents on the dollar. Bids nearly doubled when Russia began restructuring talks in 1993–94, only to slide as U.S. interest rates rose, the Mexican peso plunged, and talks stalled in late 1994.

By early 1995 prices regained steam and continued up as President Boris Yeltsin was reelected in mid-1996. Over the next fifteen months, Russian debt doubled again on hopes of a finalized restructuring and the country's announced sovereign BB credit rating. However, the October 1997 Asian crisis signaled the party's end. As metal and energy prices collapsed with contracting Asian economies, Russia began bleeding in 1998. Poor tax collection created huge fiscal and monetary holes that not even a $22 billion IMF aid package could plug in July 1998. By mid-August 1998, Russia defaulted on nearly $30 billion of local treasury bills which tanked external debt prices to default levels not seen since the early 1990s.

The market for new bank loans to developing countries was essentially dead for most of the 1980s and early 1990s, deemphasized

FIGURE 6.2

INTERNAL AND EXTERNAL VARIABLES AFFECTING RUSSIAN DEBT PRICES

Price
(% of face value)

SOURCES: Bloomberg News; ING-Barings

as the Brady Plan worked out problem assets and the new sovereign Eurobond market emerged. However, as developing countries have become creditworthy entities again, certain borrowing situations need custom-tailored finance that cannot be securitized; consequently, bank lending fills an important hole. In fact, according to Capital Data of London, more than $150 billion in new syndicated loans have been booked for developing countries in the mid-1990s. Yet trading in these loans still remains cumbersome and problematic. First, most loans can be prepaid by the borrower, making their maturity and other features crucially important to bond investors hard to determine. Furthermore, lending banks are often driven by long-standing corporate relationships; as such many are reluctant to be seen selling client loans, which might reflect badly on such relationships. This is fine when the markets are liquid and buoyant; it will be interesting to see if a new secondary market accelerates as banks get close to country limits[8] or if political trouble breaks out again as it did in the early 1980s. Some market participants believe the recent problems in Asia might give rise to greater trading of problem credits from that region. If there are any restructurings or debt securitization from the stock of nearly $300 billion in Asian loans, this asset class may dramatically mushroom in coming years.

BRADY BONDS: OLD WINE, NEW AND BETTER BOTTLES

Prior to Brady Bonds, traditional sovereign debt analysis was impossible; no one really knew what defaulted Polish or Peruvian government loans, for example, were worth. Few countries were paying a set interest rate, and most loans were past due with uncertain maturities. This confused investors, who simply need to know how much to invest today, when they'll be repaid, and what interest rate they'll receive. Believe it or not, that is the essence of bond investing. With old restructured loans, investors had none of this. Then came the Brady Plan. The Brady Plan provided a mechanism for replacing LDC debt with tradable bonds and, in doing so, gave birth to an entirely new asset class. It also sparked interest in developing countries that had been dormant for many years, while providing a quantitative basis for sovereign risk.

By defining when and how much investors would be repaid, and in some cases insuring payments through cash collateral, the Brady Plan would attract more financial investors to the developing world than ever before; finally yield-to-maturities could be calculated. By 1995, nearly 75% of all $400 billion in troubled commercial-bank loans to developing countries had been restructured under various Brady Plans in some fifteen countries, including Latin America (Argentina, Brazil, Costa Rica, Dominican Republic, Ecuador, Mexico, Panama, Peru, Uruguay, and Venezuela), Africa (Nigeria), the Middle East (Jordan), Central and Eastern Europe (Bulgaria and Poland), and Asia (Philippines).

The bonds, usually dollar denominated, were minted in maturities of between fifteen and thirty years. A menu of restructuring options was given to banks to provide the best tax relief possible, which created a variety of debt instruments. Most were coupon-bearing bonds with assortments of fixed or floating rates (or a combination), many with principal and certain interest collateralized by U.S. Treasury zero coupon bonds and other high-grade instruments.

The most common Brady Bonds outstanding today are long-dated "Par" and "Discount" issues. Par bonds were converted on a 1:1 basis relative to the original face value of the loans for which they were exchanged, and carry a below-market coupon. Discount bonds carry a floating coupon, and were converted at a discount on the original face value. Approximately 75% of all Bradies are Par or Discounts, both of which have principal and some interest guarantees. In addition, other Debt Conversion Bonds (DCBs) and Floating Interest Reduction Bonds (FLIRBs) offered interest rate reductions and shorter payments, but no collateral. Past-due interest bonds have been issued to resolve interest arrears situations. Because many countries argued that falling commodity prices were the root cause of their liquidity problems, some commercial banks also required warrants that would give them more money if prices climbed back to pre-crisis levels. In Venezuela, for example, Par and Discount bond holders can increase annual coupons by 1.5% if oil reaches $29 dollars per barrel for a sustained period.

As part of the Brady Plan, most of these bonds are fairly long dated to allow the countries time to repay the banks. This means that these bonds are highly susceptible to two things: U.S. interest rates and country-specific factors. Positive or negative developments in either could cause the bonds to rise or fall in price. Furthermore, the key to Brady Bond analysis is not a traditional yield-to-maturity calculation, but what has been dubbed "stripped yield." Given the U.S. Treasury collateral insuring principal repayment on Par and Discount bonds, Bradies are true hybrids—a mixture of U.S. and emerging market risk. Traders are forced to dissect the cash flows to understand what the true return is on the emerging market component (see Figure 6.3). In fact, because of the zero coupon and collateral, some Bradies have a "Default Return," a positive spread even if the country defaults and never makes another payment.

Investors have been interested in Bradies because of their relatively high stripped rates of return compared to U.S. high-yield (a.k.a. "junk") bonds. While for most of the 1990s the average spread on U.S.

FIGURE 6.3

ANATOMY OF A BRADY BOND: VENEZUELA PAR 6.75% DUE 2020

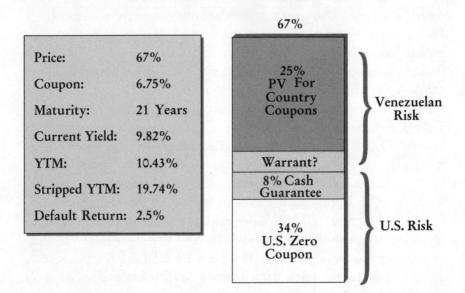

Price:	67%
Coupon:	6.75%
Maturity:	21 Years
Current Yield:	9.82%
YTM:	10.43%
Stripped YTM:	19.74%
Default Return:	2.5%

67%

25%
PV For
Country
Coupons

Warrant?

8% Cash
Guarantee

34%
U.S. Zero
Coupon

} Venezuelan
Risk

} U.S. Risk

SOURCE: J.P. Morgan (January 8, 1999)

high-yield bonds was 463 basis points per annum above comparable U.S. government Treasuries, Bradies have averaged 481 nominal and 795 stripped with similar credit ratings.[9] Therefore, compared to many high-yield corporate bonds, Bradies have looked relatively cheap to the market. Moreover, Brady Bonds offer a minimum default yield—basically, the principal and interest collateral—which adds to their attractiveness. In addition, as some of these countries become more creditworthy over time, these relatively wide spreads may indeed tighten. For example, typical borrowings by Germany or Sweden, for example, would be done at spreads of less than twenty-five basis points over U.S. Treasuries. Therefore, long-dated Brady debt offers not only relatively high current yields but also the potential for capital gains as certain countries increase their creditworthiness. Some smaller Brady countries like Ecuador and Bulgaria have bonds yielding approximately 600 to 700 basis points per annum over U.S. Treasury bonds, while others such as Poland trade at spreads closer to 100. But at a current average of approximately 500 basis points per annum more

FIGURE 6.4

HISTORICAL SPREAD COMPARISON

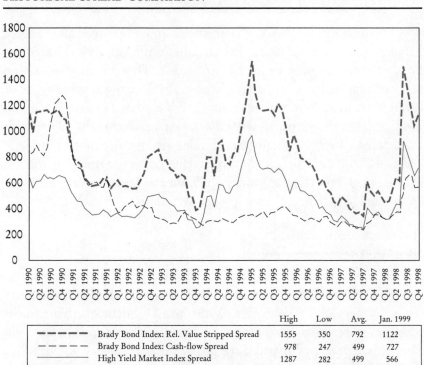

	High	Low	Avg.	Jan. 1999
Brady Bond Index: Rel. Value Stripped Spread	1555	350	792	1122
Brady Bond Index: Cash-flow Spread	978	247	499	727
High Yield Market Index Spread	1287	282	499	566

SOURCES: Lehman Brothers; Solomon Smith Barney; Bloomberg News

than U.S. government bonds, Bradies as an investment class are capable of delivering returns that rival U.S. stock investments.

The $180 billion Brady market is extremely liquid, with turnover of nearly $2 trillion or more than ten times market capitalization, making it the second most liquid bond market after U.S. Treasuries. However, the political risks inherent in Bradies make the market more volatile than that of First World bonds. Prices have moved wildly during chaotic periods such as the Mexican peso crisis, scaring away some pension funds, insurance companies, and other more conservative asset allocators. According to Bloomberg, in the first ten months of 1997, Brady Bond ten-day volatility was a mere 7%—comparable to that of U.S. bonds. However, during the Asian crisis in late October 1997, the figure jumped to more than 50% for this bond index composed of some fifteen developing countries. While this volatility is aberrant, it underscores what can happen when investor confidence is shaken.

Fortunately, the market is mainstreaming. Historically, only a handful of commercial banks held Bradies until Moody's re-rated the bonds, elevating some to investment grade. This put Bradies within reach of a far wider investor class who is also looking at other types of emerging market debt. And investors have been handsomely rewarded. Bradies have outperformed several asset classes during the 1990s, with the Salomon Brothers Brady Bond index rising more than many U.S. and global equity indices and even the IFC Index for emerging market equities in certain years. As mentioned, success breeds greater investor confidence, which begets even greater investment.

NEW ISSUES

For much of the 1980s, there were few fresh dollar-denominated bond issues by developing countries. With the LDC debt overhang, most investors were petrified of sovereign defaults and, as a result, less than $1 billion a year was issued during that decade. However, ever since the first Brady Plan in 1989, the perceived fears of sovereign default have diminished dramatically. As a result, one of the ripest areas for growth on Wall Street is new bond issues for emerging market countries and companies, with an estimated $90 billion being raised in 1997. Increased issues also bring greater liquidity. As of year-end 1996, the volume of emerging market traded new issues (also known as Euro-bonds because they are predominantly issued in the Euromarkets) was nearly $650 billion in a universe of debt that is estimated at more than $250 billion (larger than that of the U.S. high-yield market). This includes straight bonds, but also certificates of deposit from developing country banks and convertible bonds.

New issues carry high coupons for emerging market entities, typically 1% to 5% more per annum than U.S. government and corporate bonds. While this may not seem significant to laymen, returns of this magnitude are very attractive for professional bond investors who have been known to kill relatives for an extra ⅛% or

¼% in yield. It is a huge premium relative to the broader investment-grade world. Moreover, as some of these entities are just beginning the ratings process, many developing country borrowers have upgrade potential, making initial issuance spreads relatively cheap.

Such capital market instruments are being utilized by sovereign, public sector, and corporate borrowers. In contrast to Bradies, new issues inject new money into countries, which helps bolster hard currency reserves. Though certain emerging market Eurobonds and Brady Bonds are issued by borrowers in the same country (and should, therefore, carry the same credit risk), the Euros have traded at tighter spreads. This is largely due to the market's higher expectation of default on the longer-dated Bradies: new issues are generally one to ten years, whereas Bradies are five to thirty years in maturity. Often there has been a 1% to 1.5% annual yield difference in some overlapping maturities, creating interesting arbitrage opportunities and relative value trades between certain sovereign issues. While it may seem counterintuitive, smaller Eurobond deals in the $100–$300 million range typically trade tighter than the Brady issues, which can be $15 billion in size. This is largely because Bradies trade in more speculative circles like hedge funds, whereas new issues are often bought by

FIGURE 6.5
GROWTH IN EMERGING MARKET EUROBOND ISSUANCE

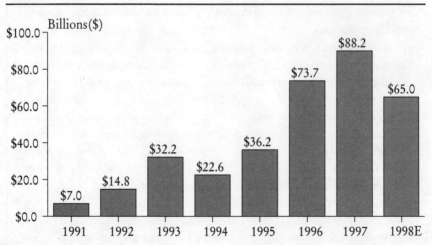

SOURCE: Merrill Lynch, author's estimates, Bloomberg News

longer-term investors—like mutual funds—which intend to hold bonds until maturity rather than trade them.

THE RATINGS GAME: HOW STANDARD & POOR'S RATES COUNTRIES

The traditional world of bond investing is dominated by professional fiduciary firms, organizations such as pension planners and insurance companies that manage other people's money. As such, most of these institutions are highly regulated in what they can buy, and most are restricted from investing in below-investment-grade or "junk" bonds. This places enormous importance on the credit rating debt issuers; without a credit rating, it becomes nearly impossible to access the trillions of dollars in fiduciary funds. Like companies, countries need to be rated by one of the major bond rating firms, Moody's or Standard & Poor's (S&P). In addition to helping the country access capital, a sovereign rating also helps determine the risk of corporate debt issued from that country. These ratings indicate each government's capacity and willingness to repay debt. S&P uses a ratings system of AAA (highest) to C (lowest), with distinctions in categories of AA or lower made by a plus (+) or a minus (−). A country that has received a credit rating of BBB or higher is considered *investment grade,* and the market for investment-grade debt could be twenty times the size of the junk bond market in the U.S.

To determine a country's rating, S&P assesses the risk—economic and political—involved with a country's credit. Economic risk estimates whether or not the government has the means to repay its debt on time. Political risk ascertains the sovereign's willingness to repay the debt as a function of political stability, regardless of whether or not it has the financial means. During its analysis, S&P typically sends a team to a country for two to four weeks to analyze economic and financial data. More important, the team meets with a cross section of the country's key players—businessmen, bankers, academics, union leaders, and opposition party members—in order to assess political risk.

S&P uses several criteria to determine a country's risk: the stability of the political institution; the country's income and economic structure; the government's fiscal policy, monetary policy, budgetary flexibility, and inflation pressures; and the country's public debt burden, external financial position, international liquidity, and debt service track record (David T. Beers and Marie Cavanaugh, "Sovereign Credit Ratings: A Primer," *Standard & Poor's,* April 1997, p. 3). S&P considers a country's annual inflation rate to be the most important component of a sovereign rating. Countries with inflation of 25% to 100% probably have unsound monetary policies and less stable governments and are, therefore, more likely to receive a below-investment-grade rating. Countries with inflation of 0% to 10% typically have stronger governments and economic policies and, therefore, are more likely to be rated as investment grade (David T. Beers, "Credit Comment," *Standard & Poor's Criteria,* March 27, 1995, p. 6).

Playing the ratings games is like walking a tightrope for many developing country politicians. Tight fiscal policies—loved by the credit rating agencies—typically mean less spent on social services and welfare, programs that are politically popular in poorer nations. Governments, therefore, must have the ability to persuade the population to adopt strict measures for some time and build a *willingness* to repay external debt. For those who have the grit and determination, billions of development dollars await to help fuel the virtuous circle of reform and prosperity.

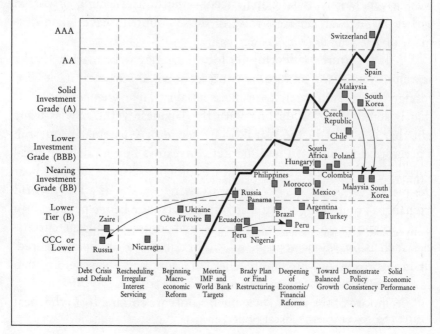

LOCAL CURRENCY

Local currency–denominated debt is one of the fastest-growing sectors in emerging market investing, mushrooming by more than $25 billion per annum.[10] This is a healthy sign, as governments rely more on domestic savings (generated by economic growth), which helps foster the culture of money. It also reflects the creation of new currencies and monetary systems. For example, in 1990 no money market existed in the Soviet Union. When it splintered into some twenty countries, twenty new currencies and money markets were created. In the future, such markets will begin to broaden and deepen as pension, insurance, and banking sectors develop—sectors that never existed in most statist economies.

In the past, local money markets offered investors high interest rates—sometimes more than 100% per annum—because of high inflation. For example, in 1990, the average inflation rate in the developing world was more than 50%, according to the World Bank. By 1997, that number had declined to approximately 10%. The fall was driven largely by the macroeconomic housecleaning discussed earlier. As a result, interest rates in those countries have fallen dramatically.[11]

A key feature of developing local currency debt markets is the scarcity of forward or futures contracts on the currency itself. For foreign investors, forwards are an essential risk management tool, one that is standard when dealing with the Japanese yen or Swiss franc but that is absent in the Kazakhstani tenge or Guatemalan quetzal. Therefore, in many of these markets, investors buying debt in local currency must speculate on the future foreign exchange rate and bear the market risks. This is beginning to change, and many First World exchanges are looking to offer investors currency hedge products. In Chicago and London, for example, several contracts on large currencies such as the Mexican peso and the Brazilian real are being offered. In Hong Kong and Singapore, there are contracts for several Asian currencies.

Yet more of the risk management tools are coming from the local markets themselves. In Brazil, for example, interest rate futures, currency and gold futures, stock index futures, and stock options are traded, and small but growing futures markets are emerging in South Africa, the Philippines, Hungary, China, Russia, and Slovakia. Demand for such futures and forward products also comes from the real economy; importers and exporters need them for hedging out risks related to their underlying businesses. As global trade accelerates, one can expect to see a greater number of futures markets develop over time.

With the growth in emerging market currency instruments, there comes a need for performance benchmarks and reference assets for First World investors. To some extent, the Bradies have become a hard currency benchmark for pricing new issues in international capital markets, as well as setting reference levels of interest rates for domestic money market instruments. In June 1996 J. P. Morgan launched its Emerging Market Local Market Index (ELMI), which tracks total returns for local currency–denominated emerging market instruments.[12] The index focuses on some of the largest and most liquid markets accessible to international investors: Mexico (22%), Malaysia (17%), Thailand (15%), Indonesia (12%), South Africa (8%), Turkey (7%), Poland (5%), Philippines (5%), and the Czech Republic (4%).[13] This is a dynamic and potentially huge growth area for global bond investors (as well as Wall Street), particularly if the European monetary union materializes and the Continent loses more than ten traded currencies.[14]

While few formal futures markets exist for emerging market currencies, over-the-counter (OTC) products are often bought and sold to hedge rate exposure. Certain MNCs with local operations in developing countries buy and sell forward currencies, and many local banks informally offer such hedges to clients. Sometimes local central banks will offer limited coverage, often tied to a specific investment or transaction deemed to be important. Some arbitrages arise from these contracts, allowing investors to earn yields greater than comparable U.S. dollar rates, something rarely seen in First World currency markets.[15]

THE ASIAN FINANCIAL FLU: ARE BONDS THE CURE?

The causes of the unexpected currency crises that swept across North and Southeast Asia in late 1997 will preoccupy scholars and bankers for some time. Some will cite opaque Asian business practices, rampant economic "cronyism," asset bubbles, failures to maintain productivity, and limits of export-driven models, among others, as the causes of financial panic. While these appraisals seem reasonable, I would argue that Asia's currency woes are largely rooted in embryonic financial marketization. Over time, it will be seen that the crises had less to do with Asian culture or poor macroeconomics than with the conspicuous lack of Asian bond markets, the corporate overreliance on bank credit, and the distortions created by these factors.

In First World countries like the U.S. or Germany, the bond markets are enormous and liquid. In the U.S., for example, bond market capitalization totals some 120% of GDP with annual turnover of nearly 1500%, meaning that bonds are very readily bought and sold by investors. In developing East Asia, however, the average bond market size is approximately 30% of GDP, with turnover of less than 50%. Relative to its economy, the U.S. bond market is five times as large and thirty times more liquid than those in East Asia. It is supported by a broad and deep base of institutional and individual investors, who choose from a vast range of products and prices from sellers who make required financial disclosure and representations.

Because most Asian countries have not run fiscal deficits (like most have in the West), government bond markets never took root. Even though savings rates in Asia have been notoriously high, myopic governments have failed to promote bond markets, believing that they were not needed. Without a proper sovereign yield curve, corporate bonds could not be effectively priced, which led to an underdeveloped corporate debt market. With no investment alternatives, thrifty Asians channeled savings through banks or finance companies, who amassed unchecked power over capital flows in their respective economies. These financial institutions could be influenced by governments to invest in sectors deemed important regardless of economic viability. There was also room for corruption. The only other Asian investment alternative was stock markets, another bubble that grew because of a lack of debt options for investors.

Why are bond markets important? Without them to measure risk, bank loans are prone to mispricing. Plentiful savings lead banks to lend at cheap rates, which encourages excessive borrowing. In the U.S., when a large company wants to raise debt for a project, rating agencies and the market act as a reality check on the project's viability. If a project is deemed risky, the cost of borrowing for the company goes up. If the cost of borrowing is too high, projects are scrapped; this curbs excessive borrowing. Not so in Asia. With banks having seemingly endless capital pools, along with heavy-handed government policies to influence where such money was to be lent, financial bubbles had been built in all sectors, from real estate (Thailand, Malaysia, and Indonesia) to computers (South Korea). Moreover, without bond markets, Asian companies had been forced to borrow short term from banks to invest in longer-term assets like real estate and factories. In total, this created huge asset/liability mismatches and distorted corporate viability, and left many banking systems and economies vulnerable to liquidity shocks.

These problems were complicated by the fact that many First World banks felt very comfortable lending in hard currency to Asian banks. During the 1990s, loans from the OECD to developing Asian banks totaled more than $300 billion, with more than half coming from slow-growing Japan. Because banking is considered a "protected" industry—that is, deemed too important to fail—"moral hazard" risks were distorted. No First World banker could believe an Asian government would allow their banks to default, because of the financial panic that would ensue. As a result, liquidity flowed to Asian banks unchecked, further increasing the banking system's vulnerability.

This was a recipe for disaster: First World banks lend to Asian banks in hard currency, and Asian banks lend to questionable projects at low rates. It looks uncomfortably similar to what happened in Latin America in the 1970s and 1980s. Had bond markets developed in Asia, financial disclosure for companies would have increased and high-risk projects could have been avoided. In addition, bond markets would have spread financial risks beyond the banking sector. Some companies would have been allowed to go bankrupt, and some investors would have lost money. This process is ultimately what makes business and capital markets efficient: healthy entities survive; stock, bond, and bank markets grow in balance; and investor bases stratify according to their risk/return profile. While not a panacea for all of Asia's financial ailments, fully functional bond markets could have curbed overborrowing, overexpansion, competitive inefficiencies, asset bubbles, and, ultimately, the crisis in confidence that destroyed more wealth more quickly than any financial Cassandra could have imagined.

Trading developing country bonds is somewhat different from investing in U.S. government or corporate bonds. As Steven Dym notes (see Table 6.1), different economic shocks may produce slightly different

Table 6.1
The Price Impact of Economic Shocks on Debt Instruments

Economic Shock	Industrialized Country Bond	Dollar-denominated Brady or Eurobond	Local Currency Emerging Market Bond
Faster growth	Yield rises; stronger currency unless inflation accelerates	Sovereign risk decreases as solvency improves; hence credit spread on borrowing narrows	Yield rises; currency strengthens
Higher inflation	Yield increases; currency *may* depreciate unless central bank tightens	Sovereign risk increases; hence credit spread widens	Yield increases; currency depreciates
Global capital tightening	Yield rises, but degree depends on the country's global sensitivity	Underlying U.S. rate rises; credit spread increases and debt service costs rise	Same as dollar-denominated bond
Trade deficit worsening	Yield may fall due to decline in economic activity; currency surely depreciates	Sovereign risk increases, raising credit spread	Yield increases; currency falls for both sovereign risk and trade reasons

Source: Steven Dym, "Integrating Emerging Market Bonds into a Global Portfolio," in Frank J. Fabozzi and Alberto Franco, *Handbook of Emerging Fixed Income & Currency Markets* (New Hope, PA: Frank J. Fabozzi Assoc., 1997), p. 38.

price outcomes for emerging market instruments and industrialized country bonds. When analyzing and selecting emerging markets, therefore, an investor needs a solid understanding of the macroeconomic environment both in the emerging market itself and around the globe.

EMERGING EQUITY MARKETS

Beyond debt opportunities, greater economic growth in the long run should lead to greater stock market returns (See "The Mother of All Emerging Stock Markets," page 171). Emerging market stocks also offer investors great value through cheap earnings and assets. One would expect that higher emerging market growth would produce greater earnings acceleration, reflected in higher developing country price-earnings ratios (P/Es). However, on average, emerging market P/Es are considerably lower than those in the G7: 18 versus 26, according to the IFC in 1999. If emerging markets have greater economic growth, why the lower P/Es? Two simple reasons: first, low P/E illustrates the general scarcity of capital in developing countries; second, it reflects a naturally risk-averse, "show me" attitude of the market. In short, emerging stock markets need time to capitalize and prove themselves worthy of First World multiples.

Just how cheap are emerging market stocks? It certainly varies; remember, there are more than sixty emerging markets. However, in measuring enterprise value by dividing stock market capitalization by a respective production capacity—such as in cement (price per ton of annual production) or telephony (price per telephone line)—many emerging market companies look incredibly cheap. A dramatic example is the Russian petroleum giant LUKoil.[16] In asset size, LUKoil—with 11 billion barrels of proven reserves—would rank as the world's largest publicly-traded oil company. Yet in stock market capitalization, at $2.8 billion, LUKoil would not rate among the world's top twenty most valuable energy concerns at year-end 1998. Exxon would have been first at $178 billion, followed by Royal Dutch/Shell ($154 billion). When looking at price per barrel of proven oil reserves, investors were paying some $25 for Exxon versus only 25 cents for LUKoil. Why such a disparity?

First, let's go back to earnings. While all businesses produce different goods and services, they all should make one thing in common: *profit*. Companies are essentially money factories because investors are theoretically buying dividend streams. In this respect, Exxon is one of the world's great profit machines, with decades of proven profitability and netting $8+ billion after taxes in 1998. At 1998 year-end stock prices, investors were paying approximately 28 times Exxon's projected earnings—a highly confident view of the company's future. In contrast, LUKoil has only been a private enterprise for a few years; there's no real track record for investors to analyze. In terms of earnings, LUKoil netted only $300 million in 1997 and lost money in 1998. Obviously, while LUKoil professes to have huge reserves, the company cannot seem to extract, refine, and ship oil as efficiently as Exxon; thus, the difference in earnings.

There are other country-specific factors that also cap LUKoil's stock price. Its home market—Russia—has seen GDP and energy demand plummet more than 50% over the 1990s. Moreover, investors fear future Russian political risks that may impair LUKoil's profitability—everything from nationalization, dividend remittance controls, a reversion towards communism, and general economic chaos. In short, LUKoil—and more importantly, Russia itself—has much to prove to investors before the stock can be bid at anything close to G7 multiples.

So why buy LUKoil at all? Simple. Investors look forward to the day when LUKoil pumps out the same amount of oil as it did in the Soviet era—more than double its current production. With further modernization and help from its U.S. partner, Atlantic Richfield, analysts believe LUKoil could earn $1–2 billion by 2002. Moreover, when the Russian economy accelerates, so will demand for LUKoil's energy. Therefore, by buying LUKoil, investors are also buying into Russia at (hopefully) the bottom of a cycle. Indeed, before the Asian crisis investors were far more optimistic about LUKoil's future: the stock peaked at $116 per share (October 1997). After Russia's August 1998 crisis it bottomed out at $8 (October 1998) and rebounded to around $20 by early 1999—but still off 80% from the highs. Therefore, if LUKoil and Russia get their acts together, and the market steps up and pays even one-quarter of Exxon's P/E multiple, LUKoil's stock

THE MOTHER OF ALL EMERGING STOCK MARKETS: JAPAN

When trying to understand the long-cycle attractions of emerging stock markets, one needs only to look at Japan, the twentieth century's most successful developing country. While calling Japan's meteoric economic rise after World War II successful is a dramatic understatement (regardless of its recent economic troubles), few words adequately describe the great bull run of Tokyo's stock exchange—undoubtedly one of the century's most profitable investments.

With few natural resources and a land leveled by war, Japan was forced to rebuild itself using wits and hard work. Thanks to high literacy rates and a strong work ethic, Japan's economy grew by approximately 4.5% annually compounded from 1945 to 1995, more than double America's 2+% rate. When the country's stock market was reopened in May 1949, it chose to begin its index—the Nikkei—at 176.52. While most indexes begin with a base number of 100 or 1,000, the Nikkei was set at the *exact* number of the Dow Jones index of U.S. industrials—a gesture that should have alerted the world of Japan's aspirations. While few realized it at the time, the Japanese clearly looked at this situation as a footrace. Who won?

As of March 1999, the Dow Jones index—riding the crest of a fifteen-year bull cycle—has hit 10,000. Meanwhile, the Nikkei has settled in near 16,000—a dramatic drop from its 39,000 peak in 1989—but still 60% more than the Dow. However, the Japanese yen actually appreciated during this period, from the mid 300s to 120 against the U.S. dollar. Therefore, one U.S. dollar invested in the Nikkei in the late 1940s would be worth nearly *300* times its original investment, while only 60-odd times for the Dow Jones—a remarkable outperformance by a factor of 5.

Will *all* emerging stock markets do as well as Japan's did in the postwar period? Probably not. However, a few may. Brisk compounded economic growth over fifty years can unleash massive investment returns. In this respect, it would seem inherently more risky *not* to invest in emerging markets as we approach the twenty-first century. Fortunes undoubtedly will be made in select markets of Asia, Latin America, the former Soviet Union, and Africa.

could rise five- to twenty-fold in a couple of years. That return potential simply does not exist with a G7 company like Exxon or Royal
Dutch/Shell; their current operating efficiency and high stock valuations lack that return potential. In summary, emerging market stocks
like LUKoil have three key upsides: (1) benefits of greater operating
efficiency; (2) expansion within increasingly attractive country factors;
and (3), more favorable multiple expansion in the stock market.

When investing in emerging market equities, country factors are
most important, as Figure 6.6 indicates. Accordingly, investors should
take a top-down approach and focus on country selection, something
that has accounted for approximately 46% of emerging market equity
returns (50% more than in developed markets), according to IFC/
Barra. This is followed by sector selection (38%) and then by actual
company selection (only 16%).

FIGURE 6.6
FACTORS OF EQUITY RETURNS IN EMERGING AND DEVELOPED MARKETS

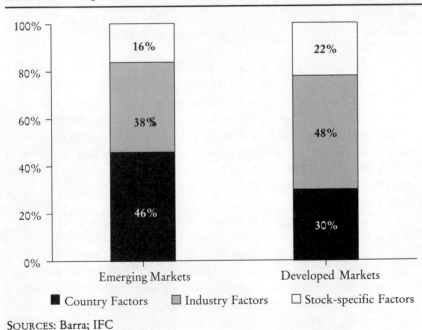

SOURCES: Barra; IFC

Country selection seems to make sense. According to the IFC/ Barra study, in a typical year in a single country stock market, the return difference between companies in the seventy-fifth percentile of performance and those in the twenty-fifth percentile is marginal— possibly a few percentage points. Both are close to the 50% percentile. However, when comparing the returns of countries in the seventy-fifth percentile of global stock performance and those in the twenty-fifth percentile, the results can vary by huge margins: Malaysia up 50%, Poland down 50%. From my experience, it is not nearly as important to pick a Cementos Mexicano over Cementos Apasco, but rather to decide whether to be in Mexico at all. And it is a country's economic and political policies that often draw liquidity in and out of markets, all of which affect price formation.

With country factors playing such an important role in stock performance, it should come as no surprise that emerging stock markets individually carry higher volatility than most First World stock markets, with some, like Poland's market, approaching a remarkable 80%, according to the IFC. However, the IFC index, in which twenty-six emerging stock markets are pooled together, has registered volatility of only 15%, just slightly ahead of the index for Morgan Stanley's EAFE index for Europe, Japan, and Oceania (14%).[17] This reaffirms the importance of country selection for overall return and risk management. However, if your goals are merely broad exposure, a pool of emerging market equities has risk comparable to many individual First World stock markets.

For the above-mentioned reasons, emerging stock markets will become an increasing component of First World portfolios. According to the IFC, total market capitalization for emerging markets grew nearly ten-fold from 1985 to 1996. At projected economic growth rates, emerging stock markets could rise from approximately 15% of global market capitalization in 1996 to 35% by 2020.[18] How can investors profit from such growth? Just as in debt, not all emerging market equity opportunities are created equal. There are several ways to play these countries, some easier than others. As a result, there are situations that offer huge risk/reward potential and others that offer crafty arbitrage opportunities and relative value plays.

Local Equities

Emerging stock markets are like grass-roots movements; they start small and grow. Most begin through government privatizations, as discussed earlier. As of 1996 there were approximately sixty-four emerging market stock markets around the world.[19]

Trading locally in Third World countries is more complicated than investing in the United States or other First World countries. Often investors in embryonic markets must deal with local brokerage houses to buy and sell shares, because the large U.S. and European players have yet to establish coverage of those markets. While some of these local players may have a better understanding of their markets and be privy to more and better information, there are potential trouble spots. Local firms have less at stake than large established First World firms, which are subject to onerous home-market securities regulations. That means that research and advice from such local players must be carefully studied and scrutinized. One never knows for whom a local is really working. For example, a local brokerage house might actually be controlled by a wealthy family that also owns several industrial companies, and its coverage of such companies might be biased. Remember, regulatory environments are also different from the First World. Many emerging markets have weak laws and enforcement regarding "insider trading." Moreover, local players might also take advantage of foreign investors through "front-running" or other practices that are forbidden in most First World stock markets.[20] This is not to say that every emerging market broker is a crook; on the contrary, my experience to date has been remarkably problem-free. However, a lack of experience and knowledge about what is customary in the West can often create an uneven playing field for a First World investor in an emerging market. Therefore, two words of advice: caveat emptor.

Trading costs—brokerage commissions and other related administrative fees—are often higher in developing countries, which adds risk to investors' portfolios. On average, the IFC estimates the costs to be four times higher than in the United States. Investors from industrialized countries often have to engage in foreign exchange, which also carries costs. This often steers investors toward a few large-capitalization stocks that have high correlation with the broader market. By concentrating exposure, investors can execute larger block trades to reduce costs. And, because market concentration is typically high in an emerging market, this can be a practical issue as well. The top ten stocks in most emerging markets typically account for some 80% of trading volume and market capitalization, versus less than 10% in the First World.

While opening an account and trading in exotic markets like Morocco or Bangladesh may seem exciting, local markets often have restrictions on foreign investors, limiting ownership and minority rights. Many countries also lack electronic settlement, which makes registration and custody issues more difficult. Time zone differences also make local trading more risky, unless one trades around the clock. Thus, local equities can be a difficult way for foreign investors to access these markets, even for large institutions that have an overseas presence and experience.

There are also trading restrictions that can hamper a foreign

FIGURE 6.7

TRADING COSTS IN EMERGING MARKETS

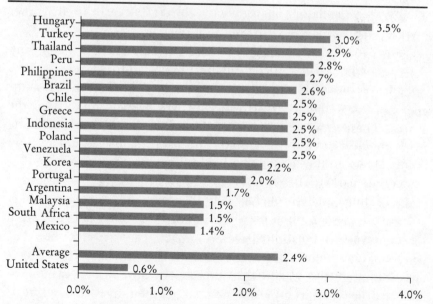

SOURCE: IFC/EMDB survey of brokers and fund managers, January 1996

investor's ability to trade overseas. For example, certain markets require foreign investors to keep their money in the country for a specified period of time. Chile, for example, has recently maintained a one-year hold period. There are also limitations on "short-selling"—that is, speculating that a market may drop—and the ability to borrow against shares. These leverage trades are the cornerstone of many aggressive First World "hedge funds," some of the biggest players in the developing world, and these restrictions can greatly reduce an investor's flexibility in trading the markets.

DEPOSITORY RECEIPTS

Just as certain select minor league baseball players make it to the major leagues, some Third World companies reach world-class status by listing outside the home country on an internationally recognized exchange through a Depository Receipt program. Under such a scheme, a block of local shares is bundled and held by a named custodian (often a big U.S. or European bank), and the receipts of that pool are listed. American Depository Receipts (ADRs) are listed in New York, and Global Depository Receipts (GDRs) are listed in other markets such as Luxembourg and London.

There are great advantages to listing overseas. Once a company issues an ADR or a GDR, the large First World investment banks often begin securities coverage and research. This broadens the audience of buyers and sellers, which improves overall liquidity for the shares. These stocks are also user-friendly. Unlike local emerging market equities, ADRs are quoted and paid for in U.S. dollars, and dividends are paid in U.S. dollars as well.

While such depository receipts are listed in the industrialized markets, one must remember that they are still emerging market stocks. Just because the stock price is quoted in dollars does not mean local currency fluctuations have no impact. Theoretically, the ADR price will reflect the local prices *and* the foreign exchange rate. However, it is interesting to note that companies whose shares get bundled in depository receipts typically broaden out their investor base, creating greater liquidity and price action for the stock than those not listed abroad. In this respect, an ADR program can prove to be a huge boost to a local company's share price.[21]

The fact that depository receipts trade in First World markets gives investors more flexibility. Shares can be borrowed against, and short positions can be constructed for hedging (against local positions that can be locked in for a period of time) or speculating. In some cases, ADRs and GDRs allow for relative value opportunities between local stocks and depository receipts. Often the overseas stock tends to be more expensive than the underlying local shares for a number of reasons. Frequently, accessing local shares is highly regulated, discouraging foreign participation. In India, for example, only qualified overseas institutional investors can play locally and avoid paying certain withholding taxes. Yet many Indian stocks trade in GDR form in London. Because of the local restrictions, Indian GDRs trade at substantial premiums—sometimes as high as 50%—over their local equivalent shares. Over time, there is a good chance that such local restrictions will fade away. Therefore, for skillful investors, who can figure how to get in locally and go long, while short-selling the comparable GDRs overseas, there are opportunities for arbitrage profits. Such situations exist in many emerging markets.

But not all depository receipts are created equal either. In the U.S. there are different levels of ADRs for companies, depending on whether or not they can comply with strict SEC disclosure and accounting requirements. Rule 144a ADRs represent companies that issue equity through private placements only to large institutional investors, although non-U.S. citizens can invest. Through this vehicle, foreign companies are able to avoid many regulatory hurdles involved in a public listing and have an opportunity to present themselves to U.S. investors before making a full public offering.

COUNTRY FUNDS

One of the simplest and most common ways for individual investors to access emerging stock markets is through country funds. Managed by professional fiduciaries, such pools are aggregates of stocks that attempt to represent the local market of a specific country. The funds can be actively or passively managed, the major difference being that actively managed funds strive to outperform the market index, while passive strategies try to mirror an index's performance.

Country funds can provide wide exposure to a nation's market (or regional market), enabling investors to own a portfolio of stocks from a given country without having to buy each stock individually. One caveat is that some country funds have more concentrated exposure than others, while index funds provide the most expansive coverage. Obtaining the same diversification with individual securities or ADRs would require a larger investment, since country funds essentially enable investors to hold fractions of foreign securities. Funds also provide professional management for specific stock selection, obtaining usable information, providing relatively safe custody, hedging against foreign currency depreciation, providing dividend remittances, abiding by local tax laws and restrictions on foreign ownership, and repatriating dividends and capital gains. Therefore, individual investors do not have to become expert in these areas. A country fund can often provide a comparatively hassle-free, cost-effective means of tapping into restricted markets. This is particularly attractive to retail investors, who can access these funds by simply calling their local stock broker.

Frequently, country funds are the only way for foreigners to obtain access to a given market. For example, in the 1980s South Korea allowed only two reputable Western mutual funds to participate in the Seoul stock exchange. The government stated it wanted only sophisticated investors in its market who understood the inherent risks. The last thing South Korea wanted was to develop a bad reputation as a market in which foreigners lost money.

While they may provide easy entry for retail investors, country funds are often not the cheapest way to access markets, particularly for large investors. Funds for countries with difficult access—like Russia or other nascent markets—may carry steep premiums. Many are loaded with high broker and filing fees. Some may trade only a finite number of shares and often trade at a discount or premium to net asset value (NAV); that is, the share price might actually be higher or lower than the underlying value of the fund's assets. Discounts to NAV are often comments on a manager's poor performance, but could also reflect restrictions of the underlying market, availability of alternative

investments, tax liabilities, exchange controls, or merely bearish sentiment on a country. However, country funds offer interesting features.
Discounts can erode or even become premiums when the market or a
sector returns to favor. There are many sophisticated investors who
look for relative value and arbitrage opportunities through the
premium/discount phenomenon with country funds and ADRs and
local shares. They don't care whether stocks go up or down; they care
only about the spreads widening or tightening. Country funds also
allow investors opportunities to find pre-ADR companies, hidden
jewels that may skyrocket in price when a depository receipt program
is initiated in that stock.

Index products are vehicles related to country funds. In the spring
of 1996 the American and New York Stock Exchanges introduced
local index products for several countries. Like a country fund, these
instruments—which trade like stocks—let investors buy a replicated
local stock market in one neat package. Unlike country funds, index
products intend to replicate the performance of a local market "passively" with no day-to-day manager. Many Wall Street houses are
developing similar products with acronyms like WEBs (World Equity
Baskets) in an attempt to provide a cheaper, easier play on a given
emerging market. Such passive strategies are also gaining footholds in
the institutional investors' world because of their cost effectiveness.

Like depository receipts, country funds can also be borrowed
against and short-sold. That opens opportunities to use country funds
in combination strategies with local shares, as well as with depository
receipts. If a country fund is trading at a steep premium, for example,
an investor may go long on a local share or ADR of the same country,
short-sell the country fund, and play for a relative spread profit. The
investment choices—long only, short only, or a combination—
become endless, which is what makes emerging market trading such a
fascinating realm of Wall Street.

The fact that there are so many options in the emerging markets,
as well as greater volatility, has drawn the attention of the so-called
hedge funds, the private pools of money that roam the world looking
for high returns. Hedge funds typically employ leverage, often bet that
markets will drop, and seek to make money on short-term momentum
in a given marketplace. Some seek relative value opportunities—long

something, short another—in the hopes of capturing a predefined spread. Often this includes both debt and equity. However, most hedge funds are not long-term investors; they are often called "hot money" because they come in and out of markets quickly and opportunistically. While some may "like" a country, most hedge funds invest in places where they smell profit, not tasty food. And half the time that profit might be derived from actually betting *against* a market. Regardless of their intentions, hedge funds do serve a vital purpose in financial marketization. Because this money will go into relatively risky situations, hedge funds provide small markets with capital, liquidity, and greater efficiencies—often the critical mass that is needed to broaden and deepen an emerging market. However, there is a price to be paid: the volatility created by such funds moving in and out of small markets often can produce destabilizing price swings that can undermine long-term confidence. This is the unfortunate price many developing countries pay in the early stages of financial marketization.

PRIVATE EQUITY

Unlisted shares in companies provide an opportunity to invest in that significant portion of economic activity in developing countries not captured by stock markets. In many countries with embryonic stock markets, private equity is the only way to build meaningful equity exposure. As mentioned in chapter 5 (Figure 5.1), stock market capitalization in developing countries is often only 20% to 50% of GDP. That means that more than half of many developing countries' economies lie outside the listed stock universe. Some formerly closed economies are still dominated by old patriarchal enterprises, privately held by families for generations. Moreover, certain newer industries, like telecom, are created by granting concessions, investment opportunities that also fall outside stock markets. Furthermore, as mentioned earlier, multinationals are plowing billions into local assets and in some cases private equity investment to facilitate their expansion throughout the emerging world, helping to finance everything from Kentucky Fried Chicken stores in Eastern Europe to mines in Central Asia and Fotomats in sub-Saharan Africa. These opportunities, coupled with the privatization of state-owned companies through commercial tenders, still offer investors excellent plays on the economy—in many ways, the best access to the real economy. Although private equity is inherently less liquid than listed stocks, few emerging market stock markets offer liquidity comparable to First World exchanges. In addition, steep transaction costs on traded emerging market stocks (often four times that in the U.S.) make private securities even more attractive. As a result, many of the world's leading global investors, such as George Soros, are devoting more capital and manpower to pursuing such private opportunities.

The private nature of this sector requires a lot of homework and due diligence. Investors must not only know the country but also sift through the company's financials (if they exist) and meet with the management (often the most important consideration is their reliability) in order to understand the industry and assess the company's potential. Because of the work required to be successful in this area, private equity investment is often done through limited partnership funds managed by specialists. Some are country or region specific, while others focus on a key sector. Often such funds have long lock-up periods, some for up to ten years. Therefore, investors who go this route must be extremely comfortable with both the countries that are being targeted by such a fund and, more important, the fund manager.

However illiquid such investments are, investors should realize that these unlisted opportunities should track the parallel stock market in a country. In this respect, think of private equity as venture capital in the U.S.; investors are getting in before the company goes public. Often the primary goal of such funds is to flip out companies onto the country's exchange once they have grown in terms of capitalization and liquidity, or even on major exchanges in New York or London. As a result, country factors should still play an important part in private equity investment decisions.

REAL ESTATE

Unlike most investments in operating businesses through public or private securities, investments in real estate require a direct play on property, whether involving land or buildings. Because most of these investment opportunities will be unlisted, many investors see it as a form of private equity. The main attraction of Third World real estate is the fundamental supply-demand imbalance. Most developing countries lack sufficient modern infrastructure such as office buildings, and in formerly statist economies, the real estate market has historically been distorted, as rents were often set by governments. Furthermore, the build-out time in real estate creates an odd supply-demand tension in these countries, one in which rents are equal to or greater than those in some prestigious First World markets, such as New York and London. Real property is important to an improved business infrastructure. First World MNCs, for example, cannot ask expatriate employees to work in substandard space. In many locales, particularly in former Soviet bloc countries, there is little suitable space to meet the needs of MNCs. What little supply exists primarily consists of older residential and government buildings adapted for office use and an even smaller number of business-specific properties. At present rents for these limited spaces in these emerging marketplaces are high, in many cases higher than rents for Class A space in highly developed markets (see Table 6.2). Thus MNCs that want to establish a business presence in certain markets are often forced to pay years of rent in advance, which makes the deals very lucrative for developers.

These real estate imbalances may last for some time. There are substantial barriers to entry in these markets, including arcane property law; in some cases there are restrictions on foreign ownership of land. Moreover, long-term finance—a key to real estate—is not easy to obtain for prospective buyers. Currently, there are few local lenders for such projects in developing countries, as traditional providers of this type of long-term capital—pension funds and insurance companies—are fledgling sectors in most of these countries. Eventually, as economies grow and incomes rise, residential and commercial markets will develop. Until then, scarce capital and increased demand for space mean that there are often great financial opportunities for foreign investors in the real estate sector.

TABLE 6.2
PRIME OFFICE RENTS IN MAJOR INTERNATIONAL CITIES (1996)

City	$/square foot
Tokyo	121.3
Hong Kong	81.6
Moscow	75.4
St. Petersburg	70.8
Warsaw	60.2
Mexico City	58.5
Sydney	42.0
London	37.2
Washington	37.0
Prague	35.6
New York	34.0
Budapest	32.6
Buenos Aires	27.8
Amsterdam	23.4
San Francisco	23.0

SOURCE: WPEM

NO FREE LUNCH: RISKS IN EMERGING MARKETS

To think that blindly investing in emerging markets will produce immediate, consistent, and endless profits would be a huge mistake. Having traded some $50 billion worth of instruments throughout the developing world, I myself and other professionals still get burnt in markets from time to time. What has yet to be discussed in detail is *risk,* particularly the unique types investors assume and must manage in nascent markets.

This recent wave of investor capital from wealthy countries to less developed ones is not the first of its kind. For ages investors have been seduced by investment opportunities in exotic locales such as Casablanca, São Paulo, and Shanghai. While many such waves of interest

THE LIFE CYCLES OF EMERGING MARKETS*

Like Schumpeter and Kondratieff, Hong Kong–based fund manager
Marc Faber is a wave man. With wit and anecdotal observance, Faber
believes that the key to investing wisely in emerging stock markets is to
identify where countries are in their individual social, political, and
economic developmental cycles.

Phase Zero: This phase is categorized by economic stagnation,
unstable economic and social conditions, and little foreign direct or
portfolio investment. Headlines are negative, hotel occupancy and tourism are low, and the stock market is cheap and illiquid. *Examples:*
Argentina in mid-1980s, Phillipines 1985–90, Russia 1991–93.

Phase 1: A significant positive change—such as a new government or new economic policies—occurs. General economic conditions
improve, and consumption rises, as does capital spending and corporate
profits. Exports increase, capital is repatriated, and foreign direct investments flow in. Stocks, along with tourism, begin to pick up as foreigners
become interested in joint ventures and other investments, while tax
laws are changed to encourage and attract these entities. *Examples:*
Argentina after 1990, Mexico after 1984, China after 1978, Russia 1993.

Phase 2: Economic expansion leads to lower unemployment,
higher wages, and more foreign funds. Positive sentiments prevail,
perhaps to a fault, as the improvements are perceived to be everlasting,
and capital spending to expand capacity soars to dangerous levels. Great
expectations fuel the boom, and everyone jumps on the bandwagon.
This period is characterized by a proliferation of thick country research
reports, packed hotels, and construction everywhere. Meanwhile,
markets are soaring. But like human babies, these markets are
"accident-prone" and susceptible to crashes. *Examples:* Japan and Thailand between 1987 and 1990, Russia in mid-1990s.

Phase 3: Although the boom seems ongoing, ultimately overinvestment leads to excess capacity and real estate, infrastructure problems, and strong inflation pressures, all of which culminate in a shock
and an unexpected decline in stock prices. This marks the beginning of a
mature stage, where markets lose energy and gain volatility. *Examples:*
Thailand, Japan, and Indonesia after 1990, Russia 1997.

Phase 4: While the economy appears to be fine, profit margins
are decreasing, and growth is slowing. Stocks revive as new foreign

investors, thinking the slowdown is temporary, seek "missed" opportunities. Stocks fail to reach new highs as the large numbers of new issues outstrip demand, while political and social conditions start to deteriorate, and hotels are forced to offer discounts with declining tourism. *Examples:* Japan and Thailand in 1991, Russia early 1998.

Phase 5:   Corporate profits and stocks plummet, and consumption grinds down. As markets turn bearish, investors finally recognize their past miscalculations, realize that they have overpaid for stocks, begin to unwind leveraged positions, and accelerate the decline by rushing to get out of the market. Capital spending and real estate prices fall. A regression, or perhaps progression, to Phase 1 or 2 is around the corner. *Examples:* Japan and Thailand in 1992, Russia mid-1998?

Phase 6:   Investors abandon stocks, capital spending falls, foreigners exit the local markets (and begin speculating against them), and the currency weakens or is devalued. Compared to Phase 3, the mood is pessimistic, confidence fades, and fear takes over. In the prosperous phases, everyone wanted in; now everyone wants out. *Example:* Asia in the 1990s?, Russia 1998?

There is some wisdom in Faber's approach, which underscores the importance of country analysis and timing. The trick is to accurately identify when the overall trend in confidence has shifted, which ultimately will affect liquidity and price formation. What is interesting is how Faber's framework seemed to predict the downturns in Asia and Russia years before the markets actually fell hard in 1997 and 1998. But rest assured, as the markets rise in some countries, they fall in others. Identifying such cycles, therefore, can undoubtedly help in country selection and boost returns.

* This theory was first published in *Barrons* in 1992. "The International Trader" (July 13, 1992), pp. 20, 22, 64.

had legitimate economic rationales, some did not. And fortunes have been lost pursuing the latter.

Some of these waves have been part of what historian Charles Kindleburger calls "panics, crashes, and manias," odd situations in which eager investors get caught up in irrational speculation. One of the most notorious such panics started in the early eighteenth century in something known as the South Sea Company, an entity that was set up to assume government debts of England in exchange for rights to mine and trade throughout South America. In 1720 the company issued stock that skyrocketed from 128 pounds to 1,000 in a panic over six months, only to collapse by autumn of that year. No profits had ever been earned by this paper company, but investors were seduced by visions of gold and silver. This is one of countless Ponzi-type schemes and general investor frenzies over developing countries throughout history.[22]

On the whole, I would say that the current wave has little to do with the speculative bubbles of the South Sea Company or the Dutch tulipomania in the seventeenth century. However, that does not imply that certain emerging markets are not prone to spurts of insanity or that investors can operate risk-free in these countries. Investors in foreign debt, for example, have been faced with periodic defaults throughout history. Max Winkler's 1933 classic *Foreign Bonds: An Autopsy* covers a range of situations in which governments have defaulted on debt obligations from ancient Greece through the early twentieth century.[23] The Brady Plans were sovereign defaults in some respects; many banks and investors lost billions in those restructurings. Moreover, Russia's default and restructuring in mid-1998 also underscore the risks that still exist in cross-border finance.

MNCs have also had their problems. There are many companies that lost millions in property when Cuba nationalized in the late 1950s, and there have been isolated incidents of nationalization in Peru, Chile, and several African countries in the 1970s and 1980s. War and embargoes also produce commercial losses, and many doing business in the former Yugoslavia, Libya, Iraq, and in other Middle Eastern hotspots in the last two decades have taken financial hits. But there is, I believe, a fundamental change in this kind of developing country risk heading into the new millennium.

THE NEWEST AND MOST PREVALENT RISK

Historically, the most common form of risk faced by investors in developing countries has been political risk; that is, risk of loss due to direct government action such as nationalization or expropriation of assets in one form or another. Remember, in the past there has been precious little financial market investing in the Third World; most capital flow has been dominated by foreign direct investment. However, as countries adopt free-market reforms—and as the First World presses for and nurtures such reforms—increasingly the greatest risk for MNCs and overseas financial investors will become *market* risk.

Market risk, also known as systematic risk, is one that cannot be diversified away in a given country. In any country, whether industrialized or developing, financial opportunities tend to be a reflection of economic activity. While investors can diversify across industrial sectors, there are broad tides that lift and sink all boats. For example, during the autumn 1987 stock market crash in the United States, no major stock finished up on Monday, October 19. The whole market sank. Similarly, in December 1994 and early 1995, few Mexican stocks rose during the peso crisis. The daily price fluctuation in a market is known as *volatility,* and developing markets, in general, have much more of it than First World markets. The historic volatility of First

FIGURE 6.8

EMERGING STOCK MARKET VOLATILITY

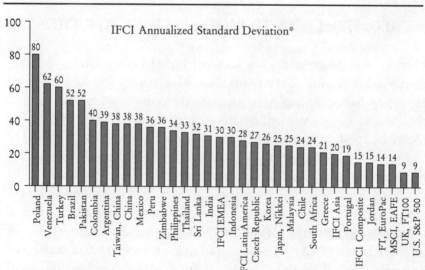

* *In most cases, results are based on five years of monthly data, measured in U.S. dollars, through August 1996.*

SOURCE: IFC

World stock markets is somewhere in the 15% per annum range, as measured by standard deviation of daily returns. Very few of the G7 markets would experience greater volatility because most of their economies are relatively balanced and predictable. On the other hand, the average volatility of an emerging market is more than double the First World average—in some cases, *five* or *six* times the average. Why is the volatility, and consequently the market risk, so great? When markets are nascent and thinly capitalized, a sudden rush of cash will immediately affect prices. Since much of this liquidity is sentiment driven, prices can quickly change with perceptions of political, economic, or social turbulence as the world recently witnessed in Asia. The virtuous circle of reform can be reversed, becoming the vicious cycle of poverty—sometimes in a matter of months. This is where we see the fallout from market risk. The fact is the risk of direct seizure or expropriation is considerably lower today. What has increased, however, is the *market* risk attached to today's capital flows. One of the most recent examples of such risks is a slip-and-fall situation in Mexico, a country which has experienced the highs and lows of economic reform.

MEXICO: FROM RAGS TO RICHES TO RAGS TO RICHES[24]

Mexico's rise began under the stewardship of Harvard-trained President Carlos Salinas Gortari in 1988, as privatization and inflation reduction had completely restructured the economy. Over his tenure, the number of government enterprises fell from approximately 1,110 to 220 by 1994. Inflation, which had been as high as 159% in 1987, fell to 7% by 1994. Mexico also began attracting MNCs to take advantage of the *maquiladora* assembly plants that had begun to populate northern border towns. However satisfying these macroeconomic changes were to foreign MNCs and investors, enormous social and political tensions were brewing domestically. Not more than a dozen weeks after the historic NAFTA was passed in November 1993, a small civil uprising erupted in the southern state Chiapas between the local Indian population and government troops in January 1994. In previous years, Mexico—gearing up for greater economic activity due to NAFTA—had begun importing foreign capital goods until it had amassed a huge $28 billion trade deficit; exports had yet to accelerate. To cover much of the deficit, the government issued peso debt at relatively high yields to attract foreign money. Coupled with Mexico's modest devaluation policy, this helped calm nervous foreign money. Chiapas rattled investors and jostled markets, although its long-term effects remained unclear. The government began to dollar-link its foreign borrowings through instruments called *tesobonos*, radically altering the risk profile of the country.

In March, the hand-picked successor of Salinas, Donaldo Collosio, was assassinated, some say by insiders in Collosio's own party—the PRI—Mexico's monopolistic ruling party for some seven decades. Sensing political instability, foreign investors began to leave the country, and the central bank started to use its hard currency reserves to protect the peso and the government's policy of modest devaluation. As reserves fell, overseas investors grew even more anxious. That summer, it is estimated that the Mexican government spent between $6 and $8 billion to support its peso stabilization policy. The currency's market value had become distorted, harking back to prereform days.

It became clear that Mexico had attracted the wrong type of capital to finance its trade deficits. The IMF noted that, in 1993, 77.26% of the foreign capital coming to Mexico was "hot" portfolio money and only 22.4% was in FDI. That money would leave quickly and painlessly over the subsequent months. Amid further political tension and a weak economy, confidence waned. As global interest rates began to increase dramatically in February 1994 (with the first of six rate hikes), hard currency began to migrate back to home countries in the First World, further increasing pressure on the peso.

Eventually the dike burst. No longer able to support the peso stabilization policy, newly elected President Ernesto Zedillo decided to relieve some of the market pressure with a one-time surprise mini-devaluation on December 19, 1994. Overnight the peso went from 3.5 to 4 against the dollar. That held for all of two days. Feeling betrayed by the Mexican government, overseas investors sucked out an estimated $10 billion in those forty-eight hours. By December 21, the government was forced to abandon peso support altogether and go to a free float. Within a few days foreign financial investors lost more than 50% of their money as the peso hit a rate of 6 to the dollar. By

March 1995 it approached 7. Needless to say, investors were burnt and boiling mad.

Mexico's *tesobono* crises in 1994 and 1995 were not dissimilar from problems that had plagued the country ten years earlier. In both cases, a failure to address a stubborn trade deficit made things worse. An unbalanced composition of capital, coupled with an inability to deliver economic benefits to all segments of society, caused tensions in and out of the country. While financial investors waited patiently for change, hope eventually ran out in the marketplace. It took an unpopular $50 billion bailout package supported by U.S. President Bill Clinton and the World Bank to restore confidence and get Mexico back on track and avoid defaults on nearly $30 billion in foreign borrowings.

Even with the bailout, serious money was lost in Mexico, and its crisis typifies the risks investors will face in the next century. Some eighteen months earlier, Venezuela and Turkey suffered similar macroeconomic problems. Moreover, by the summer of 1997, the long economic bull run of East Asia took a long-overdue breather. Several countries—including former miracle economies in Thailand, Philippines, Indonesia, and Malaysia—faced similar problems holding U.S. dollar pegs to their respective currencies. Rapid wage growth and slower productivity gains began to erode their competitive advantage. Increased competition from other Asian developing countries like China, Vietnam, and India—along with resuscitating former Soviet economies—began to slow growth in the former Tigers. A property bubble in Thailand, based on the belief that economic growth would continue indefinitely, forced the country to devalue its baht. Amid Thailand's problems, Malaysia, Philippines, and Indonesia were forced to relax their hard-currency pegs, all of which have cost investors billions in foreign exchange–related losses. Perhaps the biggest surprise came when South Korea—one of the Third World's great success stories and now the world's eleventh largest economy—was forced to accept massive financial assistance from the World Bank in late 1997 due to huge financial holes from years of overinvestment, overcapacity, and mounting debts. And in 1998 Russia's default/restructuring precipitated a complete meltdown of the country's markets for debt, equity, and currency.

These financial collapses will undoubtedly become more frequent in the future; it is only natural in a world of rapid marketization. Markets often get way ahead of themselves—ahead of policies, expectations, and realities. Because so many of these countries are operating at the margin, there is little room for error. Financial markets have always punished companies—or countries—that fail to deliver the goods as promised. But although risks are increasing, investors are increasingly able to gauge and manage such risks. Data on countries is readily available; the World Bank gathers and disseminates more than 140 important pieces of information monthly. News feeds provide real-time information on such countries as well. Travel and communication costs are all dropping quickly, so investors cannot readily blame foreign governments for their financial losses. Caveat emptor is the rule du jour.

As global economic integration and competition intensify, such losses may surface far more frequently than in the past. While certain types of sovereign and political risks—in the classic sense of nationalization or expropriation—may begin to wane, market risks to overseas investors should undoubtedly rise as First World countries accelerate their economic and financial involvement with the Third World. In this respect, the IMF and the World Bank may see their profiles rise dramatically in future global affairs, maybe more so than the United Nations. This may, indeed, become even more complicated as military and economic security, for example, become frequently intertwined, as was underscored recently with nuclear tests conducted by India and Pakistan in 1998. When the World Bank announced that certain moneys might be cut off from these two nations based on the tests, many analysts raised fears that both of these large IMF recipients would be tempted to peddle such technologies to raise needed hard currency. Furthermore, Russia's recent economic woes also raised proliferation concerns. The key to global security, therefore, may increasingly depend on the ability to monitor country economics and finances; to mobilize strategic capital when needed, to help stabilize markets; and to prescribe economic remedies and guidelines. The First World may be regularly summoned as mediator in economic emergencies to shore up financial confidence, as it was in past military emergencies. As we'll see in the next chapter, a greater incidence of commercial and financial diplomacy will characterize twenty-first century international affairs.

CHAPTER 7

Winners and Losers of the Future

THE PICTURE PAINTED so far has been one of bounty, progress, and upsides. True, economic growth brings improvements in living standards and health: many Third World children today are an average of four or five inches taller than they were in the 1940s, with twenty years greater life expectancy and 50% higher caloric intake. Economic growth also brings higher and more stable incomes, which means new consumer markets: today there are 200 times more TVs, telephones, and cars per household in Taiwan, for example, than in 1950.[1] And as has been argued, faster growth in developing countries brings benefits to First World countries, by offering new and hungry markets for their exports, as well as new financial markets for higher investment returns than are available at home. In Malaysia, this dynamic is in its advanced stages. In Kuala Lumpur, the eighteen to twenty-five age range has become a target population for cellular telephone marketing, with apparently 60% already signed up to cellular service.[2] This population is one of the latest additions to the growing global consumer market that has MNCs so excited.

However exciting this future may seem, the fact is that not everyone will be a winner in this global realignment of economic power. There will be, as described, a *net* gain. But this is a story about comparative advantage, and it will require the First World to cede certain lower-skilled jobs to its emerging neighbors. Despite the discomfort and challenge faced by the American, European, and Japanese workers whose jobs will migrate, there are opportunities to be seized by First World workers who exploit their home country's comparative advantage, which is increasingly in the service and technology industries, including semiconductors, telecommunications, software, biotechnology, and finance. In the United States, for example, the engine of growth is increasingly to be found in Silicon Valley and its offshoots, and on Wall Street.[3] Allowing such a dynamic to run its course will mean that, ultimately, the refrigerators that the average First World worker will buy will be cheaper, even though that worker may need to get retrained in order to remain competitive in the labor force. The average Third Worlder will now have a job, producing these refrigerators, and the value of Third World manufacturing exports will reflect production in such sectors; such goods now account for almost 60% of the exports of emerging markets, up from only 5% in 1955, and the Third World's share of world manufacture exports jumped from 5% in 1970 to 22% in 1993.[4] Eventually, the Third World worker will himself own a refrigerator from his factory. This same dynamic will be reproduced in other manufacturing sectors, and between other sets of economically differentiated countries. A new class of Third World consumers will have been created, with greater purchasing power and an improved standard of living. Indeed, developing countries are likely to account for approximately two-thirds of the increase in world imports over the next twenty years.[5]

In this way international trade can raise everyone's living standards—indeed, there is an inevitability to this process, and it is only by allowing it to run freely and by adapting to the new environment that the First World can guarantee continued improvements in living standards for its citizens, in an era of skyrocketing public deficits and competitive global labor pressures.

LEADING LAGGARDS?

> The world has become a huge bazaar with nations peddling their work forces in competition against one another, offering the lowest price for doing business. The customers, of course, are the multinational corporations.[6]

There are countries in the First World that might find the economic squeeze particularly tight. Western European economies with structurally inflexible labor markets have found, and will continue to find, that they are unable to quickly adapt to the loss of competitiveness resulting from sticky wages and the cost of running an exhaustive welfare state. Restrictive labor regulations in Western Europe may mean that low-skilled manufacturing jobs, such as the ones currently migrating south from the U.S. to Mexico, will take longer to migrate to neighboring emerging markets. This may represent temporary relief for potentially displaced workers, but it also means a loss in competitiveness for entrenched economies. Unless they wake up to the (however harsh) reality that their comparative advantage lies beyond the traditional low-skilled manufacturing industries that fueled their postwar economic success stories, these countries will truly be the lazy hares in the race against the slower, yet ultimately more dynamic tortoises of the emerging markets. Thus, largely as a result of a US$61,650 annual subsidy for each German mining job (recently increased to US$87,000 as mass demonstrations and union pressure thwarted Chancellor Kohl's attempts at reform), German coal today costs about US$180/ton, compared to the world price of US$65/ton.[7]

In Germany, home of the highest average industrial labor costs in the world, the last decade has already seen a significant migration of German jobs into countries with lower labor costs. As Table 7.1 demonstrates, German companies have adapted to their growing wage and benefit obligations at home by moving their jobs abroad.

As Table 7.1 shows, even where jobs *were* created in Germany, at least four times as many were created abroad, and in the majority of cases, the number of jobs in Germany fell. And this process is not limited to German jobs. In every First World region, jobs are moving to the peripheries where labor costs are lower, particularly jobs that do not require a sophisticated skill set. Certain American manufacturing jobs have migrated to Mexico for the last decade. Japan has aggressively relocated labor-intensive assembly work to various cheaper labor markets throughout Asia. Even South Korea, up to now one of developing Asia's success stories, has been looking at moving manufacturing jobs to various parts of the former Soviet Union.

TABLE 7.1
GERMAN CORPORATE EMPLOYMENT TRENDS

Company/Business	1985 Employment				1995 Employment					
	German	Foreign	% Foreign		German	Foreign	% Foreign	%Δ German (gross)	%Δ Foreign (gross)	
BASF/chemicals, pharmaceuticals	87,292	42,881	32.9%		63,715	42,850	40.2%	−27.00%	+0.07%	
Daimler/cars, trucks, and aerospace	257,538[1]	62,427	19.5%		242,086	68,907	22.2%	−5.99%	+10.38%	
Henkel kGaA/chemicals	16,006	15,015	48.4%		14,684	27,044	64.8%	−8.26%	+80.11%	
Hoechst/chemicals, pharmaceuticals	61,642	118,919	65.8%		39,108	122,510	75.8%	−36.56%	+3.02%	
Krupp/steel	59,978	7,424	11.0%		49,112	17,240	26.0%	−18.12%	+132.22%	
MANGroup/capital equipment	52,264[2]	8,513	14.0%		45,085	11,418	20.2%	−13.74%	+34.12%	
Mannesmann AG/machinery	77,174[1]	32,280	29.5%		78,015	41,660	34.8%	+1.09%	+29.06%	
MG/materials	21,384	3,458	13.9%		18,571	4,870	20.8%	−13.15%	+40.83%	
SAP/software	749[3]	191	20.3%		4,345	4,851	52.8%	+480.11%	+2539.79%	
Siemens/electrical and electronic	240,000	108,000	31.0%		211,000	162,000	43.4%	−12.08%	+50.00%	
Veba/energy and transport	68,689[1]	5,361	7.2%		125,158	24,930	16.6%	+82.21%	+365.03%	

(1) Figures are for 1986.
(2) Figures are for 1987.
(3) Figures are for 1988.

SOURCE: *Forbes*, May 5, 1997, p. 131.

GERMANY: WORKING HARD OR HARDLY WORKING?

Germany's labor laws have long been one of the world's most generous, at times providing Germans with benefits that Americans would consider luxuries, rather than bare necessities. Until recently, workers could be prescribed a four-week spa holiday, which would be paid for by the employer. Dental care was similarly covered by the employer, causing the contingency of $10,000 treatments to be factored into labor costs. In 1970, contributions to social security (split 50–50 between employer and employee) were 26.5% of gross wages. This went up to 35.8% in 1990, and to 40.9% in 1996. From 1970 to 1990, the increase was mainly due to increased health care contributions. From 1990 to 1996, it was due partly to increases in unemployment contributions after unification and partly to new long-term nursing care contributions (Wendy Carlin and David Soskice, "Shocks to the System: The German Political Economy Under Stress," *National Institute Economic Review,* January 1997, pp. 57–76, at p. 60). The German workweek lasts only 37.5 hours (or 35 in the metals industry), after which overtime is paid (Howard Banks, "Deutsche Hegira," *Forbes,* May 5, 1997, p. 131). Laid-off workers are entitled to as much as 70% of their salary for at least a year (Edmund L. Andrews, "The Jobless Are Snared in Europe's Safety Net," *New York Times,* November 9, 1997). Today, one of Europe's highest rates of unemployment (unadjusted, about 12% as of April 1997) has contributed to pressure for labor reform. Labor costs are clearly a disadvantage: at $31.76 per hour, German wages are more than double those of the U.S. and Britain (Banks, "Deutsche Hegira"). Ironically, the very legislation that seems to burden employers may well be a factor in forcing employers to adjust by upskilling their workforces in response to the challenges of globalization.

Lest we forget, such labor cycles are a historical fixture. At one time 97% of the U.S. labor force were farmers. There was a period during which the U.S. economy urbanized and factory jobs began to displace farmwork, when the U.S. ceased to be principally an exporter of primary goods and began to export manufactured goods instead. At the cusp of each economic era, there is a sense of crisis, an immediate sense of insecurity that is particularly painful for the workforce caught between gears. But on the other side, once the crisis has passed its peak, we see a workforce with higher incomes, greater purchasing power, higher standards of living, and longer lifetimes, all living in a stronger global economy. A recent BBC documentary series entitled *The People's Century* explored these very issues, contrasting the experiences of two former employees of the Kaiser Steel plant, which has been not only shut down but dismantled and transported, piece by piece, to China. One former employee, now unemployed, laments the loss of the superb health plan he had at Kaiser, the friendships he built up, and the (illusory) job security that came from working for an industrial giant in the 1970s. Another, lamenting the same losses, nonetheless recounts how he went on to retrain and is now a successful real estate agent, owner of two cars and four houses. However difficult or challenging it may be in the short term for a former factory employee to seek training and relocate to another, more competitive sector of the economy, in the long run it is both possible and necessary for him to do so.

This should not be seen as the twilight of the economic gods of the twentieth century. Not only is it well within the capabilities of the First World to adapt to the new environment, but to do so is the key to its continued leadership. No one is advocating a slashing of wages to the levels of Haiti or the elimination of all labor protection altogether. Indeed, as long as the First World enjoys higher levels of education and better infrastructure and management (all contributing to a higher average productivity), wages will remain higher there. Rather, what is advocated is a deliberate political decision to shift the focus of the economy from the lower-skilled manufacturing sectors where it is clear (for instance, through the economic investment decisions of MNCs to move their plants to the emerging markets) they have lost comparative advantage, to higher-skilled sectors. There are already signs of this change in the U.S., where approximately 11 million jobs have been created since 1989, two-thirds of which are managerial and professional positions. As Michael Mandel comments with optimism, "rather than becoming a nation of hamburger flippers, we are becoming a nation of schoolteachers, computer programmers, and health care managers."[8]

From here on, in order to sustain this type of job creation and thus protect high levels of productivity and therefore wages, it will become increasingly important for First World countries to focus on education, in particular on mathematics and the sciences—the building blocks of the technology that lies behind our comparative advantage. It must be understood that global economic integration has a momentum of its own, and that the only way the First World can increase its living standards, let alone preserve its economic lead, is to adapt to the changing environment. However, a recent study reveals that some of the world's richest are currently also falling behind in technical literacy. In a ranking of computer literacy among employees across a range of countries, Iceland took the top spot, while the U.S. ranked only sixteenth, Germany ranked eighteenth, and the U.K. ranked twenty-third. Surprisingly, Singapore ranked second, Hong Kong eighth, Taiwan tenth, Chile seventeenth, and South Korea nineteenth, surpassing many members of the OECD.[9]

Clearly it is easier to catch up than to preserve one's position as leader. In the case of today's advanced countries, facing the shrinking gaps between them and the truly "emerging" markets, and given what we know about the migration of employment opportunities, national goals should include investment in education. The key to national security is to be found far more readily in an intelligent, healthy, happy, productive populace, than in a spotless fleet of F-17 fighter planes.

Education cannot be overemphasized. Japan, a country with a dearth of natural resources and minimal arable land, was the first emerging market to join the ranks of the First World, and its investments in human capital are largely the reason why. South Korea similarly has none of the natural riches that have traditionally been credited with pulling countries out of economic wells. Both countries' indigenous cultures emphasize education and a respect for learning, and indeed both countries have stressed the importance of acquiring technical skills. In South Korea, for instance, there are as many engineering students as in the United Kingdom, West Germany, and

Sweden combined.[10] These examples should serve as early warnings of our shortcomings in the First World. It is clear that any remaining complacency toward the massive changes facing our economic environment must be quickly replaced by a constructive engagement.

LOSING IN THE THIRD WORLD

Just as not all First World countries will prosper in the future, not all developing countries will thrive in the global realignment. The process described above is not one of generalized global convergence, but rather one of continual differentiation. In Akamatsu's model, at no point do all the geese fly at the same height. The countries that will experience the highest indices of growth in the present wave are those that already have developed the infrastructure necessary to take over the manufacturing industries described above. Sub-Saharan Africa, for instance, is only beginning to enter its own "virtuous" circle of development: as aid and loans become conditional on foreign approval of economic (and sometimes, political) reform, and as the cost of borrowing is seen to be clearly linked to creditworthiness, the carrot of economic success seems ever closer.

In Akamatsu's model, a regional economic pole (for instance, Japan in East Asia) will begin to send lower-skilled jobs abroad when they become too expensive at home. In this way, for example, once South Africa cements its position as sub-Saharan Africa's economic pole, it will move jobs to neighboring Zimbabwe and Botswana, drawing them into the regional economy directly and the global economy indirectly. Those swept along by this wave of growth will benefit from technology transfers and the spillovers associated with closer trade integration. As these peripheral countries enjoy higher employment rates, they develop more stable consumer markets and are increasingly able to absorb exports, thus benefiting the regional economic pole. As salaries stabilize, savings rates slowly rise, increasing the availability of low-interest capital for investment and planting the seeds for a country's own capital market, offering neighbors with excess capital yet another opportunity to find higher rates of return, while providing the rising periphery with much needed foreign exchange and additional capital for investment at home. This is how Mexico is being brought into the ranks of the First World (it is already a member of the OECD), as well as South Korea, the Czech Republic, Brazil, and the Philippines, to name a few.

And as places such as Turkey import the manufacturing sector jobs from Western Europe, those on the next rung down acquire the primary goods trade from Turkey. This mechanism will (and should) continue to take effect in order to avoid the inertia and dependence that plagued the developing countries earlier this century. And this mechanism has operated throughout history. As Paul Kennedy notes, "the prosperity gap in the seventeenth century between, say, Amsterdam and the west coast of Ireland or between such bustling Indian ports as Surat and Calcutta and the inhabitants of New Guinean villages must have been marked, although it probably did not equal the gulf between rich and poor nations today."[11] Differentiation is the secret behind understanding capitalism as a positive-sum game. Total global convergence is therefore undesirable—not to mention unlikely.

Indeed, economic differentiation will increase between those at the bottom and those at the top, and there will be some countries that will get lost in the shuffle if they fail to make themselves hospitable hosts to foreign trade and investment interest. Much of sub-Saharan Africa is being abandoned even by aid organizations, whose tireless efforts have been thwarted by tribal warfare, "cleptocratic" regimes, and the lack of state investment in education and infrastructure. But as regional economic poles such as South Africa develop, neighboring countries may stand a chance at integration, swept up by the flying geese next door. Still, to benefit from successful economic poles, countries currently suffering from political disorganization, a lack of infrastructure, and a lack of any prospect of economic reform will have much homework to do. In particular, countries that need a World Bank or an IMF lifeline will be forced to swallow the bitter medicine of the economic reform programs long peddled by those organizations. Some skeptics may contend that certain countries are geographically inhospitable to economic development—too little rain in some, too much in others, no arable soils, or perhaps simply too much hot weather. Although this may partly explain why these countries have been so late to develop, the example of Japan, a perfectly inhospitable mountainous archipelago with virtually no arable land and millions to feed, offers sure signs of hope for the future.

THE PLAGUE OF PROTECTIONISM

But just as Depression-era protectionism crippled the economies of single-product exporters in the developing world, protectionism by any of the participants in the latest wave of growth would be fatal to the momentum of differentiation, which is a critical motor for spreading global wealth. And indeed, this is the intuitive response of anyone beginning to lag. We have already seen signs of protectionist tendencies around the globe, particularly from the potential First World laggards. In fact, "not since the Great Depression, when Congress passed the Smoot-Hawley Tariff Act of 1930, not even during the mid-1980s, when trade deficits ballooned, has opposition to an open international economy [in the U.S.] been so prevalent. The long-standing pro-trade coalition on Capitol Hill has all but dissolved, and important elements in both parties now dismiss trade liberalization as a major goal of U.S. foreign policy."[12] And we should be wary and heed the lessons of the Smoot-Hawley tariff—argued by some to be not *a* cause of the Great Depression, but *the* cause. Slapping import taxes on thousands of foreign goods, the tariff reduced purchasing power, caused unemployment, shriveled consumer markets, and contracted international business—not to mention the added damage that came from the retaliation by those whose goods were taxed—all of which culminated in the stock market crash, the near-destruction of the U.S. banking system, and arguably even the collapse of some European democracies.[13]

CULTURAL PROTECTIONISM

In 1892, the Republican Party platform called for the imposition of an import duty on all imports competing with U.S. production, equal to the difference between wages abroad and in the U.S.[14] Today, as migrant workers create domestically differentiated labor markets,

The IMF: To Bail or Not to Bail?

During the recent Asian financial crisis, conservative skeptics have lambasted the IMF over $100+ billion financial packages for the region, calling them unnecessary bailouts of underregulated national banking systems, as well as circumventions of the moral hazard present in financial markets. Meanwhile, skeptics from the opposite end of the political spectrum continue to denounce the austerity-inducing programs (on which aid and loans are traditionally made conditional) as consigning their "beneficiaries" to eternal poverty, rather than casting them an effective lifeline, while lining the pockets of the First World bankers and MNCs.

Both may be right. By providing Asian debtors (largely domestic banks) with the necessary dollars to repay their creditors abroad, First World lenders' own imprudent lending practices will have gone unpunished. Banks will get repaid, and MNCs with high levels of foreign direct investment in Asia will be further protected. Moreover, IMF austerity programs that are part of bailouts often inflict economic hardship on Third World citizens.

But regardless of which camp one aligns oneself with, the answer to the question of whether these institutions should continue in their role as financial doctors making emergency house calls is indisputably "yes." The potential imprudence of a handful of creditors is a very small price to pay for the preservation of confidence in the international financial system and the world's globalizing economy.

In 1994 the liquidity crisis that shook Mexico's peso was assuaged by a $40 billion injection, which carried out the important task of restoring investor confidence in the currency. Foreign money that had once sustained the growth of what had become an OECD economy, and which had then fled amid fears that national hard-currency reserves would be unable to service short-term foreign debt, began to return, giving Mexico a second chance. One year after the currency crisis, Mexico was able to borrow directly from the marketplace again, and FDI hit record levels. The quick-response rescue of the Mexican currency served to patch up a tear in the fabric of economic globalization, restoring confidence in the Mexican economy (and by extension in the rest of the emerging markets) and in the belief that economic integration produces net gains for all involved.

The Asian crisis is similar. Left unchecked, the currency runs were extremely contagious and spread to more than six countries. Without intervention, the bug may have spread globally, ultimately affecting weaker First World currencies. But however improbable such a systemic crisis may be, the danger remains that an entire region (which, let us not forget, has been the fountain of riches for many investors over the last 15 years) will be allowed to sink back to levels of unemployment, inflation, and poverty not seen since the 1960s. This will affect not only the quality of outstanding loans but also past and future First World FDI expansion plans, projects which generate high profits for MNCs, increasing their share value and ultimately benefiting economies at home.

Moreover, "moral hazard" risks can be addressed pre-emptively. First World governments could increase capital requirements on their banks that make such cross-border loans, forcing them to price loans higher to Third World customers. This would have a dual effect in curbing such lendings: it would make imprudent lenders think twice about the risks, and it would force Third World borrowers to seek out alternative (and hopefully domestic) forms of finance. And as has been argued earlier (see box page 166), one of the main causes of the Asian crisis was the lack of such alternatives, and in particular the under-development of Asian bond markets.

In any case, the Asian crisis will not be the last. As integration accelerates, and as capital becomes increasingly mobile and volatile, financial emergencies are sure to erupt. However, if the First World wants to keep the "virtuous circle" of financial and trade liberalization moving forward, it must be willing to support such trends at critical times. The highway of globalization is littered with ditches and potholes, and in order to prevent potential investors from staying at home, they must be periodically filled.

immigration issues have become similarly politically charged, both in Europe and in the United States. Were the Akamatsu dynamic allowed to run its course unhampered by protectionism, these workers would not have to migrate at all, as the jobs would come to them. To the

German worker, it seems to be a catch-22: either his job will migrate or his national identity will be "threatened" by a growing proportion of immigrant Turks. Indeed, this concern for cultural integrity seems little more than an expression of economic insecurity, and, were Turks flooding to Berlin to retire and to shop, it is far from clear that Germans would feel as threatened.

Similarly, in France, the pressure of a sclerotic labor market has more than just economic consequences. France has suffered chronic, record unemployment in recent years, peppered with strikes by unions protesting the Chirac government's attempts at trimming one of Europe's more generous welfare states, and immigration policy has largely been behind Jean-Marie Le Pen's rise to stardom, the right-winger gaining 15% of the presidential vote in 1995.[15] His National Front party, with its extreme right-wing anti-immigration policies, is increasingly appealing to blue-collar workers (30% of whom voted for him in 1995), the hardest-hit victims of France's official unemployment rate of 13% (though some estimates would put it closer to 20%).[16] Interestingly enough, the official unemployment rate for legal immigrants is 20%, well above the official national average, and in the Netherlands and Germany immigrants are almost three times as likely to be unemployed.[17] However, since 1983 foreigners in Europe have been getting jobs quicker, especially those in second generations who are often better educated.

This is no less the case in the U.S., where the end of the Cold War refocused our attention on the threat from the East, as Japan and its trade surplus seemed to suck the wealth out of, among other things, the American automobile industry. Americans cringed when Rockefeller Center and Pebble Beach golf links fell into Japanese hands. But the more serious cultural clash in America has been over the migrant workers from south of the border. Illegal immigrants searching for jobs regularly try to cross the Mexican border into the U.S., and now constitute 6.2% of the population of California, 2.4% of Florida, and 3.7% of Texas. Their acceptance of lower wages and employers' under-the-table dealings have annoyed many local residents. Tempers have further flared when faced with the costs to the individual states of providing social security and public school education to illegal immigrants and their families. As a result of the cost pressures, and the *domestically* differentiated labor markets, California's state legislature responded with Proposition 187—a measure aimed at excluding illegal aliens from social services, public education, and access to most medical treatment. The proposition was approved by 59% in November 1994. On the national level, immigration has also been highly controversial, as bills cracking down on illegals having been easily passed, including the Immigration Reform Bill of March 1996 approved by the U.S. Congress 333 to 87. As the economic squeeze gets tighter, such immigration issues will become more prominent in First World headlines.

BACKLASH IN THE THIRD WORLD

Clashes are not limited to the First World. When those hotly contested manufacturing jobs are prevented from migrating to the emerging markets, and indigenous goods are blocked from full participation in the global marketplace, emerging markets respond with their own cultural backlash, and this is understandable. If Singapore were pried open by MTV and McDonald's, flooding the country with what is traditionally considered American pop culture, these American exports might be seen as pure imperialism unless a Nike or an IBM were there providing employment.

Wall Street has felt the blows of such a backlash. As one observer notes, "in 1963 the Ugly American was a smug ambassador to Vietnam played by Marlon Brando. Now he is a currency trader"[18] whose day job consists of systematically undermining foreign currencies through unscrupulous speculation. When international capital flees from a place like Malaysia, the Malaysian government maligns George Soros, the quintessential Western financier, blaming his speculative investment practices for destabilizing the Malaysian economy. But whereas IBM can profitably provide jobs to make up for the erosion of Malaysian culture under the American influence, Wall Street is often dismissed as a group of opportunistic and parasitic speculators. This bizarre preference for the multinational CEO over the Wall Street speculator is easily explained, however. When an MNC sets up shop in Kuala Lumpur, its positive presence is felt directly and immediately: a factory building perhaps, two hundred jobs, a fixed and secure salary, increased purchasing power. But when a fund manager buys equity in newly listed Malaysian companies or buys the Malaysian currency, speculating on its strength, the path from their computer terminals to the pockets of the average Malaysian is anything but direct. By investing in the local stock market, Mr. Soros and other investors are pumping capital into the country, increasing capital pools and allowing productive investment to take place, which ultimately contributes to economic growth and job creation. The difference is, Mr. Soros is less forgiving of economic and political blunders that may threaten the stability of his investment, and he, not the MNC chief, is able to pull out his funds overnight and relocate them to a safer place.*

Up until the early 1980s, all an emerging economy had to do to ensure preferential treatment from the U.S. was to be "our son of a bitch." By the early 1990s, just because George Bush was John Major's staunchest ally didn't mean George Soros would not, indeed, could not, crush the British pound sterling. Today, just because the U.S. government finds strategic value in supporting a dictator, or a regime whose economic indicators are at artificially high levels, does not mean Wall Street will do the same. In many ways, foreign aid (which made up a larger percentage of capital flows into emerging markets up until the mid-1980s) was both more tolerant and forgiving of economic ill health, and less temperamental and volatile, in that it was rarely retracted. The private financial flows that have largely replaced foreign aid have limited patience for an artificially overvalued currency, and this is what Malaysia, Thailand, Brazil, Indonesia, Russia, and South Korea have recently learned. Ironically, the OECD presence, whether in the form of direct investment or speculative flows, often seems to stir a cultural backlash when it threatens to leave. But many of these countries owe their recent growth largely to 1990s-style ugly Americans' otherwise prescient investment decisions, so they are in a bind: they can't live with them, but they can't live without them. As Lawrence Summers, the Deputy Treasury Secretary, explained, "major financial disturbances almost always have deeper causes than a few speculators. . . . [Y]ou can't attack 'speculation' without also undermining the flow of capital that can finance productive investment."

There are other internal obstacles that can impede the statist-to-

---

* This is one reason why Malaysia enacted modest capital controls in mid-1998.

market progression. As traditional business patterns are disrupted by Western-style economics and finance (along with newly empowered constituencies), we have witnessed enormous social and political conflict thoughout the developing world. Moreover, as opportunities for talented (and sometimes corrupt) entrepreneurs grow, income inequalities within such countries may indeed grow wider. This could lead to further local backlash against continued market reforms and Western influences.

EXPORTING CULTURAL PROTECTIONISM

We set this nation up to make men free, and we did not confine our conception and purpose to America.[19]

—PRESIDENT WOODROW WILSON, 1919

Some in the West would argue that when low-skilled jobs migrate they also become exploitative, as labor costs are cheap and labor regulations sparse; the debate shifts from a question of job migration to a question of humanitarian work conditions abroad. And indeed, the impact of immigration and trade on labor markets, compounded by improved communications that act to raise international humanitarian concern over work conditions (what has been called the "CNN Effect"), has made the voices of many interest groups (ranging from Amnesty International to unions whose members are in a sense direct victims of this labor mobility) louder and more frequently heard. The same can be said of cries against the unfair advantages obtained by companies operating in countries with laxer, or nonexistent, environmental regulations. How readily should we heed these voices?

However loudly the unemployed in advanced countries may protest about the unethical corporate heads exploiting "sweatshop" labor abroad, and leaving them on the dole, one should not be quick to judge. The legal working age is fourteen in Honduras, where young teenage girls work seventy-five-hour weeks for a paltry thirty-one cents an hour. Yet when the American public accused Kathie Lee Gifford, whose clothing line for Wal-Mart the Honduran girls had been assembling, of this "exploitative" corporate practice, she shut down the plant. The girls were left unemployed, and are no more grateful to Mrs. Gifford for her attempt at being humane. In fact, according to Jeffrey Sachs, "sweatshop" jobs are "precisely the jobs that were the stepping stone for Singapore and Hong Kong, and those are the jobs that have to [go] to Africa to get them out of their backbreaking rural poverty."[20] And according to Richard Freeman's studies, around 80% of the variation in nominal wages among countries can be accounted for by the variation in the educational composition of the workforce and the purchasing power of wages.[21] Indeed, if we look at Hong Kong, Singapore, South Korea, and Taiwan, often known as the Four Tigers, these are fine examples of countries that once assembled stuffed animals and that today are developing and exporting their own computers and cars. According to Krugman, "a policy of good jobs in principle, but no jobs in practice, might assuage our consciences, but it is no favor to its alleged beneficiaries."[22]

More often than not such cries of conscience, when taken up by trade representatives, are little more than business's pet peeves, dressed in the more sympathetic garb of allegedly universal values. A Silicon Valley CEO calls the Commerce Department to complain of China's complacency toward the well-established practice of pirating computer software, which makes fair competition in the Chinese market effectively impossible. Similarly, a CEO in Detroit calls Washington to lobby the Chinese to reduce tariffs on American automobiles. But it is far easier for the U.S. government to garner international support for its campaign against Chinese unfair trade practices if, instead of pointing to complaints filed by the country's corporate fat cats, it targets the alleged human and civil rights violations. Such violations are not new—they have been taking place for decades. Yet they only seem to have appeared on America's political agendas once its trade deficit with China grew to billions in the 1990s. The fact is, many would argue with large MNCs about pricing and marketing, but no one would argue with the virtue of freedom of speech and the vice of child labor.

To give in to the demands of labor and human rights activists campaigning for international labor standards might jeopardize any chances those countries with lower labor costs may have to eventually join the ranks of the emerging and advanced markets. These countries have a true comparative advantage in the production of labor-intensive goods, and it is by exploiting this comparative advantage that they can maximize their wealth through trade integration. There is no reason to believe that just because Haiti's wages are among the world's lowest today, they will be among the world's lowest in twenty years. Take Korea, for instance, which in 1960 had the same GNP per capita as Ghana ($230) but is twelve times more prosperous today.[23] Whereas Korea and the other Asian Tigers concentrated their efforts on labor-intensive manufacturing industries for export (where their cost competitiveness lay), most African countries relied on optimistic projections of commodity prices, a rather unreliable fountain of wealth, as the countries of Latin America learned in the first half of the century. Partly thanks to a relatively open international economy, the success of the Tigers' export-oriented growth policies was ensured. And with wages quadrupling since 1987, South Korea has already ceded jobs in light industries such as shoe manufacturing to its lower-wage neighbors in Asia and has begun to export jobs in the automobile, electronics, and other heavier industries as well.[24] There is hope for the periphery. Meanwhile, South Korea is able to produce mid-price, mid-tech goods to feed the hungry markets of Latin America, China, and Eastern Europe while some of its slower neighbors replace it in more labor intensive sectors.

THE BOTTOM LINE

Protectionism is the biggest risk to the wave of growth on whose cusp the world is currently surfing. Protectionism would mean that the emerging markets, whose ticket into the world economy lies in their lower production costs, would be barred from full participation and their potential to grow would be stifled. The degree of a country's integration into the world economy correlates with its own economic health, fostering spillovers from research and development that ultimately contribute to the recipient country's total factor productivity. According to Jeffrey Sachs, open economies grew 1.2% a year faster than closed economies, controlling for everything else.[25] A recent study found that from 1971 to 1989, a 1% increase in developing countries' ratio of foreign direct investment to GDP was associated

SOUTH KOREA: GROWING PAINS?

Perhaps no country has better exemplified development success than South Korea, a nation that rose from ashes to become the world's eleventh largest economy in forty years. But, recently, it appears that every economic success has its limits. As South Korea's economic rise has come to an abrupt halt, its vision of vaulting into the world's elite group of economies at a record pace has been temporarily put on hold.

South Korea achieved an incredible record of growth, comparable to few, managing an 8.2% annual growth over three decades and raising annual incomes from $80 in 1960 to over $10,000 today ("Can Korea Battle Back?" *Business Week,* November 24, 1997). With a GDP per capita comparable to those in the poorer countries of Africa and Asia only a few decades back, by 1996 its GDP had reached nine times India's, fourteen times North Korea's, and close to the lesser economies of the European Union.* This growth rate has been hailed as the seventh fastest in the world. From this rapid advancement, a tremendous growth in wages also took place. From 1985 to 1995, South Korea's wages increased 279% versus 171% in Hong Kong, 142% in Taiwan, and 105% in Singapore. But having been unable to anticipate future needs and gracefully move the economy from an industrial into a high-tech one, South Korea has suffered a shift from what used to be a $10 billion per annum trade surplus in the late 1980s to a $20 billion trade deficit by 1996.

"South Korea is being sandwiched between fully industrialized economies and less developed, low-cost economies like China," says one Seoul academic. Moreover: "the development model the country has used—heavy government direction of business, tightly closed markets, export-led growth and the funneling of resources to industry at the expense of consumers—is running out of steam, just as it is in Japan, where the model was first perfected" ("South Korea's Growing Pains," *New York Times,* February 4, 1997, p. D8). Power in Korea is concentrated mostly in the hands of vast, family-run businesses, called *chaebols,* which, through ruthless and aggressive overexpansion at the expense of profit and economic prudence, have led the country into debts of over $115 billion. Consumer spending has been perennially discouraged in favor of domestic savings in order to fuel these *chaebols,* resulting in a current account deficit of $23 billion in 1997. After witnessing lesser economies cave to market pressure, South Korea has been forced to abandon its dollar-pegged currency and to ask the IMF and G7 for a nearly $60 billion financial package to restore confidence in its currency and economy.

It is hoped this crisis will initiate the painful but long-overdue process of reform and regeneration that will put South Korea back on its feet again. And the benefits of reform may be registered even sooner than expected. In less than three years after its devaluation, Mexico was able to generate 7% annualized growth and push its *bolsa* to record highs. South Korea still has world-class companies in dozens of sectors, like steel and electronics. Amid all this chaos, South Korea is expected to grow by more than 5% in 1999, a downshift from its historic expansion rate, but still almost double that of the First World. The financial bubble that fed overconfidence, overexpansion, and bad lending has now burst. With a recalibrated currency and structural reform, there is no reason why South Korea should not be able to come out of this current crisis more aware, efficient, and ready to finally join the ranks of the world's top economies, albeit a little later than planned.

* The World Fact Book Page on South Korea: www.adci.gov/cia/publications/nsolo/factbook/ks.htm.

---

with a 0.4% to 0.7% increase in per capital GDP growth.[26] And foreign investors are attracted by countries that have their economic house in order, giving rise to the "virtuous" circle of development described earlier.

Remembering that the First World relies on increasing purchasing power in the large markets of places like China, Indonesia, and India, a slowdown of growth in any of these countries would ultimately affect the First World's bottom lines as well. As for those developed countries resisting this momentum altogether by artificially protecting their manufacturing industries, they will eventually hit a budget deficit wall as the inevitability of labor and product cycles proves them globally uncompetitive. Protectionism would make victims of all of us.

TABLE 7.2

INTEGRATION POLICY AND ECONOMIC PERFORMANCE, 1984–93 (%)

	High-income countries	DEVELOPING COUNTRIES			
		Fast integrators	Moderate integrators	Weak integrators	Slow integrators
CPI inflation[1]	3.63	13.40	16.86	23.86	19.89
Change in CPI inflation	−5.22	−2.81	−0.22	8.21	19.77
CPI inflation volatility[2]	1.65	7.24	7.63	14.21	13.27
Black market premium	0.00	0.12	0.56	0.41	0.48
Real exchange rate volatility[2]	0.06	0.13	0.20	0.27	0.40
Per capita GDP	2.03	2.09	−0.40	−1.04	−0.92
GDP volatility[2]	1.89	2.61	3.09	4.39	3.60
Budget balance/ GDP	−2.45	−2.37	−6.66	−3.70	−5.92
Change in budget deficit	1.16	1.88	0.79	0.38	−2.54
Budget balance volatility[2]	2.27	2.31	2.82	2.79	4.53

[1] CPI denotes consumer price index.
[2] Standard deviation.

SOURCES: World Bank data and estimates; Milan Brahmbhatt and Uri Dadush, "Disparities in Global Integration," *Finance & Development,* September 1996, p. 49.

Note: Contains data for 88 countries for which there were adequate tariff data. The balanced data set for this sample allows comparison across policy areas, such as between macroeconomic and trade policy. Values for integration classes are medians. Changes in inflation and budget deficit are averages from 1981–83 and 1991–93.

The "fast" integrator quartile contains most of the fast-growing East-Asian exporters, as well as reformers such as Argentina, Chile, Mexico, Morocco, Ghana, Mauritius, the Czech Republic, Hungary, Poland, and Turkey. At the other end of the spectrum, the "weak" and "slow" integrator quartiles include not only most of the low-income countries in sub-Saharan Africa but also many middle-income countries in Latin America, the Middle East, and North Africa.

POSTSCRIPT: A NEW DEBATE?

I have attempted to explain the economic landscape of the future: I have argued that not only is it silly to miss the opportunity presented by the accelerating integration of developing countries into the global economy, but to seize this opportunity is to ensure that today's First World leaders do not become the laggards of tomorrow. The emerging markets' share in world wealth is growing. As schoolchildren, most of today's First World investors viewed the Third World through distorted Mercator maps conceived in 1569: Scandinavia was bigger than India, Western Europe was bigger than Latin America, and Greenland was bigger than China, when in fact two-thirds of the world's land mass is in countries of the "South."[27] This geographic myopia symbolically mirrored three hundred years of Western- and Northern-dominated economic and financial development, with the result that most of the First World thinks of the G7 as enduring world leaders. But we should be cautious in our presumptions. Measuring output on the basis of purchasing power parity, the developing countries and the former Soviet Union already account for 44% of world output.[28] At these rates, the West will account for less than half of global output by the year 2000, and by 2020, less than two-fifths. Around the corner is the new E7, the Emerging 7, to counter the current G7: Brazil, China, India, Indonesia, Mexico, Russia, and South Korea (see the text box). In fact, in recent years the G7 has already invited Russia to participate in the group's annual summit, an acknowledgment of that country's growing role in world affairs. What we may witness in two generations is a return to an economic multipolarity not seen since the thirteenth century, when several competing empires littered the globe. Perhaps the last three hundred years have been the anomaly, and the sooner the First World awakens from its pessimistic and protectionist viewpoint, the sooner it will realize that it has no choice but to ride this latest tide of growth, fueled perhaps by other nations, but ultimately able to benefit all nations.

Less tangible than the facts and figures propelling the emerging markets is the changing intensity of the cultural confrontations that lie

THE E7: A NEW GLOBAL POWER CLUB?

At the end of the twentieth century, the postwar economic and political leaders—the Group of 7 (G7)—seem strangely undeserving of their privileged status. Those countries—Canada, France, Germany, Italy, Japan, U.K., and the U.S.—have a combined population of approximately 700 million, with some small countries such as Canada totaling only 30 million. And European fertility rates have fallen below the 2.1 children per woman average needed to maintain a steady level of population.

Meanwhile, the up-and-coming economic leaders of the twenty-first century, the E7, or the Emerging 7 countries of the world—Brazil, China, India, Indonesia, Mexico, Russia, and South Korea—have already dwarfed their developed colleagues. With a combined population of 2.8 billion, the E7 is roughly four times as large as the G7, and yet its economies still total only some $3 trillion, compared to the G7's $17 trillion.

What does this mean? Keep in mind that developing countries are set to double their output over the next twenty-five years, according to the World Bank's 1997 annual report on global prospects based on an estimated 5% to 6% annual growth rate ("Developing Countries Gain Pace," *Financial Times,* September 10, 1997, p. 1). While many Asian countries currently may be experiencing a pause in growth due to financial imbalances, the World Bank believes underlying fundamentals to be quite sound. The E7 currently contribute approximately 12% of global output, and at a growth rate often more than twice that of the G7, this figure should soon double, shouldering out some of the world's current economic leaders.

Using PPP (purchasing power parity) methodology, many of the E7 are already economic powerhouses. (See Chapter 1 for a full explanation of PPP.) By 1996, China, India, Russia, and Brazil were among the top ten PPP economies, with Mexico, Indonesia, and Korea in the top fifteen. By 2020, China—currently the number three PPP economy in the world—should move past the U.S. and Japan. Old powers, such as the U.K., France, and Italy, should drift down, while Canada may drop completely from the top twenty. And as Jeffrey Garten noted in *The Big Ten*, certain other developing countries such as Argentina, Poland, South Africa, and Turkey should be considered up-and-comers. They, too, are growing in economic importance with the E7 to counter the older G7 powers of the late twentieth century.

ahead between the First and Third Worlds. The greater the degree of economic integration between countries with different cultural traditions often in stark contradiction to each other, the more frequent and the more intense will be the "clashes of civilization" between them.[29] Human rights advocates urge the White House to factor human rights abuses and routine curtailments of civil rights into their otherwise economic equations. Until now, the bottom line has prevailed. Not long ago, Shell oil company came under attack for remaining in Nigeria despite the politically motivated execution of prominent author and human rights campaigner Ken Saro-Wiwa. Shell has not moved. Despite Iran's notoriously repressive regime, its financing of Lebanese Hezbollah terrorists, and its *fatwas* on such international figures as author Salman Rushdie, Germany—at times Iran's biggest trading partner—has given a red-carpet welcome to the Iranian Intelligence Chief.

There have been cases where high-profile campaigns against human rights violations have successfully forced multinationals out. For example, Pepsi, Macy's, Columbia Sportswear, Carlsberg, and Heineken have all left Myanmar (formerly Burma) in the wake of serious civil repression. But Myanmar is still a newcomer in the international economy, with only US$3 billion in foreign investment by mid-1996, compared to Vietnam's US$20 billion.[30] The commercial stakes in Myanmar for those companies are not high enough yet. But the energy company Total of France and its U.S. partner, Unocal, account for over a third of committed foreign investments in Myanmar, and they have stayed. And ASEAN (the regional trade bloc composed of Malaysia, Singapore, Thailand, the Philippines, Brunei, Indonesia, and Vietnam) admitted Myanmar as an observer member in July 1996 despite international condemnation of Burmese repression.[31]

The strain on Sino-American relations is at an all-time high. We are already familiar with the yearly debates in political and academic circles when the U.S. has to decide whether to renew China's Most Favored Nation (MFN) status. And despite reports that China's human rights record has only gotten worse since Tiananmen Square, and includes child labor, torture, and religious oppression, the U.S. has still not imposed sanctions on China and continues to renew its MFN status. Yet this is hardly surprising, as IBM has a $500 million semiconductor plant in China, under threat of expropriation if the U.S. makes a diplomatic mistake; Boeing is coming to rely increasingly on its billions in sizable Chinese contracts; and even McDonald's, already trading in Beijing, is wary of losing one billion hamburger eaters.

But the story is not so simple. If China is not punished, for instance, for its widespread piracy of Western videos, computer software, and CDs, other U.S. corporations will feel the pinch. Purported Chinese piracy of intellectual property could cost Western companies millions in profits and billions in market capitalization. Although punishing China for failing to satisfactorily address the piracy problem may satisfy Disney and Microsoft, it might threaten the contracts of Boeing, IBM, and McDonald's. The U.S. is put in a most delicate position.

And so, American foreign policy discourse can easily be accused of being hypocritical, loud and clear, where American economic interests are sparse (as in Iran), yet muffled and strangely complacent when American interests are at stake (as in China). Indeed, there are potential deals with China in the pipeline for the exporting of nuclear power reactors worth about $15 billion through 2010, at a time when global demand for such reactors is at a low point.[32] Why did the Clinton administration refrain from threatening to impose trade-linked penalties on undemocratic China, when it continues to argue that such penalties, along with possible military action, are the only way to punish (and possibly convert?) the dictatorial and violent regime of Saddam Hussein? As the French newspaper *Le Monde* wrote shortly after China's President Jiang Zemin's recent visit to Washington, "the Chinese case destroys the American pretension to universality on human rights. Are [citizens] less trampled on in Turkey or Saudi Arabia than in Iran or Cuba? The former are allies of America, which cajoles them; the latter are enemies it is bent on punishing."[33]

It is safe to assume that as economic stakes increase, and as the First World economies increasingly rely on the emerging markets for high capital returns, cheaper labor costs, and massive consumer markets, these social and political points of tension will become both more visible and more difficult to assuage. The First World will inherit some regional conflicts: the more money it invests in India, the more of a stake it takes in India's enduring conflict with Pakistan. As it invests in Turkey, it will deepen its involvement, however inadvertently, in that country's internal religious schizophrenia. Yet while the First World may inherit some conflicts, it may lose control of others. If the E7 do indeed become serious economic players in the world, and recalling that at least three of them (Russia, India, and China) are known nuclear powers, who will be calling the diplomatic shots currently being called by the G7, and principally by the U.S.? It is partly the fear of this inevitable realignment of world leadership that has some of the permanent members of the UN Security Council staunchly opposed to the council's enlargement to reflect current world wealth and power distributions. And it is because of the power of wealth to call political shots that in the U.S. trade has become as important an issue as geopolitical security was during the Cold War. China has already amassed a large army, fired missiles on Taiwan's doorstep, and challenged the U.S. on economic and social issues. As its slice of international GDP grows, one may see China being consulted on the Korean conflict, or leading a peace-keeping effort, or, most controversially, playing a greater role in dictating the orientation of the international organizations of which it is a member.

WHAT THE FUTURE HOLDS

The fact is, capital follows the promise of high returns and is generally oblivious to civil rights records. Meanwhile, the importance of foreign aid as a source of hard currency has been reduced, thus weakening the leverage power of governments once supplying such aid. Increasingly, it seems that MNCs and investors are today's diplomats and soldiers, and international relations is becoming an area of commercial discourse. Foreign policy cannot be limited to questions of military conflicts and is gradually becoming dominated by questions of commercial and trade policy. That is why in the U.S. the debate still rages over whether to give the president "fast-track" powers in negotiating trade agreements, much as U.S. presidents in the 1980s were given powers to negotiate nuclear arms control agreements with the Soviet Union. The duration and intensity of the debate is testament to the importance that matters of trade and commerce have taken in U.S.

foreign policy. And the fact that such "fast-track" powers had been enjoyed by American presidents from 1974 until 1994, and were simply up for renewal in 1997, makes it all the more bizarre that the question should have created such a stir in Congress this time around. The main reason for the controversy was the organized and systematic opposition mounted by labor and environmental groups, which had hoped the proposal for the procedure would include mechanisms to improve labor and environmental standards abroad, thus preventing U.S. jobs from flocking to the unregulated corporate playgrounds of the South and East.[34] But the impact of the administration's defeat is more than a moral victory for these lobbyists: it is a serious setback to American efforts to preserve its leadership role in international commercial relations.

Trade and commerce are all the more critical to a country's foreign policy as they become irreversibly entwined with questions of human rights and immigration. The American debate between those who would punish China in the name of human rights, whatever the consequences for the lobbying MNCs at home, and those who would treat human rights as an internal Chinese issue will have to be resolved. First of all, yesterday's dissidents are often tomorrow's presidents and prime ministers (Nelson Mandela and Vaclav Havel, for instance), and ignoring yesterday's civil rights record can hardly make for good relations tomorrow. Second, as countries with worrying practices are becoming tomorrow's global economies, our ability to isolate them and punish them through sanctions, for instance, is being reduced. But most important, at no time in history have the countries of the world been so interconnected and so interdependent, albeit to different degrees. We may often find that we cannot afford to be out, even though being in may mean commercial and ethical sacrifice.

We cannot know whose tradition will prevail, if any, but we may draw hope from a Chinese central banker, who, when I asked about his country's human rights record, responded that human rights for China meant ensuring that everyone was fed. If the First World allows the dynamic described to run its course and spread the wealth it currently enjoys to the emerging markets, it will be easier for developing world governments to feed their people and to redefine human rights to include the political and civil rights the West holds so dear.

CONFUSION AMID PROSPERITY?

Politics aside, the economic prospects for the future seem brighter than ever for both the First and Third World. Yet in the advanced societies, citizens struggle to reconcile contradictory visions of a seemingly more prosperous world on the one hand, and a more anxious existence on the other. As one psychologist notes: "One thing we [in the First World] have lost, that we had in the past, is a sense of progress, that things are getting better. . . . There is a sense of volatility, but not of progress. When people talk of the economy being strong, they don't seem to feel that they too are better off."[35] This is understandable in $25,000 GDP per capita economies: while stock markets may boom, an extra TV, a new computer, or a vacation all seem marginal in our relatively wealthy societies. Economic encroachment by and occasional crisis in the Third World, in this respect, only adds to the complexities of modern life.

Despite this confusion, the greatest opportunities for greater prosperity—whatever the risks of uncertainties—still lie in economically enfranchising the billions of have-nots in the developing world. For them, the extra loaf of bread or new pair of jeans they now enjoy will only fuel their desire to participate in global trade. Economic differentiation has always been the essence of wealth creation, and public policies—whether domestic or international—need to acknowledge this. Culture clashes, protectionist rhetoric, trade agreements, and developing country financial panics are all positive signs that the accelerated integration discussed in this book is a slow-growing reality, not a Pollyanna dream. Sure, there are risks in this future, but the rewards seem to outweigh them by multiples; they always have. Slowly, Third World investments and products are being woven seamlessly into the fabric of the global economy and First World life, providing greater value added for all participants on the dawn of the new millennium. As Saint-Simon wisely noted at the end of the nineteenth century, "The Golden Era is in front of us, not behind."

Notes

Chapter 1

1. Please note that the following terms will be used interchangeably throughout this chapter: "the West" (although some countries, such as Australia, Japan, and South Korea, are not located in the Western Hemisphere), the "First World," and "industrialized" countries. These terms all represent the high-income members of the Organization for Economic Cooperation and Development (OECD), with average GDP per person of more than $9,385. The terms "Third World," "emerging markets," and "developing countries" will all represent nations with GDP per capita below $9,385.

2. V. I. Lenin, *Imperialism: The Highest State of Capitalism* (New York: Pluto Press, 1996), pp. 63–64.

3. Lester R. Brown, Hal Kane, and Nicholas Lessen, *Vital Signs 1995* (Worldwatch Institute) (New York: W. W. Norton, 1995), p. 71.

4. International Finance Corporation, *Emerging Markets Stock Factbook 1996* (Washington D.C.: International Finance Corporation, 1996), p. 5.

5. John Maynard Keynes, "Economic Possibilities for Our Grandchildren (1930)," in *Essays in Persuasion* (New York: W. W. Norton, 1963), p. 361.

6. "Making Waves," *The Economist*, September 28, 1996, p. 7.

7. I like Kaname Akamatsu's explanation of this process in his 1960 article, "A Theory of Unbalanced Growth in the World Economy," *Weltwirtschaftliches Archiv*, vol. 86, no. 2 (1961).

8. David S. Landes, *The Unbound Prometheus: Technological Change and Industrial Development in Western Europe from 1750 to the Present* (Cambridge: Cambridge University Press, 1969), p. 5.

9. See Karl Polanyí, *The Great Transformation: The Political and Economic Origins of Our Time* (New York: Beacon Press, 1957).

10. Landes, p. 7.

11. Alvin Toffler, *The Third Wave* (New York: Bantam, 1980), p. 40.

12. Ibid., p. 41.

13. Landes, p. 6.

14. For more on Kondratieff, see David Knox Barker, *The K Wave: Profiting from the Cyclical Booms and Busts in the Global Economy* (New York: Irwin, 1995), p. 57.

15. Toffler, p. 15.

16. This uncertainty is illustrated by the fact that there is little agreement as to when the next cycle will begin, even among adherents to Kondratieff's long wave cycle. For example, one commentator has postulated that we are currently in a global depression that will last until 2007, when a new upward wave will begin. Others have suggested that it may have already begun.

17. For a more detailed account of Ester Boserup's theories, see her book, *Population and Technological Change: A Study in Long Term Trends* (University of California, 1983) and *Economic and Demographic Relationships in Development*, with T. P. Shultz (Baltimore: Johns Hopkins, 1990).

18. Julian L. Simon, *The State of Humanity* (Cambridge: Blackwell Publishers, 1995), p. 649.

19. *The Financial Silk Road: A Fifth Wave of Global Money: Cross Border Equity Flows 1995,* vol. 1 (New York: ING-Barings, 1995), p. 19.

20. Ibid., p. 20.

21. The World Bank, *Annual Report 1996* (New York: Oxford University Press, 1996), p. 98.

22. This information and other similar data are available through the World Bank's website at www.worldbank.org.

23. *The Financial Silk Road*, p. 3.

24. International Finance Corporation, p. 6.

25. ING-Barings, *The Financial Silk Road,* p. 20.

26. See Bruce Wasserstein, *Big Deal: The Battle for Control of America's Leading Corporations* (New York: Warner Books, 1998).

27. Coca-Cola Annual Report, 1994.

Chapter 2

1. Joseph Needham, *Science and Civilization in China* (Cambridge: Cambridge University Press, 1959) cited in Samuel Y. Edgerton, Jr., *The Heritage of Giotto's Geometry: Art and Science on the Eve of Scientific Revolution* (Ithaca, NY: Cornell University Press, 1994), p. 12.

2. Paul Kennedy, *Rise and Fall of the Great Powers* (London: Fontana Press, 1988) p. 4.

3. Ibid., p. 4.

4. Needham, p. 13.

5. Oddly, Japan did not perceive the West as a legitimate threat until Commodore Perry's arrival in 1840. In the sixteenth century, Hideyoshi established Japan's rigid class system that lasted until Japan adopted a Western sociopolitical system in 1867. Until then, Japan looked inward. Its isolation retarded commerce and the flow of knowledge needed for technological leaps.

6. There were some interesting cultures in West Africa as well. Rising from the ashes of the Great Ghanese kingdom, the Mali empire in West Africa, also an Islamic civilization, flourished from 1230 to 1390, with a high culture rich in books, libraries, and architecture. Strategically positioned at the edge of the Sahara, Mali traders controlled the huge gold trade that spanned Africa from the west coast across the desert and had trading relationships with Muslim communities in North Africa. Eventually, conflicts between Muslim and non-Muslim communities in the region led to the deterioration of the Mali and the neighboring Songhai empires, which remained in disunity until the eighteenth century, when French colonists conquered the region.

7. Kennedy, p. xvii.

8. Mariano Grondona, "The Triangle of Development," cited in Lawrence E. Harrison, *Who Prospers* (New York: HarperCollins, 1992), p. 16.

9. Max Weber, *The Protestant Work Ethic and the Spirit of Capitalism* (Englewood Cliffs, NJ: Prentice-Hall, 1980).

10. Lynn White, Jr., "The Historical Roots of Our Ecological Crisis," *Science*, vol. 155 (1967), p. 1203–1207, cited in Brian Tierney, *The Middle Ages Volume II*, 4th ed. (New York: McGraw-Hill, 1992), p. 322.

11. Some cite the beginning of the Renaissance as 1397, when a scholar from Constantinople named Manuel Chrysoloras became the first professor of Greek at the university in Florence. Chrysoloras arrived with treasured Greek books, and prompted many Italian scholars to rediscover ancient classical works by Socrates, Plato, Aristotle, and Euclid—those writers and philosophers who dealt with weighty questions not answered adequately by the rigid fourteenth-century Roman Catholic Church. Spiritual scholars of the day, such as Saint Anselm and Peter Abelard, began to draw students to study divinity and the theology of the Scholasticism movement of the 1100s. Thought of as heretics by the Church, these men—heavily reliant on classical Greek thought—applied Aristotle's logic to test truths of their faith. For the first time in hundreds of years, people began to question man's fate and role on earth.

12. Joseph Needham, *Science and Civilization in China* (Cambridge: Cambridge University Press, 1959), cited in Samuel Y. Edgerton Jr., *The Heritage of Giotto's Geometry*, p. 12.

Edgerton makes a very convincing case for how geometry pushed the West forward. Geometry allowed for the mechanistic transfer of ideas from the mind's eye to paper. Its legacy is clear: it enabled artists to "tame" the nature around them, reproducing it in their work in real, proportional terms. Suddenly, thoughts and concepts could be conveyed graphically and then be disseminated to other people. This was a crucial stepping stone toward humankind's increased *understanding* of nature, starting with something as simple as the angles of the rising and the setting sun. As Joseph Needham explains, by the eighteenth century, Western Europe had, unlike the civilizations of the East, a "philosophical picture of the natural order as finite, mechanistic and susceptible to demonstration by deductive Euclidean geometry." Armed with geometry, a competitive culture, and a Christian humanist view that the world should be tamed by man, the Western Europeans sprinted to the lead in the great race to develop technology.

13. In such an inquisitive environment, this *studio humanitatis* gave rise to humanism, the belief that man, not God, controlled his own fate. In essence, humanism was born of Western Christian man's desire to understand how things in the physical world worked. It revolutionized study, shifting its focus from divinity to human nature. The intellectual freedom that humanism encouraged during the Renaissance would unleash a culture of discovery and innovation that lay at the heart of subsequent technological and financial development. However, it was the great artists and scientists in Europe during the thirteenth and fourteenth centuries who first used geometry to its full potential. Although highly trained draftsmen, Renaissance artists such as Cimabue, Giotto, Masaccio, and Della Francesca, now armed with the science of Euclidean geometry, abandoned the stiff, formal style of Byzantine and medieval art and were able to depict human forms with incredible realism through the use of perspective, vanishing points, and three dimensions, creating "a window unto God." Architects and sculptors were also able to produce more complex and intricate creations, generating logical designs and perfectly proportioned structures. Indeed, Edgerton notes that although Chinese astronomy in general was equal to that of the West at the end of the sixteenth century, it lacked a geometric system. Geometry enabled Western European artists and scientists to "reproduce on a plane surface the

basic shapes of fixed three-dimensional objects as formed by light and recorded point by point in the human optical apparatus when focused from a fixed point of view. This is an accomplishment unachieved by any other cultural art anywhere in the world" (Edgerton, pp. 15–16).

14. David S. Landes, *The Unbound Prometheus: Technological Change and Industrial Development in Western Europe from 1750 to the Present* (Cambridge: Cambridge University Press, 1969), p. 1.

15. Kennedy, p. 40.

16. U.S. Department of Commerce, Economics and Statistics Administration, *Statistical Abstract of the United States*, 115th ed. (Washington D.C.: Department of Commerce, 1996).

17. The Soviet administration was so afraid that even a notion of democracy would spoil communism forever that they instituted Article 70, under the Soviet criminal code, so that anyone who tried to "weaken" the Soviet state—e.g., by listening to Western radio programs or reading Western literature—was suspect and likely to end up in prison. Criminals charged under Article 70 were considered tantamount to murderers by the Soviet authorities.

18. A thorough examination of how information, transmitted by many technologies, contributed to the end of the Soviet Union can be found in Scott Shane, *Dismantling Utopia: How Information Ended the Soviet Union* (Chicago: Ivan R. Dee, 1994).

19. Stanley J. Stein and Barbara H. Stein, *The Colonial Heritage of Latin America: Essays on Economic Dependence in Perspective* (New York: Oxford University Press, 1970), p. 196.

20. Eliana Cardoso and Ann Helwege, *Latin America's Economy: Diversity, Trends and Conflict* (Cambridge, MA: MIT Press, 1993), p. 8.

21. Stein and Stein, p. 193.

22. Joan Edelman Spero, *The Politics of International Relations*, 4th ed. (New York: St. Martin's Press, 1990), p. 155.

23. Sebastian Edwards, *Crisis and Reform in Latin America: From Despair to Hope* (New York: Oxford University Press, 1995), p. 1.

24. Cardoso and Helwege, p. 8.

25. According to Ester Boserup, GDP growth is expected of any preindustrial economy that evolves from rural agrarian life toward a more urban industrial economy. Higher output and GDP expansion are commensurate with a change from farming to manufacturing because of the increased velocity and frequency at which capital and goods change hands in an industrial economy.

26. Peter F. Drucker, "The Changed World Economy," in Robert J. Art and Robert Jervis, eds., *International Politics: Enduring Concepts and Contemporary Issues,* 3rd ed. (New York: HarperCollins, 1992).
27. World Bank estimates.
28. "Political Economy of International Crisis." Working paper, University of Texas Economics Department, Economics 350K, Section VI.
29. Cardoso and Helwege, p. 9.
30. According to a conversation with Giacomo DeFillippis, former head of treasury for one of Argentina's major commercial banks, the failure of London banks to roll over certain deposits resulted in a major liquidity squeeze that went largely unreported in the press. Some Argentine debt at that time was even being sold off at a discount. DeFillippis believes Argentina's crisis signaled the future of much of Latin American debt, months before the Mexican liquidity crisis.
31. For a thorough history of the debt crisis, see Karin Lissakers, *Banks, Borrowers and the Establishment: A Revisionist Account of the International Debt Crisis* (New York: Basic Books, 1991).
32. Robert R. Kaufman, *The Politics of Debt in Argentina, Brazil and Mexico* (Berkeley: Institute of International Studies, 1988).
33. International Monetary Fund, *International Financial Statistics Yearbook, 1991* (Washington, D.C.: IFC, 1991).
34. "Perils of Openness: Survey of Third World Finance," *The Economist,* September 25, 1993.
35. "More Money: Survey of Third World Finance," *The Economist,* September 25, 1993.
36. Paul Krugman, "Market-Based Debt-Reduction Schemes." NBER Working Paper No. 1323 (Cambridge, MA, 1989).
37. In some cases, Brady Plans offered creditors the option of taking losses through reduced interest rates. This allowed banks to write off debt over time, an option chosen typically by commercial banks whose capital positions would not allow a one-time write-off. While the principal amount owed by a country may not have been reduced by this option, the annual debt service decreased, which served as an equally powerful form of relief.
38. Either through central banks or through government trade banks like the Export-Import Bank of the United States.
39. I find *redemption* an interestingly precise word here. It would take an American notion of bankruptcy—particularly the reorganizing principles of Chapter 11—to allow these countries the second chance that they needed to move forward economically. The admission of mistakes, the

pain taken by all, and the mission of collectively moving forward I find particularly American. Perhaps that is why it took Americans like Nick Brady and his aide David Mumford to devise such a plan.

40. "More Money: Survey of Third World Finance." *The Economist*, September 25, 1993.
41. Michael Mandelbaum, "Introduction," in Michael Mandelbaum, ed., *Post-Communism: Four Perspectives* (New York: Council on Foreign Relations, 1996).
42. Robert Skidelsky, "The State and the Economy: Reflections on the Transition from Communism to Capitalism in Russia," in Michael Mandelbaum, ed., p. 82.
43. Michael Mandelbaum, "Introduction," in Mandelbaum, ed., p. 7.
44. Ahmed Galal and Mary Shirley, eds., *Does Privatization Deliver? Highlights from a World Bank Conference* (Washington, DC: World Bank, 1994), p. 3.
45. Nancy Birdsall, "The Jigsaw Puzzle," in Galal and Shirley, eds., p. 109.
46. Jeffrey Herbst and Adebayo Olukoshi, "Nigeria: Economic and Political Reforms at Cross-Purposes," in Haggard and Webb, eds., pp. 453–502.
47. Skidelsky, "The State and the Economy," in Mandelbaum, ed., p. 79.

Chapter 3

1. John Dennis Brown, *101 Years on Wall Street: An Investor's Almanac* (Englewood Cliffs, NJ: Prentice-Hall, 1991), p. 28.
2. Alfredo G. A. Valladao, *The Twenty-first Century Will Be American* (London: Verso, 1996), p. 9.
3. Christopher Andersen, "The Accidental Superhighway—Survey of the Internet," *The Economist*, July 1, 1995.
4. Valladao, p. 129.
5. International Telecommunications Union, *World Telecommunication Development Report*, 1994.
6. Bell Atlantic Telephone company statistic.
7. International Telecommunications Union.
8. Andersen, "The Accidental Superhighway—A Survey of the Internet," *The Economist*, July 1, 1995.
9. Frost and Sullivan, *U.S. Cellular Service Markets—Executive Summary, Introduction and Total Market*, February 1997.
10. "The Frequency of the Future: Wonderful Wireless—The Death of Distance: Survey of Telecommunications," *The Economist*, September 30, 1995.

11. "Stuck in the '70s," *The Economist,* February 22, 1997.
12. ING-Barings.
13. Duncan Buckeridge, *The Role of Communications Technology in Economic and Social Development* (Cutler & Company, 1995).
14. Bell Atlantic statistic.
15. Ibid.
16. Ibid.
17. Tom Forrester, ed., *The Information Technology Revolution* (Cambridge, MA: MIT Press, 1988), p. xiii.
18. Ibid.
19. "IT's Expensive—Turning Digits into Dollars: A Survey of Technology in Finance," *The Economist,* October 26, 1996.
20. "Caught in the Net—The Valley of Money's Delight: A Survey of Silicon Valley," *The Economist,* March 29, 1997.
21. John Markoff, "As Technology Spreads, Rural Areas Not Being Left Out, Study Finds," *New York Times,* February 24, 1997.
22. International Data Corporation web site.
23. Ibid.
24. Phillips Tarifica Ltd., *The Net Effect: The Impact of the Internet on World Telecommunications Markets,* 1997.
25. U.S. Department of Transportation, Bureau of Transportation Statistics, *Transportation Statistics Annual Report 1996* (Washington, DC: 1996), p. 23.
26. Ibid.
27. Lawrence Zuckerman, "Do Computers Really Lift Productivity? It's Unclear, but Business Is Sold," *New York Times,* January 2, 1997, p. B4.
28. Ibid.
29. Dell Computer Corporation web site.
30. Zuckerman, p. B4.
31. Michael Mandel, *The High Risk Society* (New York: Times Books, 1996), p. 49.
32. International Data Communications web site.
33. "Communicating Freely: Near-zero Tariffs Will Change the World—The Death of Distance: A Survey of Communications," *The Economist,* September 30, 1995.
34. *U.S. Global Outlook 1995–2000: Toward the 21st Century.* U.S. Department of Commerce, March 1995.
35. "Communicating Freely," *The Economist,* September 30, 1995.

Chapter 4

1. V. I. Lenin, *Imperialism: The Highest Stage of Capitalism,* pp. 62, 63.
2. David Ricardo, *On the Principles of Political Economy and Taxation* (Cambridge: Royal Economic Society Press, 1962), p. 132.
3. Kaname Akamatsu, "A Theory of Unbalanced Growth in the World Economy," *Weltwirtshaftliches Archiv* vol. 86, no. 2 (1961), p. 15.
4. *Development in Practice: East Asia's Trade and Investment* (Washington, DC: World Bank, 1994), p. 28. (NIE is the abbreviation for Newly Industrialized Economies, used primarily in reference to Asian nations.)
5. Krugman P. and Cooper, R. "Growing World Trade: Causes and Consequences," Brookings Institute, *Papers on Economic Activity,* no. 1, 1995.
6. Ibid.
7. Ibid.
8. Ibid., p. 364.
9. Ibid., p. 364.
10. "Workers of the World, Compete," *The Economist,* April 2, 1994, p. 70.
11. "Emerging Nations Win Major Exporting Roles," *Wall Street Journal,* February 1, 1997, p. 1.
12. *The Financial Silk Road: A Fifth Wave of Global Money: Cross Border Equity Flows 1995,* Vol. 1 (New York: ING-Barings, 1995), p. 17.
13. Allen R. Myerson, "In Principle, A Case for More 'Sweatshops,' " *New York Times,* June 22, 1997, Week in Review, p. 5.
14. Ibid.
15. Ibid.
16. ING-Barings, p. 19.
17. Gail Fosler, "Where Workers Will Come From," *Across the Board,* World Bank, November/December 1996, p. 55.
18. Ibid.
19. World Bank, "Workers in an Integrating World," *World Development Report 1995* (Washington DC: World Bank, 1995).
20. Textiles and Clothing: Shift to Low Wage Economies." See www.fair trade.org.
21. Bloomberg News.
22. Henry Gibbon, ed., *Privatisation Yearbook* (London: Privatisation International Ltd., 1996), p. 19.
23. Ibid.
24. Ibid.

25. World Bank, *Privatization: Principles and Practice* (Washington, DC: World Bank, 1995), p. 9.
26. Ibid., p. 9.
27. John Whitley, *Consumer Spending Forecasts for the World's Largest Economies* (London: Economist Intelligence Unit, 1995), p. 45.
28. Whitley, p. 68.
29. According to Wasserstein Perella Emerging Markets in New York.
30. Coca Cola Annual Report, 1994.
31. Ibid.
32. Anheuser-Busch Annual Report, 1994.
33. "Emerging Market Indicators," *The Economist,* May 24, 1997, p. 106.
34. Stanley Ziemba, "Motorola to Open Plant in Mexico," *Chicago Tribune,* August 29, 1996, Business, p. 1.
35. See Whitley.
36. Marshall N. Carter and William G. Shipman, "The Coming Global Pension Crisis," *Foreign Affairs,* vol. 75, no. 6 (December 1996).
37. Ibid.
38. Ibid.
39. Economist Intelligence Unit World Statistics.
40. Ibid.
41. Haig Simonian, "Motown's New Eldorado," *Financial Times,* January 7, 1997, p. 13.
42. John Griffiths and Shiraz Sidhva, "Ford to Make Fiestas and Escorts in India—U.S. Car Giant in Joint Venture with Local Producer," *Financial Times,* September 15, 1995, p. 5.
43. Katherine Young, "Ford, Mazda Will Produce Second Car Model in New Thailand Plant," *Detroit News,* July 24, 1996, p. B3.
44. "Ford Seizes Ground in China's Auto Market," *Chicago Tribune,* July 21, 1995, Business, p. 1.
45. Ibid.

Chapter 5

1. Bagehot, one of the first editors of the *Economist,* wrote a seminal work, *Lombard Street,* in 1873 in which he postulated that financial development is greatly impacted by social, political, and cultural factors, all of which will dramatically affect a country's development.
2. See Ross Levine and Sara Zervos, "Stock Markets, Banks and Economic Growth" (World Bank, unpublished, October 1996).

3. It is interesting to note that I have often traveled to countries early in the reform process where the "buzz" is at first nonexistent, but develops just a couple of years later. Such was the case in several former Soviet Union countries in the early to mid-1990s, as well as in Latin America in the late 1980s and the early 1990s.

4. According to John Sullivan, partner at the law firm McDermott, Will, and Emery.

5. A one-hundred-year deal for the Philippines was planned by Bankers Trust for spring 1997 but was actually scrapped.

6. I have added to Howell's wave theory, taken from his various writings as a strategist for ING-Barings, as well from various speeches he has made, and interwoven it with my own study of investment waves.

7. *The Financial Silk Road*, vol. 1 (ING-Barings, 1995), p. 35–36.

8. It is important to note that this was for a selected period and that the numbers change absolutely from year to year. With the bullish First World stock markets in the last two or three years, I have seen research that suggests the optimal mix has shifted down from 70/30 to 85/15.

9. In addition, plummeting U.S. interest rates during 1992–93 also forced many institutions to venture abroad in search of higher yield.

10. ING-Barings, p. 37.

11. Ibid.

12. Few know who organized the first swap. Giacomo DeFillippis of Giadefi, J. Player Crosby of Finamex, and Martin Schubert of Eurinam all claim to have been trading in 1981–82, while Bob Smith of Turan is known to have brokered some Turkish government notes in the late 1970s. In any event, these four firms all contributed significantly to the birth of the debt market, and possibly even to the entire emerging market investment community, well ahead of Wall Street's more prominent houses.

Chapter 6

1. See Burton Malkiel's classic *A Random Walk Down Wall Street: Including a Life-Cycle Guide to Personal Investing* (New York: W. W. Norton, 1995) for an excellent discussion of the random nature of price movement in financial markets.

2. Michael Howell was one of the first to note this in his discussions on emerging stock markets. I believe the theory has great merit throughout the emerging marketplace, including its application to debt instruments, and much of the following discussion has been shaped by his thoughts in a London discussion in November 1992.

3. Ibid.
4. While most of Latin America, Eastern Europe, and Africa suffered under debt, much of Asia escaped the trap. However, not all the Asians were fortunate; Vietnam and the Philippines were forced into Brady-style restructurings like many other developing countries. It will be interesting to see if such plans will be used with Asia's current financial problems.
5. Interest rate parity theory states that an investor should not be able to invest in foreign treasury bills, simultaneously sell forward the currency, and lock in a higher rate of return than in the home currency. If that situation arises, investors increase exposure to such a trade until the locked-in rate is equal to the home currency investment. In fact, forward currency prices are actually calculated by the interest rate differentials between countries. While the forward prices in the First World rarely offer an opportunity to lock in a greater return than in the home market, sometimes it can be done in the Third World. I believe the extra profit from emerging markets comes from assuming political risks such as convertibility, risks that are perceived to be small in the First World.
6. Such problems with hard currency were the root causes of the old LDC debt crisis, as well as Mexico's recent peso crisis in late 1994 and early 1995. Mexico owed more than $25 billion in so-called *tesobonos,* peso-denominated but dollar-linked bonds. In these instruments, investors would be repaid a certain amount of pesos to lock in a positive dollar rate of return. During the crisis, investors worried whether Mexico would have enough dollars to exchange for the pesos.
7. Emerging Market Traders Association Annual Volume Survey, 1996.
8. Most international commercial banks operate with country exposure limits, particularly in the case of developing countries. This is their primary cross-border risk management tool.
9. Given the recent strength in the U.S. bond market, spreads for both had dwindled to record lows of 300 for U.S. high yields and 327 for stripped Bradies, according to Salomon Brothers by the second quarter of 1997. However, after the Asian financial crisis in late 1997, spreads widened 50 basis points for U.S. high yields and more than 200 basis points for stripped Bradies, representing a flight to quality during this nervous period.
10. Estimate includes certain local-currency debt markets, such as China's, which may preclude foreigners from investing.
11. World Bank.
12. "Introducing the Emerging Local Markets Index (ELMI)," J. P. Morgan, June 24, 1996, p. 1.

13. 1996 target weights.
14. At this point in time, it is difficult to speculate on the fate of the Euro, the planned future currency of the European Community. However, its introduction will effectively eliminate many of the currency markets that now exist.
15. Much of this premium, I believe, is derived from the convertibility risks investors assume. For example, an investor earns no premium from investing in German deutsche marks because the perceived risk that the Bundesbank will prohibit currency conversion is nonexistent. In the case of the Ukrainian hyvrnia (introduced in September 1996), an investor may need a premium because of a lack of experience in that currency or concerns over the country's financial footing.
16. The prices and values discussed herein were obtained from Bloomberg L.P. and Morgan Stanley Dean Witter. Please note that any reference to stock price and valuations is often outdated before it goes to print. While prices in this discussion change materially each day, the concept is still applicable to the energy sector and many other industries.
17. Based on monthly data from August 1991 through August 1996 measured in dollars.
18. Please note: the International Finance Corporation has published many different types of research in 1997 that may document similar findings. For more in-depth information, I recommend the *IFC Stock Markets Factbook 1997*.
19. Ibid.
20. Front-running is when a brokerage firm buys and sells ahead of a customer order. In this respect, the firm can profit from the knowledge that some stock is being bought and sold. This is particularly important in thin, illiquid markets.
21. There are several studies on the impact of ADR programs on share price and liquidity that illustrate this point. My own anecdotal experience has proved this to be correct, particularly with a large capitalization stock like Telebras of Brazil, which trades $1 billion worth of ADRs some days on the NYSE, which is surprisingly more than IBM.
22. For more on this subject, see John Kenneth Galbraith's slender *A Short History of Financial Euphoria* (New York: Viking, 1990), which recounts the South Seas incident and many other financial manias.
23. It is interesting to note that Russia in 1996 actually settled a French class action suit against the Russian government to pay back an estimated $2 billion in czarist debt. Boris Yelstin approved a $400 million settlement check for investors who filed such claims.

24. For an in-depth study of Mexico's development, see two Harvard Business School case studies: "Mexico: Escaping the Debt Crisis" by Helen Shapiro, HBS 9-390-74, revised January 24, 1994; and "Mexico 1995: The Crisis Returns" by George C. Lodge, HBS 9-795-126, March 30, 1995.

Chapter 7

1. "Taiwan and Korea: Two Paths to Prosperity," and "South Korea: A New Society," *The Economist,* April 15, 1989, pp. 19, 23–25, cited in Paul Kennedy, *Preparing for the Twenty-First Century* (New York: Vintage Books, 1994), p. 200.
2. Bernard Wysocki, Jr. "The Global Mall: In Developing Nations, Many Youth Splurge, Mainly on U.S. Goods, *Wall Street Journal,* July 26, 1997, pp. A1, A11.
3. Although the United States leads the world in software development, and the meteoric rise of the Internet here and around the world promises a steady demand for associated programs, it should be noted that the U.S. is already facing competition from lower-paid Indian, Filipino, and Irish programmers.
4. "War of the Worlds: A Survey of the Global Economy," *The Economist,* October 1, 1994, p. 3.
5. Ibid., p. 5.
6. Statement by Thomas R. Donohue in Werner Sengenberger and Duncan Campell, eds., *International Labor Standards and Global Economic Integration* (Geneva: International Institute for Labor Studies, 1994), p. 80, cited in Dani Rodrik, "Labor Standards in International Trade: Do They Matter and What Do We Do About Them?" in Robert Z. Lawrence, Dani Rodrik, and John Whalley, *Emerging Agenda for Global Trade: High Stakes for Developing Countries* (Baltimore: Johns Hopkins University Press, 1996), p. 46.
7. Howard Banks, "Deutsche Hegira," *Forbes,* May 5, 1997, p. 132.
8. Michael Mandel, *The High-Risk Society* (New York: Random House, 1996) p. 5.
9. See *The World Competitiveness Report 1995.*
10. R. N. Gwynne, *New Horizons? Third World Industrialization in an International Framework* (New York: 1990) p. 199, cited in Paul Kennedy, *Preparing for the Twenty-First Century* (New York: Vintage Books, 1994) p. 198.
11. Kennedy, p. 194.

12. Marc Levinson, "Kantor's Cant: The Hole in Our Trade Policy," *Foreign Policy*, March/April 1996, p. 2.

13. Malcolm S. Forbes Jr., "Protection Produces Poverty," *Forbes*, February 14, 1994, p. 25.

14. Steve Charnovitz, "Fair Labor Standards and International Trade," *Journal of World Trade Law*, vol. 20, no. 1 (January/February 1986), note 44, cited in Rodrik, p. 35.

15. Paul Klebnikov, "France's Political Paralysis," *Forbes*, May 5, 1997, p. 138.

16. Ibid.

17. "Less Separate, More Equal," *The Economist*, April 5, 1997, p. 46.

18. David E. Sanger, "Bashing America for Fun and Profit," *New York Times*, October 5, 1997, p. 1.

19. "A Suitable Target for Foreign Policy?" *The Economist*, April 12, 1997, p. 15.

20. Allen R. Myerson, "In Principle, A Case for More Sweatshops," *New York Times*, June 22, 1997, page E5.

21. Richard Freeman, "A Global Labor Market? Differences in Wages Among Countries in the 1980s," unpublished paper, July 1994, cited in Rodrik, p. 39.

22. Myerson, p. E5. As Dani Rodrik reminds us in his article (see Note 14, above), there is a difference between uniformly lower labor standards and exemptions from national labor standards, the latter sometimes found in special export-processing zones, and open to classification as export subsidization, in breach of WTO rules.

23. Paul Kennedy, *Preparing for the Twenty-First Century*, p. 193.

24. Andrew Pollack, "South Korea's Growing Pains," *New York Times*, February 4, 1997, pp. D7–8.

25. Jeffrey Sachs, "The Limits of Convergence: Nature, Nurture and Growth," *The Economist*, June 14, 1997, p. 19.

26. Eduardo Borensztein, José de Gregorio, and Jong-Wha Lee, "How Does Foreign Direct Investment Affect Growth?" Working Paper No. 5057 (National Bureau of Economic Research: Cambridge, MA, 1995). Cited in Milan Brahmbhatt and Uri Dadush, "Disparities in Global Integration," *Finance & Development*, September 1996, p. 48.

27. See the map on page viii of this book.

28. "War of the Worlds: A Survey of the Global Economy," *The Economist*, October 1, 1994, p. 4.

29. Samuel P. Huntington, *The Clash of Civilizations and the Remaking of World Order* (New York: Simon & Schuster, 1996).

30. "Caged Tigers," *Business Asia,* July 29, 1996, p. 2.

31. Jennifer Humphreys, "Bolting from Burma," *International Business,* October 1996, p. 48.

32. Steven Erlanger, "U.S. Says Chinese Will Stop Sending Missiles to Iran," *New York Times,* October 18, 1997, p. A1.

33. Craig R. Whitney, "Carrots-for-China Policy Haunts U.S. in the Gulf," *New York Times,* p. 1.

34. Interestingly enough, President Clinton's strongest opponents came from the Democrats themselves, and in particular from the House Minority Leader, Richard A. Gephardt, who very openly stated that "the real question before us now is whether we can connect our values of environmental quality and worker and human rights to our economic policy" (Alison Mitchell, "Clinton Retreats on Trade Power; Prospects Slight," *New York Times,* November 18, 1997, p. A1). But the most bizarre linkage of policies was made by a handful of right-wing conservatives in the Republican Party, who made their votes conditional on President Clinton's agreement to change his policy of allowing U.S. funds to go to international family planning organizations that counsel abortions.

35. Louis Uchitelle, "Confusion As an Economic Indicator," *New York Times,* November 2, 1997, p. D1.

Appendix I

RELATED WEB SITES

Economic Development
http://www.worldbank.org/html/extdr/thematic.htm (Topics in Development)

International Affairs
http://www.economist.com (The Economist)
http://www.foreignaffairs.org (Foreign Affairs Journal)
http://www.foreignrelations.org/ (Council on Foreign Relations)
http://www.refdesk.com/inter.html (My Virtual Reference Desk)
http://www.worldbank.org (World Bank)

International Business and Finance
http://www.barrons.com/ (Barron's)
http://www.bloomberg.com/bbn/index.html (Bloomberg News)
http://www.uschamber.org (U.S. Chamber of Commerce)
http://www.forbes.com/ (Forbes)
http://www.newsday.com/ap/financex.htm (Newsday)
http://www.usa.ft.com/ (Financial Times)
http://update.wsj.com/ (The Wall Street Journal)
http://www.uschamber.org (U.S. Chamber of Commerce)
http://www.emgmkts.com/ (Emerging Markets Companion)

Regional Information
http://www.census.gov/main/www/stat_int.html (Index Of Statistical Agencies and Data By Country—Hosted by the Census Bureau, U.S.)

http://www.chinavista.com/business/desk.html (China Business Reference Desk)

http://satellite.nikkei.co.jp/enews/ (Business News in Japan)

http://www.duke.edu/~charvey/Country_risk/couindex.htm (Country Risk Analysis)

Statistics

http://www.bea.doc.gov/ (Bureau of Economic Analysis—an agency of the U.S. Department of Commerce, providing key national, international, and regional aspects of the U.S. economy)

http://stats.bls.gov/ (Bureau of Labor Statistics)

http://www.bog.frb.fed.us/releases (Federal Reserve Board: Statistical Releases)

http://bos.business.uab.edu/charts.htm (Economic Chart Dispenser: Over 80 Economic Interactive Charts/Interactive Calculations)

http://www.census.gov/stat_abstract/ (Statistical Abstract of the United States)

http://www.fedstats.gov/FedStats (maintained by the Federal Interagency Council on Statistical Policy)

http://www.whitehouse.gov/fsbr/esbr.html (The Economic Statistics Briefing Room)

http://www.moodys.com/cgi-bin/pr.exe (Moody's Investors Service Real-Time Rating Actions)

Appendix II

WORLD ECONOMIC STATISTICS

World Economic Statistics
World Economies in 1995

Economy	GNP/a (Millions) (US$) 1995	GNP PER CAPITA US$/a 1995	GNP PER CAPITA Real growth rate (%) 1985–95	GNP PER CAPITA PPP/b intl. dollars 1995	Average inflation rate (%) 1985–95	PERCENTAGE OF GDP Agriculture 1995	PERCENTAGE OF GDP Trade 1995	PERCENTAGE OF GDP Investment 1995
Afghanistan	–	c	–	–	–	–	–	–
Albania	2,199	670	–	–	29.7	56	52	16
Algeria	44,609	1,600	(3)	5,300 d	23.1	13	57	32
American Samoa	–	e	–	–	–	–	–	–
Andorra	–	f	–	–	–	–	–	–
Angola	4,422	410	(6)	1,310 d	169.5	12	132	27
Antigua & Barbuda	–	e	3	–	4.4	4	217	22
Argentina	278,431	8,030	2	8,310	255.4	6	16	18
Armenia/g	2,752	730	(15)	2,260	179.4	44	85	9
Aruba	–	f	–	–	4.5	–	–	–
Australia	337,909	18,720	1	18,940	3.7	3	40	23
Austria	216,547	26,890	2	21,250	3.2	2	77	27
Azerbaijan/g	3,601	480	(16)	1,460	279.3	27	66	16

Bahamas	3,297	11,940	(1)	14,710 d	3.2	–	–	–
Bahrain	4,525	7,840	1	13,400 d	0.4	1	191	27
Bangladesh	28,599	240	2	1,380	6.4	31	37	17
Barbados	1,745	6,560	(0)	10,620 d	2.5	5	96	13
Belarus/g	21,356	2,070	(5)	4,220	309.4	13	–	25
Belgium	250,710	24,710	2	21,660	3.1	2	143	18
Belize	568	2,630	4	5,400 d	3.5	20	109	26
Benin	2,034	370	(0)	1,760	2.9	34	64	20
Bermuda	–	f	(1)	–	5.3	–	–	–
Bhutan	295	420	4	1,260 d	8.4	40	84	32
Bolivia	5,905	800	2	2,540	18.5	–	47	15
Bosnia and Herzegovina	–	c	–	–	–	–	–	–
Botswana	4,381	3,020	6	5,580	11.6	–	5	101
Brazil	579,787	3,640	(1)	5,400	873.8	14	15	22
Brunei	–	f	–	–	0.3	3	–	–
Bulgaria	11,225	1,330	(2)	4,480	45.3	13	94	21

Note: The number 0 means zero more or less precisely. a. Atlas method; b. Purchasing power parity; c. Estimated to be low income ($765 or less); d. Obtained from regression estimates; e. Estimated to be upper-middle income ($3,036 to $9,385); f. Estimated to be high income ($9,385 or more); g. Estimates for the economies of the former Soviet Union are preliminary; h. Estimated to be lower-middle income; i. References to GNP relate to GDP; j. Data cover mainland Tanzania only.
SOURCE: *World Bank Atlas 1997* (Washington DC: World Bank).

| | GNP / a | GNP PER CAPITA | | | | PERCENTAGE OF GDP | | |
| | (Millions) (US$) 1995 | US$/a 1995 | Real growth rate (%) 1985–95 | PPP/b intl. dollars 1995 | Average inflation rate (%) 1985–95 | Agriculture 1995 | Trade 1995 | Investment 1995 |
Economy								
Burkina Faso	2,417	230	(0.1)	780 d	2.5	34	45	22
Burundi	984	160	(1)	630 d	6.1	56	43	11
Cambodia	2,718	270	2	–	70.5	51	36	19
Cameroon	8,615	650	(7)	2,110	2.0	–	–	–
Canada	573,695	19,380	0	21,130	2.9	13	71	19
Cape Verde	366	960	2	1,870 d	7.2	13	75	45
Cayman Islands	–	f	–	–	–	–	–	–
Central African Republic	1,123	340	(2)	1,070 d	3.7	44	46	15
Chad	1,144	180	1	700 d	3.1	44	46	9
Channel Islands	–	f	–	–	–	–	–	–
Chile	59,151	4,160	6	9,520	17.9		54	27
China	744,890	620	8	2,920	9.5	21	40	40
Columbia	70,263	1,910	3	6,130	25.2	14	35	20
Comoros	237	470	(1)	1,320 d	4	39	64	17
Congo	1,784	680	(3)	2,050	2.2	10	128	27
Costa Rica	8,884	2,610	3	5,850	18.5	17	81	25

Côte d'Ivoire	9,248	660	(4)	1,580	2.1	31	76	13
Croatia	15,508	3,250	–	–	–	12	93	14
Cuba	–	h	–	–	–	–	–	–
Cyprus	–	f	5	–	4.3	5	99	22
Czech Republic	39,990	3,870	(2)	9,770	12.2	6	108	25
Denmark	156,027	29,890	2	21,230	2.8	4	64	16
Djibouti	–	h	–	–	–	3	101	12
Dominica	218	2,990	4	–	4.4	21	109	26
Dominican Republic	11,390	1,460	2	3,870	26.3	15	55	20
Ecuador	15,997	1,390	1	4,220	45.5	12	56	19
Egypt, Arab Republic	45,507	790	1	3,820	15.7	20	54	17
El Salvador	9,057	1,610	3	2,610	14.7	14	55	19
Equatorial Guinea	152	380	2	–	4.1	50	112	23
Eritrea	–	c	–	–	–	11	104	20
Estonia/g	4,252	2,860	(4)	4,220	76.2	8	160	27
Ethiopia	–	100	(1)	450	5.9	57	39	17

Note: The number 0 means zero more or less precisely. a. Atlas method; b. Purchasing power parity; c. Estimated to be low income ($765 or less); d. Obtained from regression estimates; e. Estimated to be upper-middle income ($3,036 to $9,385); f. Estimated to be high income ($9,385 or more); g. Estimates for the economies of the former Soviet Union are preliminary; h. Estimated to be lower-middle income; i. References to GNP relate to GDP; j. Data cover mainland Tanzania only.
SOURCE: *World Bank Atlas 1997* (Washington DC: World Bank).

Economy	GNP/a (Millions) (US$) 1995	GNP PER CAPITA			Average inflation rate (%) 1985–95	PERCENTAGE OF GDP		
		US$/a 1995	Real growth rate (%) 1985–95	PPP/b intl. dollars 1995		Agriculture 1995	Trade 1995	Investment 1995
Faroe Islands	–	f	–	–	–	–	–	–
Fiji	1,895	2,440	2	5,780 d	4.9	–	104	14
Finland	105,174	20,580	(0)	17,760	3.8	6	68	16
France	1,451,051	24,990	2	21,030	2.8	2	43	18
French Guiana	–	f	–	–	–	–	–	–
French Polynesia	–	f	–	–	–	–	–	–
Gabon	3,759	3,490	(2)	–	4.8	–	101	26
Gambia, The	354	320	0	930 d	10.3	28	103	21
Georgia/g	2,358	440	(17)	1,470	310.0	67	46	3
Germany	2,252,343	27,510	–	20,070	–	–	46	21
Ghana	6,719	390	2	1,990 d	28.4	46	59	19
Greece	85,885	8,210	1	11,710	15.1	21	57	19
Greenland	–	f	–	–	–	–	–	–
Grenada	271	2,980	–	–	5.3	11	47	32
Guadeloupe	–	e	–	–	–	–	–	–
Guam	–	f	–	–	–	–	–	–

Guatemala	14,255	1,340	0	3,340	18.6	25	47	17
Guinea	3,593	550	1	–	16.8	24	46	15
Guinea-Bissau	265	250	2	790 d	62.8	46	48	16
Guyana	493	590	1	2,420 d	51.1	36	159	19
Haiti	1,777	250	(5)	910 d	14.7	44	17	2
Honduras	3,566	600	0	1,900	14.2	21	80	23
Hong Kong/i	142,332	22,990	5	22,950	8.7	0	297	35
Hungary	42,129	4,120	(1)	6,410	19.9	8	67	23
Iceland	6,686	24,950	0	20,460	11.8	–	70	15
India	319,660	340	3	1,400	9.8	29	27	25
Indonesia	190,105	980	6	3,800	8.8	17	53	38
Iran, Islamic Republic	–	h	1	5,470	24.2	25	39	29
Iraq	–	h	–	–	–	–	–	–
Ireland	52,765	14,710	5	15,680	2.5	–	136	13
Isle of Man	–	e	–	–	–	–	–	–
Israel	87,875	15,920	3	16,490	17.1	–	69	24

Note: The number 0 means zero more or less precisely. a. Atlas method; b. Purchasing power parity; c. Estimated to be low income ($765 or less); d. Obtained from regression estimates; e. Estimated to be upper-middle income ($3,036 to $9,385); f. Estimated to be high income ($9,385 or more); g. Estimates for the economies of the former Soviet Union are preliminary; h. Estimated to be lower-middle income; i. References to GNP relate to GDP; j. Data cover mainland Tanzania only. SOURCE: *World Bank Atlas 1997* (Washington DC: World Bank).

Economy	GNP / a (Millions) (US$) 1995	GNP PER CAPITA US$/a 1995	Real growth rate (%) 1985–95	PPP/b intl. dollars 1995	Average inflation rate (%) 1985–95	PERCENTAGE OF GDP Agriculture 1995	Trade 1995	Investment 1995
Italy	1,088,085	19,020	2	19,870	6.0	3	49	18
Jamaica	3,803	1,510	4	3,540	28.3	9	145	17
Japan	4,963,587	39,640	3	22,110	1.4	2	17	29
Jordan	6,354	1,510	(3)	4,060 d	7.1	8	121	26
Kazzastan/g	22,143	1,330	(9)	3,010	307.3	12	69	22
Kenya	7,583	280	0	1,380	13.0	29	72	19
Kiribati	73	920	(0)	–	3.8	–	–	–
Korea, Dem. Rep.	–	h	–	–	–	–	–	–
Korea, Rep.	435,137	9,700	8	11,450	6.8	7	67	37
Kuwait	28,941	17,390	1	23,790 d	–	0	104	12
Kyrgyz Republic/g	3,158	700	(7)	1,800	172.3	44	58	16
Laos PDR	1,694	350	3	–	22.6	52	–	–
Latvia/g	5,708	2,270	(7)	3,370	73.2	9	91	21
Lebanon	10,673	2,660	3	–	45.8	7	70	29
Lesotho	1,519	770	2	1,780 d	13.6	10	138	87
Liberia	–	c	–	–	–	–	–	–

Libya	–	c	–	–	–	–	–	–
Lichtenstein	–	f	–	–	–	–	–	–
Lithuania/g	7,070	1,900	(12)	4,120	151.0	11	108	19
Luxembourg	16,876	41,210	1	37,930	4.7	–	184	–
Macao	–	f	–	–	9.3	–	111	31
Macedonia, FYR	1,813	860	–	–	–	–	86	15
Madagascar	3,178	230	(2)	640	17.9	34	54	11
Malawi	1,623	170	(1)	750	22.0	42	69	15
Malaysia	78,321	3,890	6	9,020	3.3	13	194	41
Maldives	251	990	7	3,080 d	9.2	–	–	–
Mali	2,410	250	1	550	151.9	46	60	26
Malta	–	e	5	–	2.9	3	198	29
Marshall Islands	–	h	–	–	5.4	–	–	–
Martinique	–	f	–	–	–	–	–	–
Mauritania	1,049	460	1	–	1,540 d	6.9	27	104
Mauritius	3,815	3,380	6	13,210	8.8	9	120	25

Note: The number 0 means zero more or less precisely. a. Atlas method; b. Purchasing power parity; c. Estimated to be low income ($765 or less); d. Obtained from regression estimates; e. Estimated to be upper-middle income ($3,036 to $9,385); f. Estimated to be high income ($9,385 or more); g. Estimates for the economies of the former Soviet Union are preliminary; h. Estimated to be lower-middle income; i. References to GNP relate to GDP; j. Data cover mainland Tanzania only. SOURCE: *World Bank Atlas 1997* (Washington DC: World Bank).

Economy	GNP / a (Millions) (US$) 1995	GNP PER CAPITA				PERCENTAGE OF GDP		
		US$/a 1995	Real growth rate (%) 1985–95	PPP/b intl. dollars 1995	Average inflation rate (%) 1985–95	Agriculture 1995	Trade 1995	Investment 1995
Mayotte	–	e	–	–	–	–	–	–
Mexico	304,596	3,320	0	6,400	36.7	8	48	15
Micronesia, Fed. sts.	215	2,010	–	–	4.5	–	–	–
Moldova/g	3,996	920	(8)	–	–	50	78	7
Monaco	–	f	–	–	–	–	–	–
Mongolia	767	310	(4)	1,950 d	51.6	–	62	–
Morocco	29,545	1,110	1	3,340	4.8	14	62	21
Mozambique	1,353	80	4	810 d	52.2	33	102	60
Myanmar	–	c	0	–	26.4	63	4	12
Namibia	3,098	2,000	3	4,150 d	10.5	14	110	20
Nepal	4,391	200	2	1,170 d	11.6	42	60	23
Netherlands	371,039	24,000	2	19,950	1.7	3	99	22
Netherlands Antilles	–	f	–	–	–	–	–	–
New Caledonia	–	f	–	–	–	–	–	–
New Zealand	51,655	14,340	1	16,360	3.9	–	62	24
Nicaragua	1,659	380	(6)	2,000 d	963.7	33	76	18

Niger	1,961	220	(2)	750 d	1.3	39	30	6
Nigeria	28,411	260	1	1,220	33.0	28	81	25
Northern Mariana Is.	–	f	–	–	–	–	–	–
Norway	136,077	31,250	2	21,940	3.1	–	71	23
Oman	10,578	4,820	0	8,140 d	(0.2)	–	89	17
Pakistan	59,991	460	1	2,230	9.3	26	36	19
Panama	7,235	2,750	(0)	5,980	1.7	11	79	24
Papua New Guinea	4,976	1,160	2	2,420 d	4.6	26	106	24
Paraguay	8,158	1,690	1	3,650	24.9	24	82	23
Peru	55,019	2,310	(2)	3,770	398.5	7	30	17
Phillipines	71,865	1,050	2	2,850	9.8	22	80	23
Poland	107,829	2,790	(0)	5,400	91.8	6	53	17
Portugal	96,689	9,740	4	12,670	11.2	–	66	28
Puerto Rico	–	e	2	–	2.9	1	–	17
Qatar	7,448	11,600	(3)	17,690 d	–	–	–	–
Reunion	–	f	–	–	–	–	–	–

Note: The number 0 means zero more or less precisely. a. Atlas method; b. Purchasing power parity; c. Estimated to be low income ($765 or less); d. Obtained from regression estimates; e. Estimated to be upper-middle income ($3,036 to $9,385); f. Estimated to be high income ($9,385 or more); g. Estimates for the economies of the former Soviet Union are preliminary; h. Estimated to be lower-middle income; i. References to GNP relate to GDP; j. Data cover mainland Tanzania only.
SOURCE: *World Bank Atlas 1997* (Washington DC: World Bank).

| | GNP/a | GNP PER CAPITA | | | | PERCENTAGE OF GDP | | |
| | (Millions) (US$) | US$/a | Real growth rate (%) | PPP/b intl. dollars | Average inflation rate (%) | Agriculture | Trade | Investment |
Economy	1995	1995	1985–95	1995	1985–95	1995	1995	1995
Romania	33,488	1,480	(5)	4,360	69.1	21	60	26
Russian Federation/g	331,948	2,240	(5)	4,480	148.9	7	44	25
Rwanda	1,128	180	(5)	540	10.4	37	32	13
São Tomé and Principe	45	350	(2)	–	40.1	23	108	50
Saudi Arabia	129,218	6,810	(2)	8,820 d	2.7	–	70	20
Senegal	5,070	600	(1)	1,780	3.7	20	69	16
Seychelles	487	6,620	4	–	3.3	4	129	26
Sierra Leone	762	180	(3)	580	61.5	42	40	6
Singapore	79,831	26,730	6	22,770 d	3.9	–	–	33
Slovak Republic	15,848	2,950	(3)	3,610	10.4	6	124	28
Slovenia	16,328	8,200	–	–	–	5	113	22
Solomon Islands	341	910	2	2,190 d	11.7	–	–	–
Somalia	–	c	–	–	–	–	–	–
South Africa	130,918	3,160	(1)	5,030 d	13.7	5	44	18
Spain	532,347	13,580	3	14,520	6.3	3	47	21
Sri Lanka	12,616	700	3	3,250	11.1	23	83	25

St. Kitts and Nevis	212	5,170	5	9,410	5.5	6	–	39
St. Lucia	532	3,370	4	–	3.2	11	141	25
St. Vincent and Grenadines	253	2,280	4	–	3.6	11	–	–
Sudan	–	c	1	–	63.2	–	–	–
Suriname	360	880	1	2,250 d	48.5	26	11	23
Swaziland	1,051	1,170	1	2,880	11.7	9	186	17
Sweden	209,720	23,750	(0)	18,540	5.5	2	77	14
Switzerland	286,014	40,630	0	25,860	3.4	–	68	23
Syrian Arab Republic	15,780	1,120	1	5,320	15.8	–	–	–
Tajikistan/g	1,976	340	(13)	920	146.6	–	228	17
Tanzania/j	3,703	120	1	640	32.3	58	96	31
Thailand	159,630	2,740	8	7,540	5.0	11	90	43
Togo	1,266	310	(3)	1,130 d	3.0	38	65	14
Tonga	170	1,630	0	–	7.9	36	–	–
Trinidad and Tobago	4,851	3,770	(2)	8,610 d	6.8	3	68	14
Tunisia	16,369	1,820	2	5,000	6.0	12	93	24

Note: The number 0 means zero more or less precisely. a. Atlas method; b. Purchasing power parity; c. Estimated to be low income ($765 or less); d. Obtained from regression estimates; e. Estimated to be upper-middle income ($3,036 to $9,385); f. Estimated to be high income ($9,385 or more); g. Estimates for the economies of the former Soviet Union are preliminary; h. Estimated to be lower-middle income; i. References to GNP relate to GDP; j. Data cover mainland Tanzania only.

SOURCE: *World Bank Atlas 1997* (Washington DC: World Bank).

	GNP / a	GNP PER CAPITA				PERCENTAGE OF GDP		
Economy	(Millions) (US$) 1995	US$/a 1995	Real growth rate (%) 1985–95	PPP/b intl. dollars 1995	Average inflation rate (%) 1985–95	Agriculture 1995	Trade 1995	Investment 1995
Turkey	169,452	2,780	2	5,580	64.6	16	45	25
Turkmenistan/g	4,125	920	(10)	–	381.4	–	–	–
Uganda	4,668	240	3	1,470 d	65.5	50	33	16
Ukraine/g	84,084	1,630	(9)	2,400	362.5	18	–	–
United Arab Emirates	4,280,666	17,400	(4)	16,470 d	–	2	139	27
United Kingdom	1,094,734	18,700	1	19,260	5.1	2	57	16
United States	7,100,007	26,980	1	26,980	3.2	2	24	16
Uruguay	16,458	5,170	3	6,630	70.5	9	41	14
Uzbekistan/g	21,979	970	(4)	2,370	239.0	33	125	23
Vanuatu	202	1,200	(1)	2,290 d	5.5	–	–	–
Venezuela	65,382	3,020	1	7,900	37.6	5	49	16
Vietnam	17,634	240	4	–	88.3	28	83	27
Virgin Islands (U.S.)	–	f	–	–	–	–	–	–
West Bank and Gaza	–	h	–	–	–	–	–	–
Western Samoa	184	1,120	(0.4)	2,030 d	10.6	–	–	–
Yemen, Rep.	4,044	260	–	–	–	22	88	12

Yugoslavia Fed. Rep.	–	h	–	–	–	–	–	–
Zaire	5,313	120	(9)	490 d	–	–	–	–
Zambia	3,605	400	(1)	930	91.6	22	71	12
Zimbabwe	5,933	540	(1)	2,030	21.0	15	74.3	22

Note: The number 0 means zero more or less precisely. a. Atlas method; b. Purchasing power parity; c. Estimated to be low income ($765 or less); d. Obtained from regression estimates; e. Estimated to be upper-middle income ($3,036 to $9,385); f. Estimated to be high income ($9,385 or more); g. Estimates for the economies of the former Soviet Union are preliminary; h. Estimated to be lower-middle income; i. References to GNP relate to GDP; j. Data cover mainland Tanzania only.

SOURCE: *World Bank Atlas 1997* (Washington DC: World Bank).

Index

Industrial Revolution, 4, 20, 22, 25, 26
  history of, 41
Industrialization, affluence level required for, 33
Industrialized countries, defined, 221
  See also First World
Inflation, effects of, 168
Information Revolution, 4, 5
Information Technology (IT)
  applications of, 66
  business of, 85
  consequences of, 84
  current state of, 78–82
  economic impact of, 26, 28, 66
  evolution of, 68–70
  and globalization, 81–82, 84–86
  growth of, 73, 81
  hardware for, 65–66
  and productivity, 80
  telecommunications. *See* Telecommunications
  and Third World, 83
  and transportation, 77–78
Institute for Historical Review, 3
Integration policy, and economic performance, 212
Intel, market capitalization of, 68
Interest rate parity theory, 232
Intermediate goods, production of, 92, 93
International affairs, web sites relating to, 237
International finance, web sites relating to, 237
International Financial Corp. (IFC), 130

International Monetary Fund (IMF), 53
  bailouts by, 202–203
Internet, 7, 76
  activity on, 77
Investment grade, defined, 162
Iran, economic sanctions against, 125
Iraq, economic sanctions against, 125
Islamic culture, history of, 39
Italy, membership in G7, 214
Ivory Coast, credit crisis in 1980s, 53

Japan
  automotive market in, 114
  class system of, 223
  consumer market growth in, 107
  demographics of, 112
  economic colonialism of, 204
  economic rise of, 51
  economy of, 16
  factors fueling economy of, 171
  GDP/capitalization ratio in, 122
  high-tech industry in, 82
  human capital investment of, 198
  labor costs in, 98, 99
  labor relocation and, 194
  membership in G7, 214
  savings rates of, 135
  stock market of, 171
Jiang Zemin, 216
Johnson Act of 1940, 125
Junk bond markets, 142

Kaiser Steel, 197
Kay, John, 41